AUTOCAD® 2009
ESSENTIALS

AutoCAD® 2009
Essentials

By
Munir M. Hamad
Autodesk Approved Instructor

JONES AND BARTLETT PUBLISHERS
Sudbury, Massachusetts
BOSTON   TORONTO   LONDON   SINGAPORE

World Headquarters

Jones and Bartlett Publishers
40 Tall Pine Drive
Sudbury, MA 01776
978-443-5000
info@jbpub.com
www.jbpub.com

Jones and Bartlett Publishers
 Canada
6339 Ormindale Way
Mississauga, ON L5V 1J2
CANADA

Jones and Bartlett Publishers
 International
Barb House, Barb Mews
London W6 7PA
UK

Jones and Bartlett's books and products are available through most bookstores and online booksellers. To contact Jones and Bartlett Publishers directly, call 800-832-0034, fax 978-443-8000, or visit our website at www.jbpub.com.

Substantial discounts on bulk quantities of Jones and Bartlett's publications are available to corporations, professional associations, and other qualified organizations. For details and specific discount information, contact the special sales department at Jones and Bartlett via the above contact information or send an email to specialsales@jbpub.com.

The publisher recognizes and respects all marks used by companies, manufacturers, and developers as a means to distinguish their products. All brand names and product names mentioned in this book are trademarks or service marks of their respective companies. Any omission or misuse (of any kind) of service marks or trademarks, etc. is not an attempt to infringe on the property of others.

ISBN 978-0-7637-7377-9

Cover Design: Tyler Creative
Text and cover printing: Malloy, Inc.

Library of Congress Cataloging-in-Publication Data

Hamad, Munir M.
 AutoCAD 2009 essentials / by Munir M. Hamad.
    p. cm.
 ISBN 978-1-934015-28-5 (hbk.)
 1. Computer graphics. 2. AutoCAD. I. Title.
 T385.H32932 2008
 620'.00420285536—dc22

                        2008028729

6048
Printed in the United States of America
13 12 11 10 09   10 9 8 7 6 5 4 3 2 1

PURPOSE & OBJECTIVES

This courseware is for novice users of AutoCAD 2009. It covers the beginner and intermediate levels. The courseware demonstrates in a very simple step-by-step procedure how to create an engineering drawing, modify it, annotate it, dimension it, and finally print it. At the completion of this book, the reader will be able to:

- Understand AutoCAD and how to deal with its basic operations including its filing system

- Draw different objects quickly and precisely

- Set up drawings

- Construct drawings in a few simple steps

- Modify any object in a drawing

- Create, insert, and edit blocks

- Hatch using different hatch patterns and methods

- Create text and tables

- Insert and edit dimensions

- Prepare and plot a drawing

TABLE OF CONTENTS

PREFACE

- AutoCAD has been the de-facto PC-based drafting tool since 1982. Millions of engineers, draftsmen, project managers, engineering students, and anyone dealing with drawings use AutoCAD on a daily basis.

- This book is ideal for both new and seasoned users of AutoCAD 2009, but it will not teach you engineering drafting. You should already know the science behind drafting.

- This courseware can be used as instructor-led courseware or teach-yourself courseware:
    - For the first option, the estimated time to complete the course is three eight-hour days.

- As for the second option, the reader can take to his/her time completing the course. At the end of each chapter you will find "Chapter Review Questions," which will help test your knowledge of the covered subject areas.

- There are 38 exercises spread throughout the book to help you implement what you've learned.

- There are also 21 workshops, which will complete a full (small) project starting from creating the project to plotting the project. Completing all workshops will help you to:
    - Simulate a real life project from beginning to end, helping you to learn practical skills.
    - Organize information in a very logical order.
    - Learn the basic and necessary commands and functions in AutoCAD 2009.

- This courseware will cover the basic and intermediate levels of knowledge in AutoCAD 2009.

ABOUT THE DVD

- The DVD, included with this book, contains:
  - The AutoCAD 2009 Trial version, which will last for 30 days starting from the day of installation. This version will help you complete all exercises and workshops.
  - All exercise and workshop files included in the book.
- Copy the folder named "Exercises & Workshops" into one of the hard drives of your computer. As for workshops, you will find two folders inside. The first one is named "Metric" for the metric units workshops, and the second one is named "Imperial" for the imperial units workshops.
- If you are a teacher or instructor, you will find the DVD to be a great tool to help conduct a course using this book. There is a full presentation slide show included on the DVD, which covers the whole course from start until finish.

PREREQUISITES

- The author assumes that the reader has enough experience using computers, and has working experience using the Windows operating system.
- Also, the reader should know how to start a new file, open an existing file, save and use save as, close files with or without saving, and exit the software.
- These commands are almost the same in all software packages. With this said, the author will not go through these subjects except to show some specific features of AutoCAD.

Chapter **1**

INTRODUCTION TO AutoCAD 2009

In This Chapter

◊ What is AutoCAD?
◊ Starting AutoCAD
◊ AutoCAD Interface
◊ Things you should know about AutoCAD defaults
◊ Viewing commands
◊ Creating a new file and opening an existing file

WHAT IS AUTOCAD?

- AutoCAD was one of the first CAD (Computer Aided Design/Drafting) software applications to come on the market.
- The first version of AutoCAD was released at the end of 1982, and it was designed to be used only on PCs. Since then AutoCAD use has increased dramatically on a global scale.
- Users can draw both 2D drawings and 3D designs in AutoCAD. There is another version of AutoCAD, called AutoCAD LT, which is for 2D drafting only.
- In this book we will cover AutoCAD 2009.

STARTING AUTOCAD 2009

- There are two ways to start AutoCAD 2009:

AutoCAD 2009

  - While installing AutoCAD 2009, the program will create a shortcut on your desktop. To start AutoCAD you can simply double-click this icon.
  - From the Windows taskbar click Start/All Programs/Autodesk/AutoCAD 2009/AutoCAD 2009.

- AutoCAD will start with a new drawing file opened, which will look like the following:

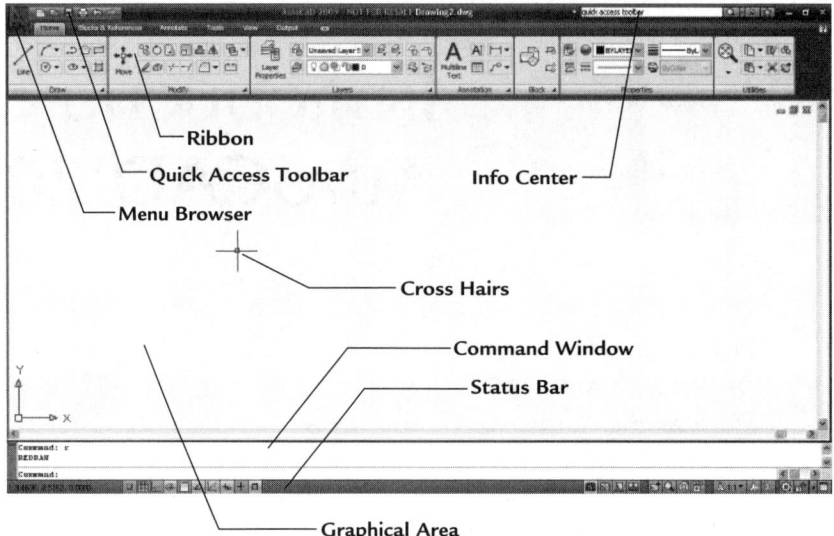

UNDERSTANDING THE AUTOCAD 2009 INTERFACE

- AutoCAD 2009 has "almost" the same interface as Microsoft Office 2007.
- You will use the **Menu Browser** instead of the usual pull-down menus.
- You will use **Ribbons** instead of toolbars.
- The new interface gives you more space in the **Graphical Area**, which is your drawing area.

Menu Browser

- Click on the **Menu Browser**, and you will see the following:

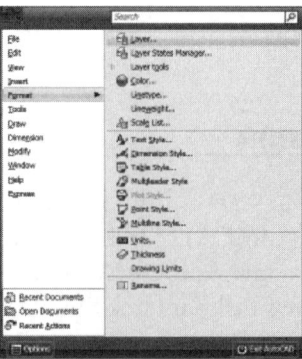

- You will see all the menus as well as all the submenus. You don't need to click to see the submenus; whenever you stop over one menu, the submenu appears automatically.
- At the bottom of the **Menu Browser**, you'll see five items:
  - Recent Documents, the files you've recently opened.
  - Open Documents, the files currently open.
  - Recent Actions you've performed.
  - Options dialog box.
- Exit AutoCAD.

Quick Access Toolbar

- The Quick Access toolbar is the small toolbar at the top-left of the screen:

- Using this toolbar, you can:
  - Create a new file.
  - Open an existing file.
  - Save the current file.
  - Print the current file.
  - Undo & Redo.

Ribbons

- **Ribbons** have two parts:
  - Tabs
  - Panels
- For example, the tab called **Home** consists of seven panels: **Draw, Modify, Layers, Annotation, Block, Utilities,** and **Properties**.
- In each tab you will see different panels.
- The following is the **Draw** panel:

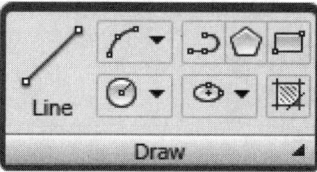

- Some panels (such as the Draw panel) have a small triangle in the bottom right-hand corner, which indicates that there are more buttons available. If you click on it you will see the following:

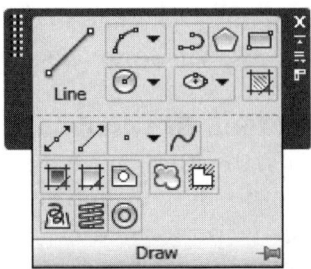

- At the lower right-hand corner of the panel you will see a small push pin. If you click on it, this will be the default view. To go back to the previous view, simply click the push pin again.
- Some buttons inside panels have a small triangle in the lower right-hand corner, which means there are additional options, as shown here:

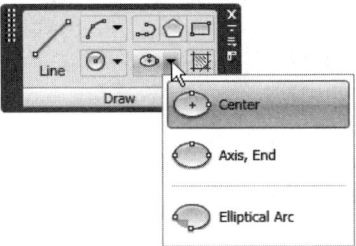

- If you rest your cursor over any button for one second, a small help screen appears. If you rest your cursor for five seconds, however, you will see an extended help screen. See the following two illustrations:

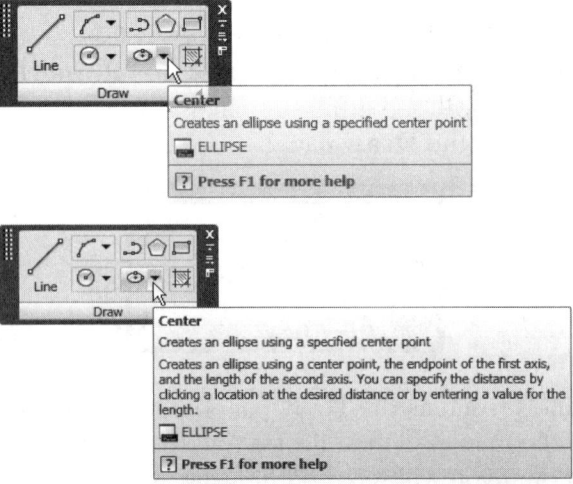

- Panels can be docked or floating. By default all panels are docked. To make a panel a floating panel, simply click the name of the panel, hold it, and drag it to where you want it to be. This is how a floating panel looks:

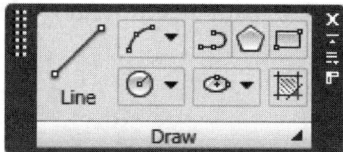

- The handle of the panel is in the left-top corner. At the right, you can close the panel, send it to the **Ribbon**, see more options, or change the orientation of the panel.
- If you close any panel, you can retrieve it by simply right-clicking any existing panel, selecting the **Panel** option, and then selecting the desired panel you want to show, as shown here:

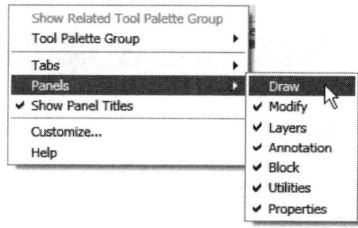

InfoCenter

- At the top-right part of the screen, you will see the InfoCenter:

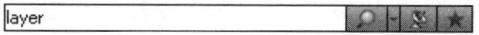

- The InfoCenter gives you the opportunity to search for answers to questions in multiple places such as Help, the New Features Workshop, as well as the Web. Type in the keyword you want to know more about, click the magnifying glass, and you will see a list of related help topics.

Command Window

- If you used AutoCAD 25 years ago, the only way to input commands was to use the Command Window. You had to memorize all of the AutoCAD commands, and type them in. There were no menus, no toolbars, no panels, no **Ribbons**, the only way was to type the commands. This method it still an option, but we don't recommend it.

Graphical Area

- The Graphical Area is where you do your actual drawing. You will use the cross hairs to specify points in the XY plane.
- You can monitor the coordinates of the cross hairs using the left part of the Status Bar.

Status Bar

- The Status Bar in AutoCAD contains many functions that will help you draft more precisely. We will discuss most of the buttons on the Status Bar throughout the chapters of this book. There are two view options for the Status Bar:
  - By default (Icons)

  - Buttons

    ■   To switch views, right-click the Status Bar and select the **Use Icons** option to switch from buttons to icons or vice versa.

POINTS IN AUTOCAD

- Points are defined (and saved) in AutoCAD using the **Cartesian** coordinate system.
- The coordinates will look something like **3.25, 5.45**, which is the **X, Y** format.
- So the first and most traditional way of specifying points in AutoCAD is to type the coordinates, whenever you are asked to do so, by typing X,Y (pronounced X comma Y). See the following illustration:

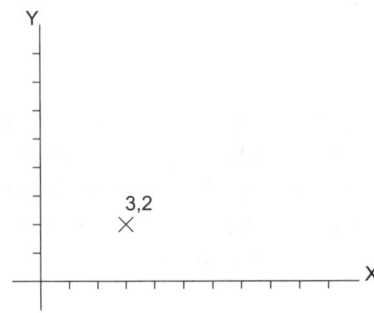

AUTOCAD DEFAULT SETTINGS

- Sign convention: positive is up and right.
- Angle convention: positive is CounterClockWise (CCW) starting from the East (i.e., 0 angle). See the following illustration:

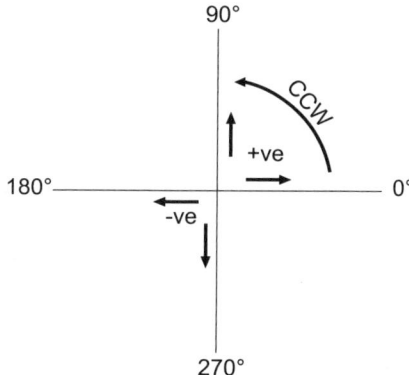

THINGS YOU SHOULD KNOW ABOUT AUTOCAD

- The mouse is the primary input device.
- The left mouse button is always used to select as well as to click.
- The right mouse button, when clicked, offers a drop-down menu.
- The mouse wheel has zooming functions:
  - Zoom in on your drawing by moving the wheel forward.
  - Zoom out of the drawing by moving the wheel backward.
  - Pan (i.e., move through the drawing) by pressing the wheel and holding it and then moving the mouse.
  - Zoom to the edges of your drawing by double-clicking the wheel.
- If you type an AutoCAD command or any input in the Command Window you have to press [Enter] key to execute it.
- [Enter] = [Spacebar] in AutoCAD.
- To repeat the last AutoCAD command, press [Enter] or [Spacebar].
- To cancel any AutoCAD command, press [Esc].

DYNAMIC INPUT

- By default Dynamic Input is turned on, so anything you type in the Command Window will appear in the screen beside the AutoCAD cursor. See the following:

- For example, if you type the word LINE, here's how it will look on the screen:

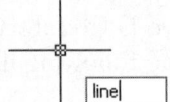

- When you press [Enter], the following will appear:

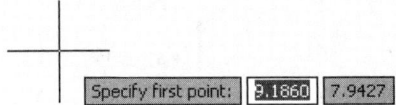

- You can now type the X coordinate, press the [Tab] key, and then input the Y coordinate.
- When you specify the first point and the second point, you will see something similar to the following:

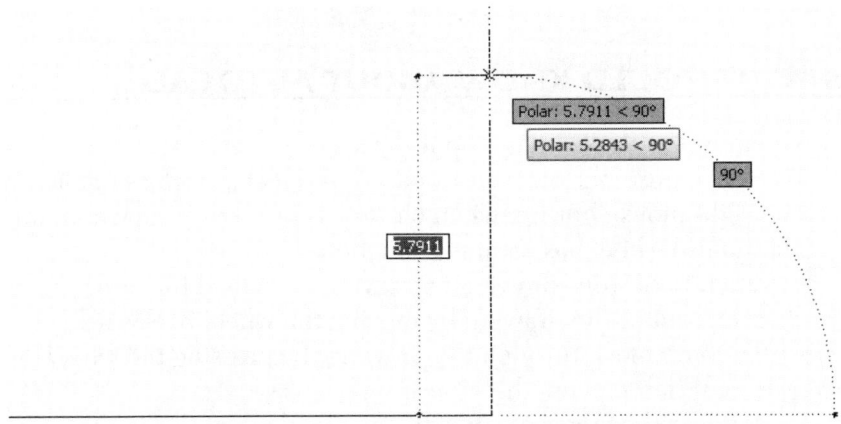

- Because of Dynamic Input you will be able to see the length of the line and its angle East (i.e., Angle = 0.0).

DRAWING LIMITS

- AutoCAD offers the user an infinite drawing sheet on all sides.
- When you start a new AutoCAD drawing, your viewpoint will be at 0,0,1.
- You are looking at the XY plane using a camera's lens; hence, you will see part of your infinite drawing sheet. This part is called the **limits**. See the following:

- In the above example you can see that limits of the drawing are from 0,0 (lower left corner) to 12,9 (upper right corner). This is your working area.
- We will learn how to change limits in upcoming chapters.

AUTOCAD UNITS AND AUTOCAD SPACES

- AutoCAD doesn't deal with a certain length unit while drafting. Take note of the following points:
  - AutoCAD deals with AutoCAD units.
  - An AutoCAD unit can be anything you specify. It can be a meter, centimeter, millimeter, inch, or foot.
  - All of these options are correct as long as you remember your chosen option and stay consistent in both X and Y.
- Also, there are two spaces in AutoCAD: **Model Space** and **Layout (Paper) Space**. You can switch between the two spaces from the Status Bar.

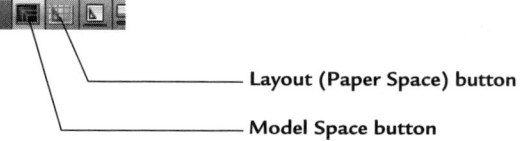

Layout (Paper Space) button

Model Space button

- By default when you start a new drawing file, you are in Model Space.
- In Model Space you can create, modify, and annotate.

- Once you are ready to make a hardcopy of your drawing file, switch to Paper Space (Layouts) so you can prepare your page setup. This is an important time to remember your chosen unit so that you can scale your drawing to the proper scale. We will discuss printing in a later chapter.

VIEWING COMMANDS

- We've already discussed the benefits of the mouse wheel for zooming in, zooming out, and panning. You can also zoom in, zoom out, and pan using the zooming and panning commands.
- Make sure you are at the **Home** tab on the **Ribbon**. Using the **Utilities** panel, select the first button at the left, or the small arrow, and a list of possible zooming commands will appear:

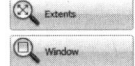

  - **Zoom Extents** used to zoom to all objects.

  - **Zoom Window** used to specify a rectangle. By specifying two opposite corners, whatever is inside the rectangle will look larger.

  - **Zoom Previous** used to restore the previous view, up to the last ten views.

  - **Zoom Realtime** is done by clicking the left button on the mouse and holding it. If you move forward, you are zooming in; if you move backward, you are zooming out.

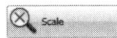

  - **Zoom Dynamic** is used with the **Zoom Window** first. You will see the whole drawing and your current place (shown as a dotted green line), then go to the new location, and press [Enter].

  - **Zoom Scale** is used to input a scale factor. If you type in a number less than 1, you will see the drawing smaller. If the scale factor you type in is greater than 1, you will see the drawing larger. If you put the letter x after the number (e.g., 2x) the scale will be relative to the current view.

  - **Zoom Center** is used to specify a new center point for the zooming, along with a new height.

  - **Zoom Object** is used to zoom to certain selected objects. AutoCAD will ask you to select objects and the selected objects will fill the screen.

  - **Zoom In** is a programmed option, equal to **Zoom Scale**, with a scale factor of 2x.

  - **Zoom Out** is just like Zoom In, but with a zoom factor of 0.5x.

- Also on the Status Bar, you can use the following two buttons:

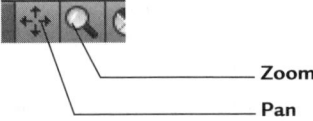

Zoom

Pan

CREATING A NEW FILE

■ To create a new file based on a pre-made template, from the Quick Access Toolbar click the **New** button and the following dialog box will appear:

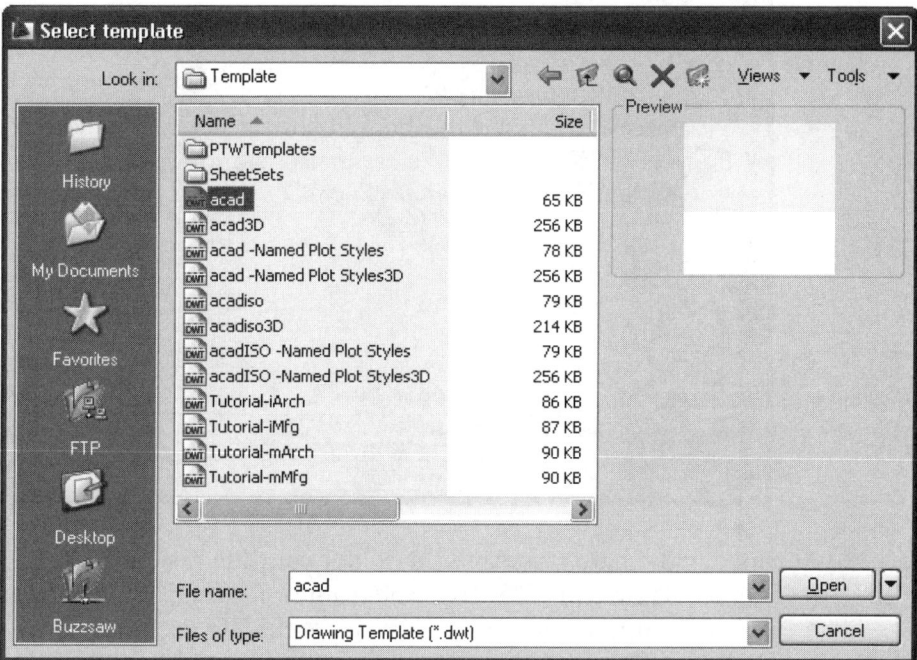

■ This dialog box will allow you to select the desired template.
■ AutoCAD template files have the extension *.dwt.
■ AutoCAD 2009 has many pre-made templates you can use, or you can create your own template.
■ For now we will use *acad.dwt* for our lessons.
■ Click **Open** to start a new file.

OPENING AN EXISTING FILE

■ To open an existing file for further editing, from the Quick Access Toolbar click the **Open** button, and the following dialog box will appear:

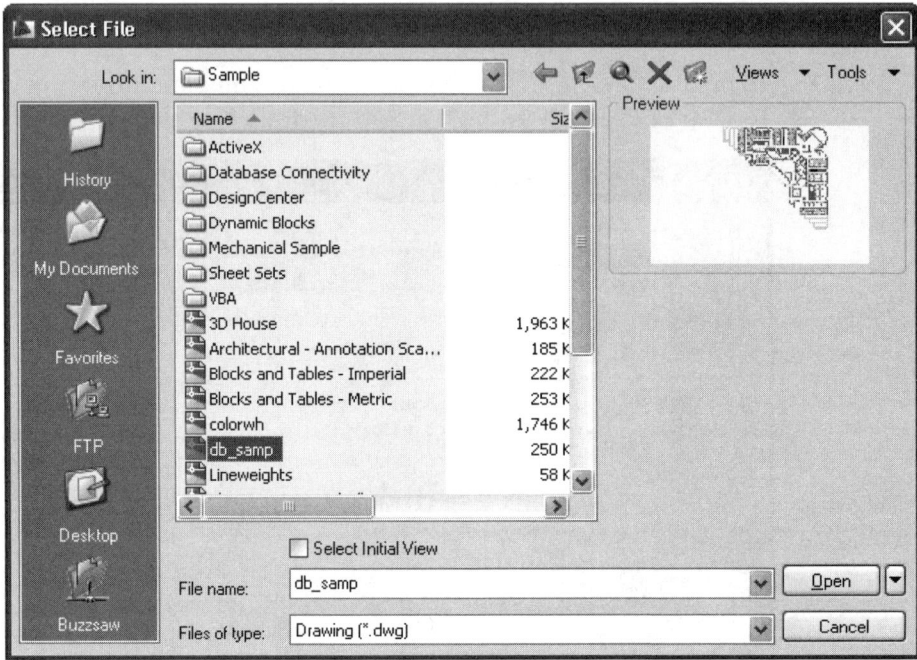

- Specify the hard drive and the folder your file resides in.
- AutoCAD drawing files have the extension *.dwg*.
- If you want to open a single file, select the file and click open (you can also double-click on the file's name).
- If you want to open more than one file, then select the first file name, then hold the [Ctrl] key on the keyboard, and click the other file names. When you are done, click **Open**. You can open as many files as you wish.

Quick View

- If you open more than one file, you can use two functions on the Status Bar: **Quick View Drawings** and **Quick View Layouts**.

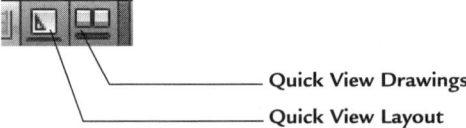

                                                         Quick View Drawings
                                                          Quick View Layout

- If these two buttons are turned on, you will see the following:

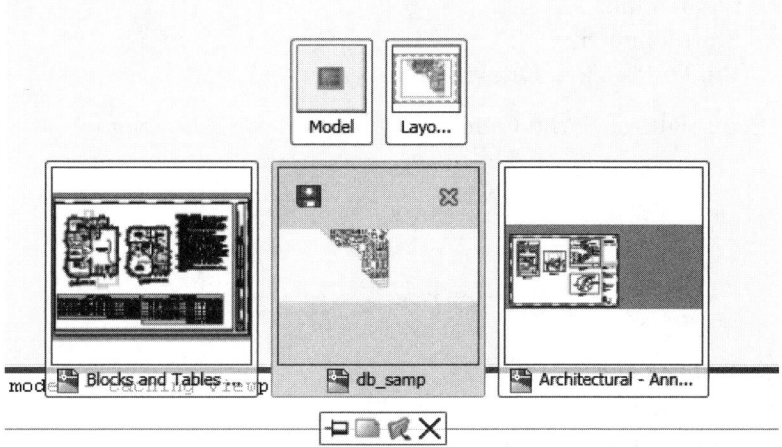

- You will see all the open files.
- In order to jump from one file to another, click the small window of the desired file.
- When you hover over any of the files, you will see the layouts of the file and the picture will change to:

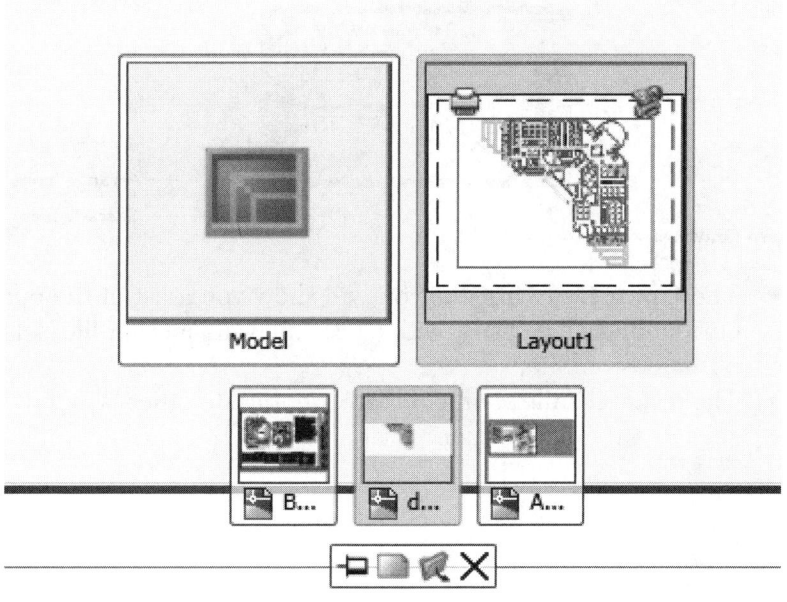

- Also, you will see a small toolbar at the bottom of the screen that allows you to:
  - Close Quick View.

- Open a file.
- Start a new file.
- Pin Quick View Drawings.

■ If you right-click the Quick View button, the following menu will appear:

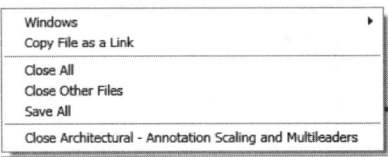

- You can close all files.
- Save all files.
- Close the current file.

Organizing files

- Make sure you are at the **View** tab on the **Ribbon**. There are several ways to organize files using the **Window** panel:

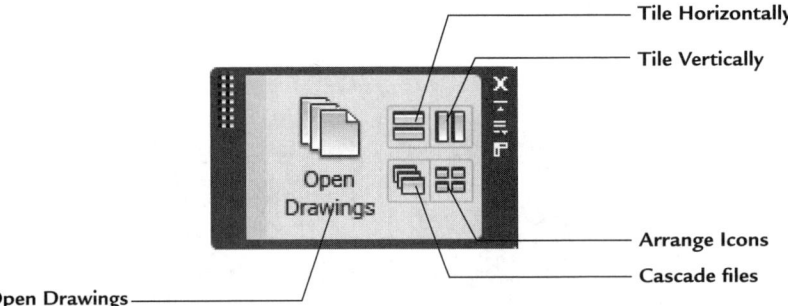

- The **Open Drawings** button will show you a list of the open files. The current file will be listed with ( ). If you want another file, select the name of the desired file.

- The rest of the file commands are identical to other Windows applications such as Save, Save As, and Exit.

NOTES:

INTRODUCING AUTOCAD 2009

 Exercise 1

1. Start AutoCAD 2009.
2. From the Quick Access Toolbar click the **Open** button.
3. Go to the **Samples** folder in the AutoCAD 2009 folder. Open the following three files:
   a. Blocks and Tables – **Metric.dwg**
   b. dbsamp.dwg
   c. Architectural – Annotation Scaling and **Multileader.dwg**
4. Using Quick View drawings, jump from one file to another. Using Quick View layouts, take a look at the layouts in each file.
5. In one of the open files, use your mouse wheel and zoom into the drawing, zoom out (using any of the methods discussed), and pan.
6. Using the right-click menu on the Quick View drawings, **Close All** files without saving.

CHAPTER REVIEW

1. You can close all open files using one command:
   a. True
   b. False
2. CAD stands for _____
3. In AutoCAD, there are two available spaces: Model Space and Paper Space. Which of the following statements is true:
   a. You draw on Model Space and print from Paper Space.
   b. You draw in Paper Space and print from Model Space.
   c. You cannot draw in either space.
   d. Model Space is only for 3D design.
4. Positive angles start from the North:
   a. True
   b. False
5. AutoCAD, unlike most software, allows you to:
   a. Connect to the Internet.
   b. Type commands using the keyboard.
   c. Accept Cartesian coordinates.

      d. Create positive angles that are CCW.

6.   _____ is a tool in AutoCAD that allows the user to see all open files in small windows.

CHAPTER REVIEW ANSWERS

1. a
2. Computer Aided Design/Drafting
3. a
4. b
5. b
6. Quick View Drawings

In This Chapter

◇ Line command, and two precision methods
◇ Arc and Circle commands
◇ Object snap (OSNAP)
◇ Object Tracking (OTRACK)
◇ Pline command
◇ Polar Tracking (POLAR)
◇ Erase, and basic selecting methods

INTRODUCTION

- In drafting, the two most important things are precision and speed.
- You want to finish your drawing as fast as possible, but you don't want to undermine your drawing's precision.
- It is best to learn precision before speed because it is easier to learn to speed up the creation process than it is to improve accuracy. In this chapter we will tackle many commands, but drafting with precision is most important.

LINE COMMAND

- The **Line** command is used to draw segments of straight lines.
- There are many methods available to draw precise shapes using the **Line** command (which we will learn later), but for now, we will type the coordinates in the Command Window.

- On the **Ribbon**, make sure you are at the **Home** tab. Using the **Draw** panel, click the **Line** button.
- The following prompts will appear:

```
Specify first point: (type in the coordinate of the first point)
Specify next point or [Undo]: (type in the coordinate of the second point)
Specify next point or [Undo]: (type in the coordinate of the third point)
Specify next point or [Close/Undo]: (type in the coordinate
of the fourth point)
```

- At any time you can use the Undo option to undo the last specified point, and hence, the last specified segment.
- After you draw two segments, the **Close** option will be available to connect the last point to the first point and to end the command.
- Other ways of ending the command include pressing [Enter] or the spacebar. You can also press [Esc] to end the **Line** command. If you are using the **Line** command and you right-click, you will get the following menu (which is identical to the command prompt):

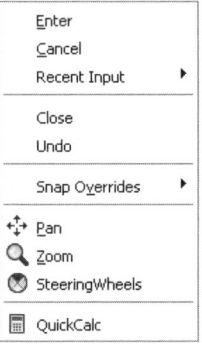

DRAFTING USING DYNAMIC INPUT

- As we learned in Chapter 1, the **Dynamic Input** button is on the Status Bar and it shows anything you type beginning when you issue the command and including the entry of the coordinates.
- In AutoCAD 2009, **Dynamic Input** has another important feature with the **Line** command. It now shows the length and the angle of the line to be drawn (the angle is measured from the East and incremented by 1 degree).
- Take a look at the following example:

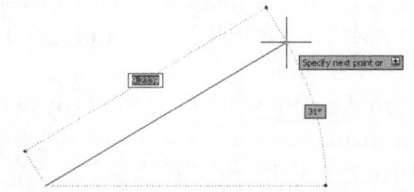

- As you can see, once you start the **Line** command and you specify the first point, if you move your mouse to the right, you will see the length of your proposed line and its angle measured from the East.
- Specify the length, press the [Tab] key, and then type the angle.

DRAWING LINES: THE FIRST METHOD

Exercise 2

1. Start AutoCAD 2009.
2. Open the **Exercise_02.dwg** file.
3. Make sure that Polar Input is off and Dynamic Input is on.
4. Draw the following lines using the **Line** command and **Dynamic Input**:

5. Save the file and close it.

- Start the **Line** command and then type the coordinates of the first point. While **Dynamic Input** is on, specify the length of the line, press [Tab], and then specify the angle. Do the same for the other line segments.

PRECISION METHOD 1: SNAP AND GRID

- As you can see the only method we used to precisely specify points in the XY plane was to type the coordinates using Dynamic Input.
- We can't depend on the mouse to specify precise points.
- In order to use the mouse precisely, we have to use tools to control its movement.
- **Snap** is the only tool in AutoCAD that can help us control the movement of the mouse.

- On the Status Bar, click the **Snap Mode** button.
- Now move to the Graphical area and watch the mouse jump to exact points.
- The **Grid** will show a grid of points on the screen similar to grid paper, which is used in drawing diagrams (these points are not real points).
- A grid by itself is not accurate, but is a helpful tool to use with Snap.
- On the status bar, click the **GRID** button.
- You can now see the points displayed on the screen.
- If the default values for either Snap or Grid do not satisfy your needs, simply right-click one of the two buttons and the following shortcut menu will appear:

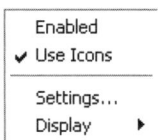

- Select **Settings** and the following dialog box will appear:

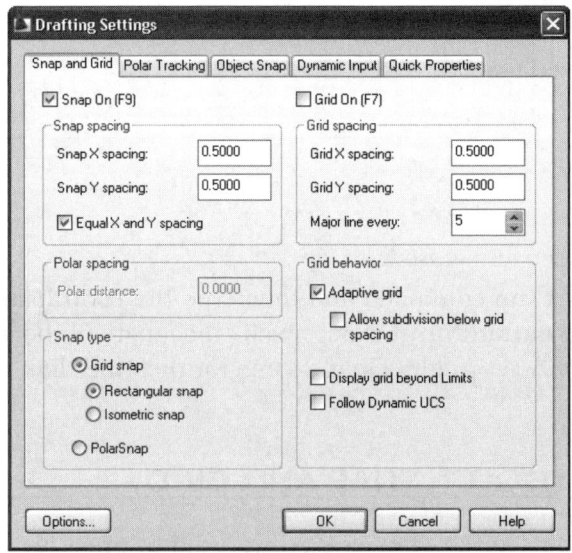

- By default, **Snap X spacing** and **Snap Y spacing** are equal; **Grid X spacing** and **Grid Y spacing** are also equal. If you want to keep this setting make sure that the **Equal X and Y spacing** box is checked.
- By default if you are working with 2D you will see only Grid dots. But if you are working with 3D you will see Grid lines, hence, set the **Major line** spacing.

- Also, all the default settings of **Grid behavior** are meant for 3D drawings.
- Make sure that the **Snap type** is **Grid Snap** (we will discuss **Polar Snap** shortly). If you are creating a 2D drawing, then select **Rectangular Snap**. If you are creating a 3D drawing select **Isometric Snap**.
- If you want the Grid to follow Snap, set the two Grid values to zero.

- You can use function keys to turn on both Snap and Grid:
  - F9 = Snap on/off
  - F7 = Grid on/off

SNAP AND GRID

Exercise 3

1. Start AutoCAD 2009.
2. Open the **Exercise_03.dwg** file.
26. Using **Dynamic Input, Snap**, and **Grid** draw the following lines without typing any coordinates with the keyboard (don't draw the dimensions):

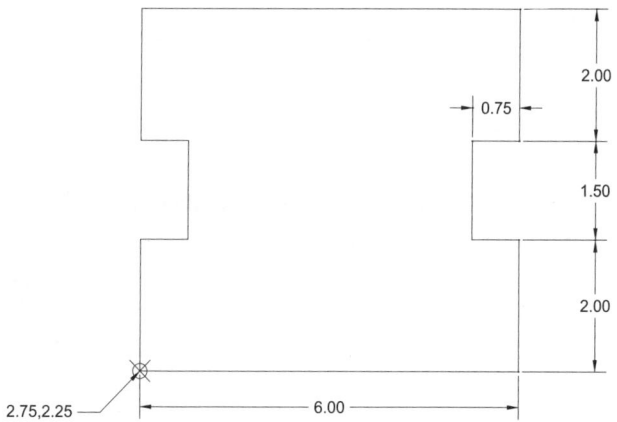

27. Save the file and close it.

- Change the Snap X spacing to 0.25 first, and set the Grid values to 0. Switch both Snap and Grid on, and draw the lines as required.

PRECISION METHOD 2: DIRECT DISTANCE ENTRY AND ORTHO

- Because we know that lines in AutoCAD are *vectors*, which means we need to specify a length and an angle to successfully draw them, we appreciate this method.

- **Ortho** is a tool that will force the cursor to always give us orthogonal angles (i.e., 0, 90, 180, and 270).
- **Direct Distance Entry** is also a very handy tool in drafting; if the mouse is already directed toward an angle, just type in the distance and press [Enter].
- Combining the two tools will allow us to draw lines with precise lengths and angles.
- Do the following:

  - On the Status Bar, click the **ORTHO** button.
  - Start the **Line** command.
  - Specify the first point.
  - Move the mouse to the right, up, left, and down, and notice how it gives you only orthogonal angles.
  - Use the desired angle, type in the distance, and press [Enter].
  - Continue with other segments using the same method.
- You can also use **Direct Distance Entry** with **Dynamic Input**.

DIRECT DISTANCE ENTRY AND ORTHO

Exercise 4

1. Start AutoCAD 2009.
2. Open the **Exercise_04.dwg** file.
3. Using **ORTHO** and **Direct Distance Entry** draw the shape below (without dimensions):

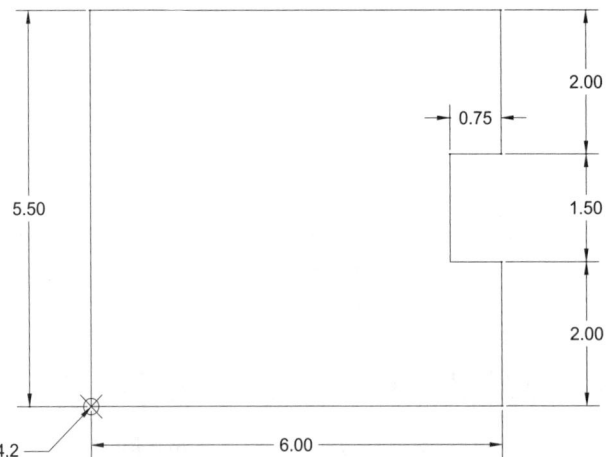

4. Save the file and close it.

ARC COMMAND

- The **Arc** command is used to draw circular arcs (the arc part of a circle).
- Take a look at the following:

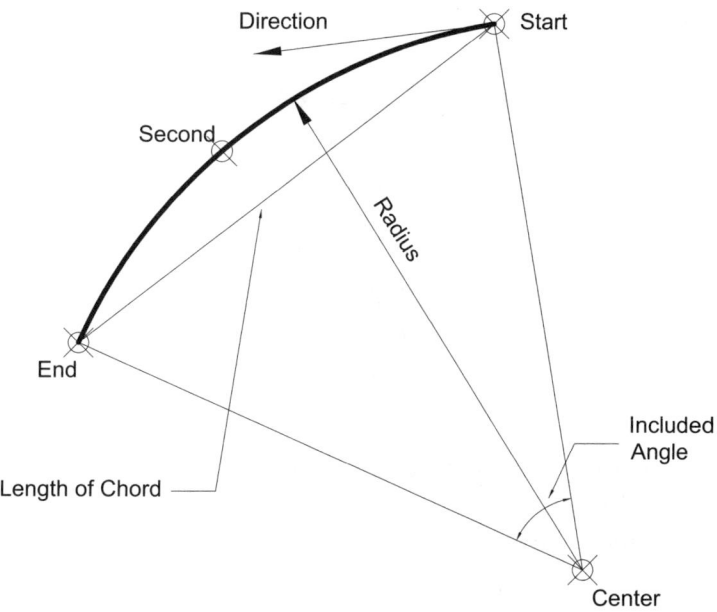

- The information that AutoCAD recognizes about an arc includes:
  - Start point
  - Second point (not necessarily the midpoint)
  - Endpoint
  - Center point
  - Radius
  - Length of Chord
  - Included Angle (angle between Start-Center-End)
  - Direction (the tangent passes through the Start point)
- AutoCAD needs only three pieces of information to draw an arc, but not just any three.
- AutoCAD will start asking you to make your first input, choosing between Start point or Center point, and based on that choice it will ask you to specify the second piece of information, and so on.
- Make sure you are at the **Home** tab on the **Ribbon**, and using the **Draw** panel click the **Arc** button (the small arrow at the right). You will see the following:

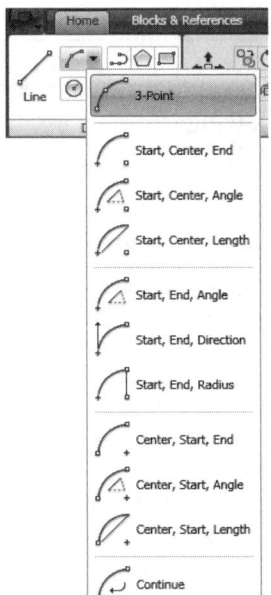

- Before you start, specify the desired method from the menu, and AutoCAD will take it from there.

 ■ Always think counter-clock-wise when specifying points.

DRAWING ARCS

 Exercise 5

1. Start AutoCAD 2009.

2. Open the **Exericise_05.dwg** file. You will see the following shape:

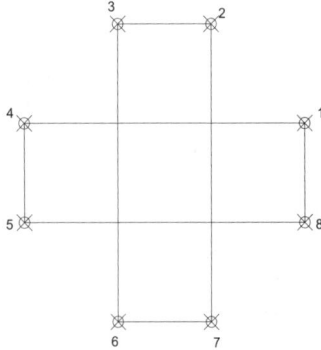

3. Turn on **Snap** and **Grid**.

4. Draw the first arc between points (1) & (2) using Start/End/Angle, where point (1) is the start point, and the angle = -90.

5. Draw the second arc between points (3) & (4) using Start/End/Direction, where point (3) is the start point, and the Direction = 270.

6. Draw the third arc between points (5) & (6) using Start/Center/End, where point (6) is the start point, and the point at the lower left is the center point (you will specify it easily using Snap and Grid).

7. Draw the fourth arc between points (7) & (8) using Start/Center/Length, where point (8) is the start point, and the point at the lower right is the center point, and the length of the chord is the distance between (8) & (7).

8. The shape should look like this:

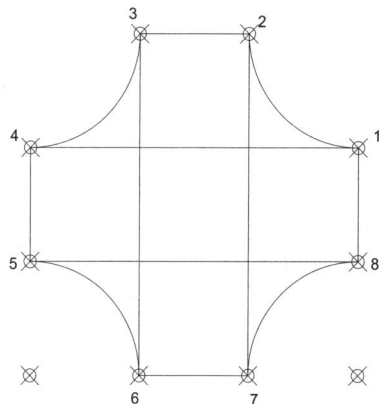

9. Save the file and close it.

CIRCLE COMMAND

- The **Circle** command in AutoCAD is used to draw a circle.
- There are six different methods available to draw a circle in AutoCAD.
- To use the first two methods you have to know the Center of the circle. They are:

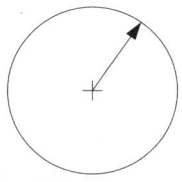
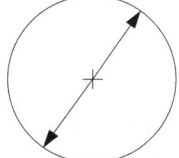

Center/Radius   Center/Diameter

- To use the third method you have to know any three points on the parameter of the circle:

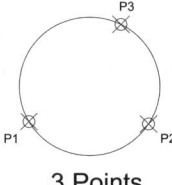

3 Points

- To use the fourth method, specify two points on the parameter of the circle, the distance between them equal to the diameter:

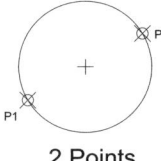

2 Points

- To use the fifth method, you should have two objects already drawn, so we can consider them as tangents, then specify a radius:

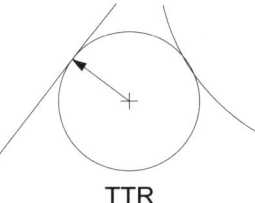

TTR

- To use the sixth method, you should specify three tangents by selecting three objects:

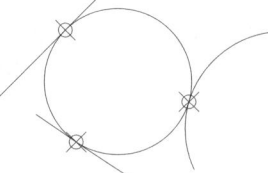

Tan, Tan, Tan

- Make sure you are at the **Home** tab on the **Ribbon**, and using the **Draw** panel click the **Circle** button (the small arrow at the right). You will see the following:

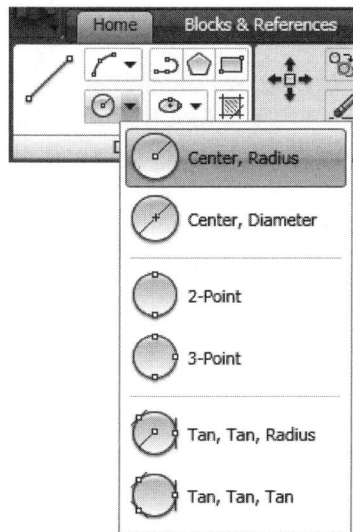

- Before you start, specify the desired method from the menu, and AutoCAD will take it from there.

DRAWING CIRCLES

 Exercise 6

1. Start AutoCAD 2009.
2. Open the **Exericise_06.dwg** file.
3. Make sure that **SNAP** and **GRID** are on.
4. Draw the five circles, which should look like the following:

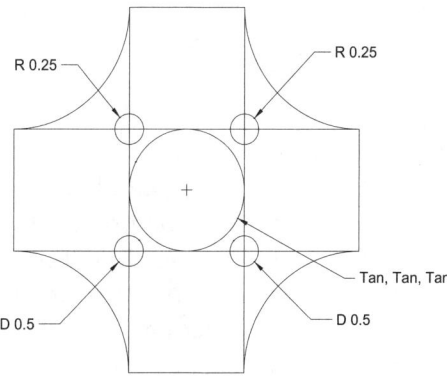

5. Save the file and close it.

PRECISION METHOD 3: OBJECT SNAP (OSNAP)

- AutoCAD keeps a full record of each object in each drawing.
- **Object Snap** (**OSNAP**) is a tool that helps to utilize this record when you need to specify points on objects already drawn precisely without knowing the points.
- For example, assume we have the following shape:

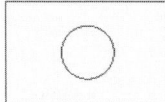

- We have no information about any object in the above shape.
- We were asked to draw a precise line from the mid of the right line to the right quadrant of the circle.
- The command to draw is **Line**. AutoCAD asked us to specify the first point, and we typed **mid** and pressed [Enter] (or the spacebar), then directly went to the upper line and a yellow triangle appeared. We clicked:

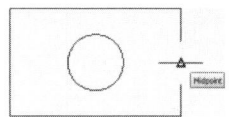

- AutoCAD then asked us to specify the next point. We typed **qua** and pressed [Enter] (or spacebar), then directly went to the right part of the circle and a yellow polygon appeared. We clicked it, and then pressed [Enter] to end the command:

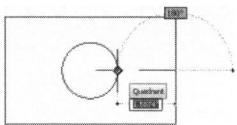

- Mission accomplished.
- Some Object Snaps are used to:

End	• Catch the Endpoint of an object.
Mid	• Catch the Midpoint of an object.
Intersection	• Catch the Intersection of two objects.
Center	• Catch the Center of an arc, or a circle.
Quadrant	• Catch the Quadrant of an arc, or a circle.
Tangent	• Catch the Tangent of an arc, or a circle.
Perpendicular	• Catch the Perpendicular point on an object.
Nearest	• Catch a point on an object Nearest to your click point.

• We will discuss more Object Snaps as we learn additional commands.
- There are three ways to use the Object Snaps whenever you are asked to specify a point. These include:

Typing

- Type the first three letters of the desired **OSNAP**, such as end, mid, cen, qua, int, per, tan, nea. This is a very old method, but often used among seasoned users of AutoCAD.

Shift+Right-click

- Hold the [Shift] key and right-click. The following menu will appear. Select the desired **OSNAP**.

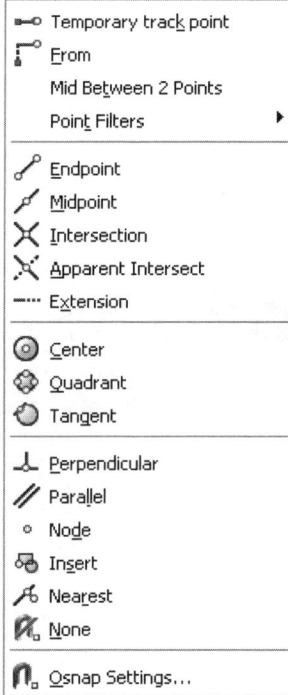

Running OSNAP

- This method is the most practical method of all of the above.
- You will select an **OSNAP** and it will run all the time. So the next time you are asked to specify an endpoint, for instance, simply go to the desired point, and it will be immediately acquired.
- There are two ways to activate **OSNAP**:

- On the Status Bar, right-click the **OSNAP** button. The following menu will appear:

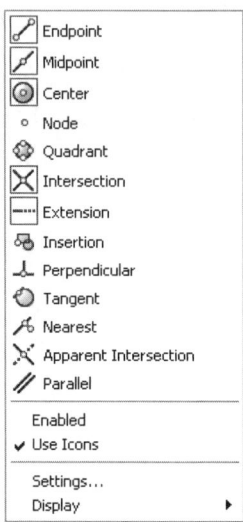

- In the above example, End, Mid, Center, Intersection, and Extension, are all running (there is a frame around each icon).
- Also, you can select **Settings**, and the following dialog box will appear:

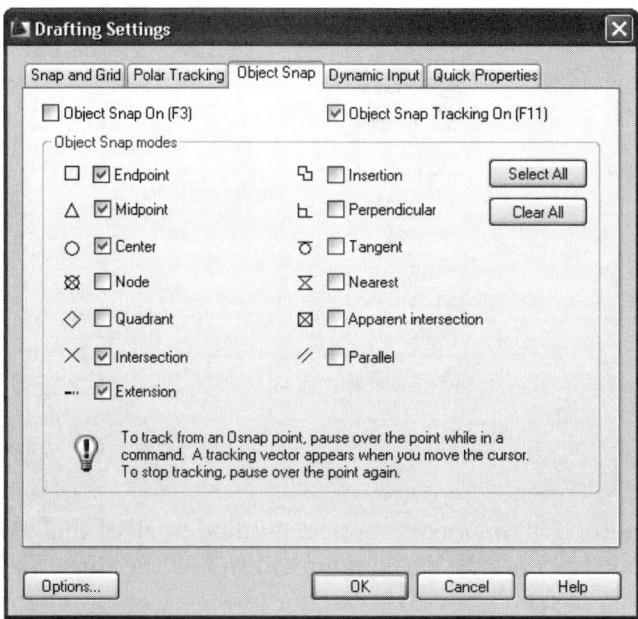

- Switch on the desired **OSNAP** and click **OK**.

OBJECT SNAP TRACKING (OTRACK)

- If you have a rectangle, and you want to draw a circle where its center will coincide with the center of the rectangle exactly, **OTRACK** will help you do this without drawing any new objects to facilitate specifying the exact points.
- **OTRACK** uses **OSNAPs** of existing objects to steal the coordinates of the new point.
- On the Status Bar, click the **OTRACK** button.
- Make sure that **OSNAP** is also on, as **OTRACK** alone wouldn't do anything.

Example of two-points OTRACK

- Let's look at an example where we will use two points to specify one point.
- Assume we have the following rectangle:

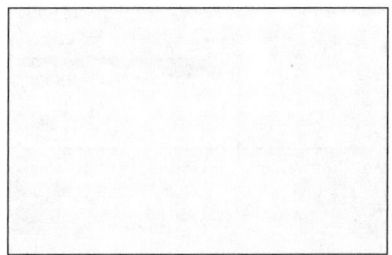

- Make sure that **OSNAP** and **OTRACK** are both turned on. Make sure that Midpoint in **OSNAP** is also turned on. Start the **Circle** command, which will ask you to specify the center point. Go to the upper (or lower) horizontal line and move to the midpoint and stay for a couple of seconds, then move up or down and you will see an infinite line extending both ways (don't click), just like the following:

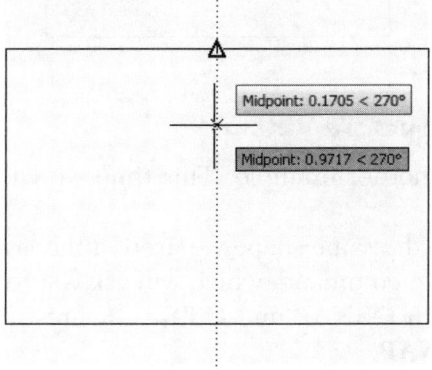

- Go to the right (or left) vertical line and move to the midpoint and stay for a couple of seconds, then move right or left and you will see an infinite line extending both ways, just like the following:

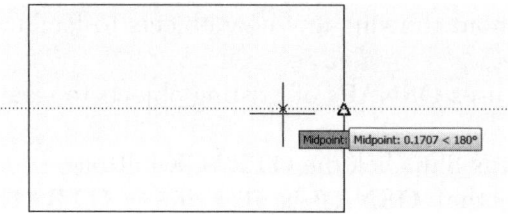

- Now go to where you think the two infinite lines should intersect:

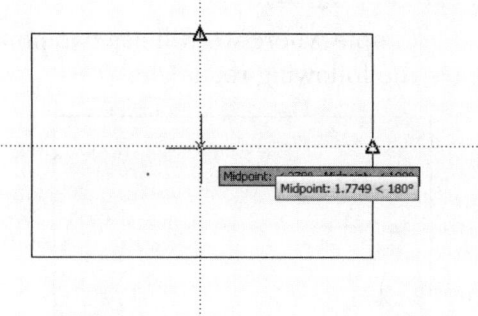

- Once you see the two infinite lines, click. At this moment you specified the center point of the circle, you can then type in the radius of the circle:

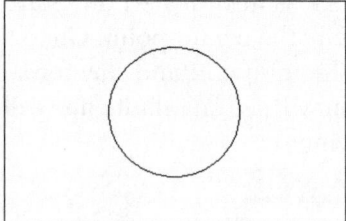

Example of one-point OTRACK

- Let's look at another example. This time we will use one point to specify one point:
- Continue with the same shape we used in the last example.
- Start the **Circle** command, which will ask you to specify the center point.
- Make sure both **OSNAP** and **OTRACK** are turned on, and also turn on Center in **OSNAP**.

■ Go to the center point of the existing circle, and stay for a couple of seconds, then move to the right. An infinite line will appear:

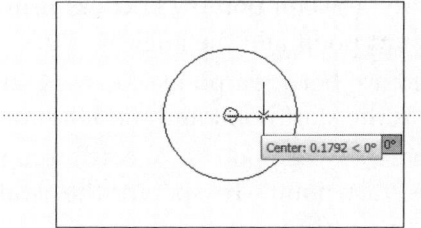

■ Type 5 (or any distance) and press [Enter]. The center of the new circle will be specified, then type in the radius. This is what you will get:

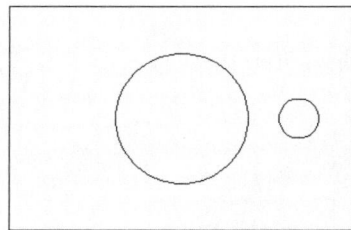

 ■ If you stayed over a point for a couple of seconds to produce the infinite line, then you discovered that this isn't the desired point. Simply go to the same point again, and stay over it again for a couple of seconds and it will be disabled.

DRAWING USING OSNAP & OTRACK

Exercise 7
1. Start AutoCAD 2009.
2. Open the **Exercise_07.dwg** file.

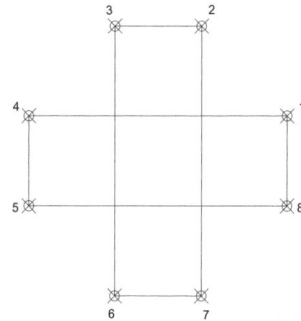

3. Make sure that Snap & Grid are both off.

4. Using **OSNAP** switch on Endpoint.

5. Draw the first arc between points (1) & (2) using Start/End/Angle, where point (1) is the start point and the angle = -90.

6. Draw the second arc between points (3) & (4) using Start/End/Direction, where point (3) is the start point and the Direction = 270.

7. Draw the third arc between points (5) & (6) using Start/Center/End, where point (6) is the start point. To specify the center point, use **OTRACK** between points (5) & (6).

8. Draw the fourth arc between points (7) & (8) using Start/Center/Length, where point (8) is the start point. To specify the center point, use **OTRACK** between points (7) & (8), and the length of the chord is the distance between (8) & (7).

9. The shape should look like this:

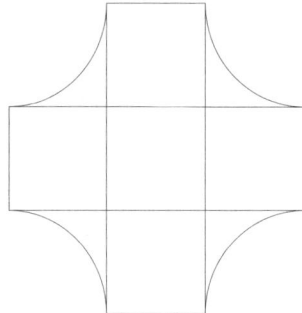

10. Using **OSNAP**, turn Intersection on, then specify five circles using Intersection to specify the center points for the small circles.

11. By default AutoCAD will activate Tangent when you use the Tan, Tan, Tan method.

12. The shape will end up like this:

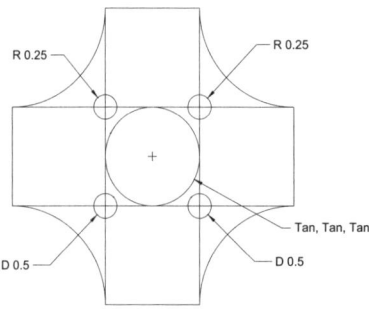

13. Save the file and close it.

DRAWING USING OSNAP AND OTRACK

Exercise 8
1. Start AutoCAD 2009.
2. Open the **Exercise_08.dwg** file.
3. Turn **OSNAP** on and set the following: Endpoint, Midpoint, and Center.
4. Turn on **OTRACK**.
5. Draw the four circles while specifying the center using **OSNAP** and **OTRACK**.

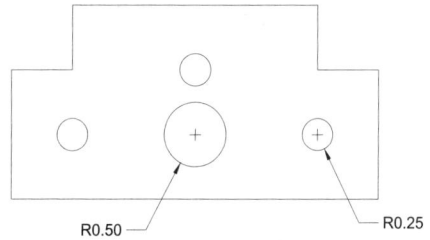

6. Save the file and close it.

PLINE COMMAND

- Pline means Polyline and Poly means many. So, if you exchange many with poly, the new name would be many lines.
- To begin, let's compare the Line command and the Polyline command.

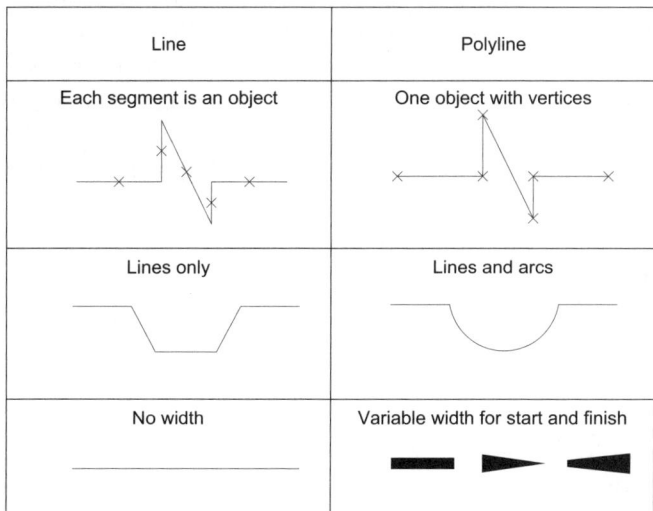

Line	Polyline
Each segment is an object	One object with vertices
Lines only	Lines and arcs
No width	Variable width for start and finish

- As you can see from the comparison there are mainly three differences between the two commands.
- Make sure you are at the **Home** tab on the **Ribbon** and using the **Draw** panel, click the **Polyline** button. The following prompt will appear:

```
Specify start point:
Current line-width is 0.9000
Specify next point or [Arc/Halfwidth/Length/Undo/ Width]:
```

- After you specify the first point, the **Polyline** command will give you the current Polyline width (in our example it is 0.90), then it will ask you to specify the next point. You can use all the methods we learned in the Line command section.
- If you don't want to specify the second point, you can choose from the following options:

Arc

- By default, the **Polyline** command will draw lines.
- You can change the mode to draw arcs by selecting this option. The following prompt will appear:

```
Specify endpoint of arc or
[Angle/Center/Close/Direction/Halfwidth/Line/Radius/Second
pt/Undo/Width]:
```

- We learned in the **Arc** command section that AutoCAD needs three pieces of information to draw an arc.
- AutoCAD already knows the start point of the arc, which is the start point of the polyline, or, the endpoint of the last line segment.
- AutoCAD will make a certain assumption and the user has the right to accept it or reject it. This assumption is the direction of the arc, which will be the same angle as the last line segment.
- If you accepted this assumption then AutoCAD will ask you to specify the endpoint of the arc.
- If you rejected this assumption, then specify the second piece of information from the following:
  - Angle of Arc, then Center or Radius.
  - Center, then Angle or Length.
  - Direction, then End.
  - Radius, then End or Angle.
  - Second, then End.

Halfwidth

- The first method is to specify the width of the Polyline.
- Specify the halfwidth of the polyline from the Center to one of its edges, something like the following:

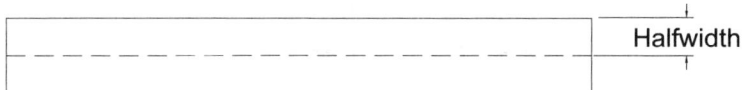

- When you select this option, AutoCAD will give you the following prompt:

```
Specify starting half-width <1.0000>:
Specify ending half-width <1.0000>:
```

■ In our above example, the halfwidth was 1.0 for both the start and end points.

Length

- In the **Polyline** command, if you draw an arc, then switch to the **Line** command to draw a line segment, and if you want the line to be tangent to the arc, then select this option.
- This option will assume the angle to be the same as the last segment, hence, you will only be asked for the length. The following prompt will appear:

```
Specify length of line:
```

Width

- Width is the same as halfwidth, but instead, you have to input the full width. See the following:

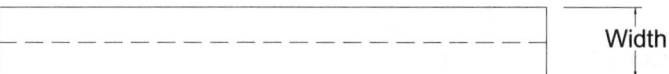

  ■ **Undo** and **Close** are the same options as in the **Line** command.
- If you choose to close in the Arc option, it will close the shape by an arc.

DRAWING POLYLINES

 Exercise 9
1. Start AutoCAD 2009.
2. Open the **Exercise_09.dwg** file.

3. Using **ORTHO** and **Direct Distance Entry**, draw the following shape (without dimensions) using the **Pline** command with width = 0.1.

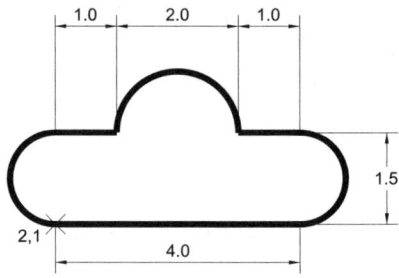

4. Save the file and close it.

■ Take note of the following tips:
    •   In order to draw the large arc, use angle = 180.
    •   Before you draw the last **arc**, change the mode to Arc and select **Close**.

POLAR TRACKING

■ We learned that we can force the cursor to give us four orthogonal angles (0, 90, 180, 270) using **ORTHO**.
■ If we want other angles such as 30 and its multiples, or 60 and its multiples, **ORTHO** wouldn't help us.
■ For this purpose the AutoCAD people invented another powerful tool called **Polar Tracking**.
■ Polar Tracking allows you to have rays starting from your current point pointing towards angles such as 30, 60, 90, 120, and so on. You can use **Direct Distance Entry**, just like we did with **ORTHO**.
■ On the Status Bar, click the **Polar Tracking** button.
■ In order to select the desired angle, right-click on the button, and you will see the following menu:

```
     90
  ✔  45
     30
     22.5
     18
     15
     10
     5
  ─────────────
     Enabled
  ✔  Use Icons
  ─────────────
     Settings...
     Display      ▶
```

- Select the desired angle and you will get it along with its multiples.
- If you want more control, right-click on the button and select **Settings**. The following dialog box will appear:

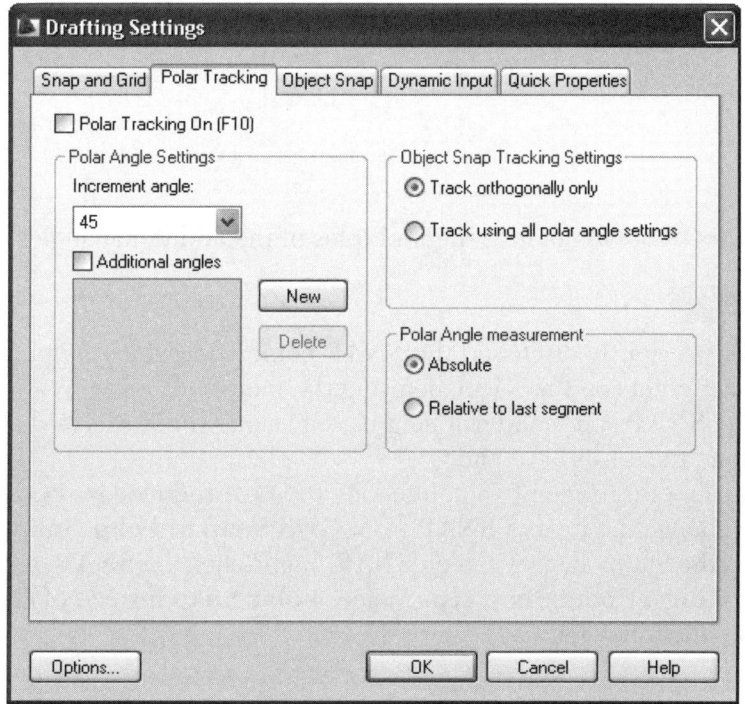

Increment Angle

- Under **Polar Angle Settings**, select the **Increment angle** pop-up list where you will find pre-defined angles. Select the desired angle.
- If the desired angle is not in the list, simply type your own angle.
- Based on the above example, the user will have rays in angles 0, 30, 60, 90, 120, …, etc.

Additional Angles

- Sometimes in the design process you will need odd angles, which the increment angle can't give you, such as 95 or 115. The option **Additional angles** will help you set these odd angles.
- Using the same dialog box, check the **Additional angles** box.
- Click the **New** button and type in the angle.
- To delete an existing additional angle, select it, and click the **Delete** button.

- You will have something similar to the following:

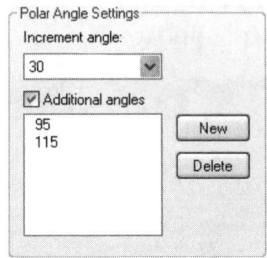

 ■ AutoCAD will not give the multiples of the additional angles.

Polar Snap

- We previously discussed the **SNAP** command, which helped us to specify exact points on the XY plane using the mouse.
- The **SNAP** command can help us only along the X axis (+ve, and –ve), and along the Y axis (+ve and –ve).
- If you want to snap to a point along the ray produced by **POLAR**, you have to change the type of **SNAP** from **Grid Snap** to **Polar Snap**.
- On the Status Bar, switch on **SNAP**. Right-click the **SNAP** button and select **Settings**. Under **Snap type**, select **Polar Snap** instead of **Grid snap**, just like the following:

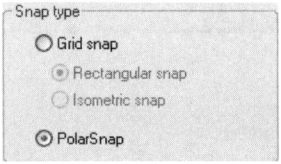

- Now set the **Polar spacing** value, just like the following:

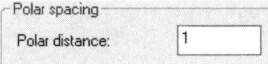

Example

- We want to draw the following shape:

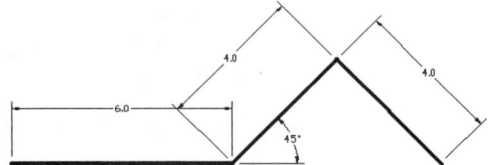

- Let's assume we set the Increment angle to 45, and we changed the type of **SNAP** to Polar Snap with Snap distance = 1.0. To draft using Polar Tracking use the following steps: Start the **Line** command, then specify a starting point.Move to the right until you see a ray coming out.Read the distance and the angle. When you reach your distance click to specify a point, just like the following:

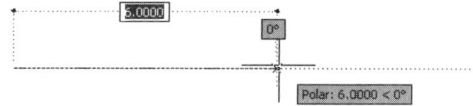

- Move the cursor toward the angle 45 until you see the ray. Now move the mouse to the desired distance and click:

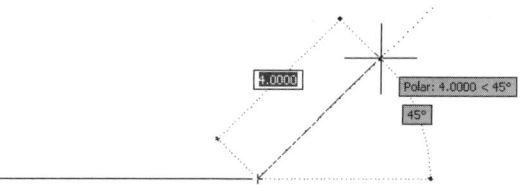

- Move the cursor toward the angle 315 until you see the ray. Now move the mouse to the desired distance and click:

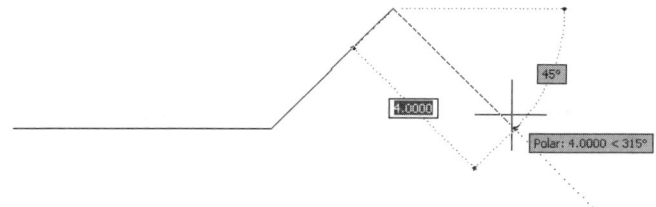

DRAWING USING POLAR TRACKING

Exercise 10

1. Start AutoCAD 2009.
2. Open the **Exercise_10.dwg** file.
3. Switch both **POLAR** and **SNAP** on, and set the following:
   a. Increment angle = 30
   b. Additional angles = 135
   c. Polar distance = 0.5

4. Draw the following shape (without dimensions) starting from 3,2:

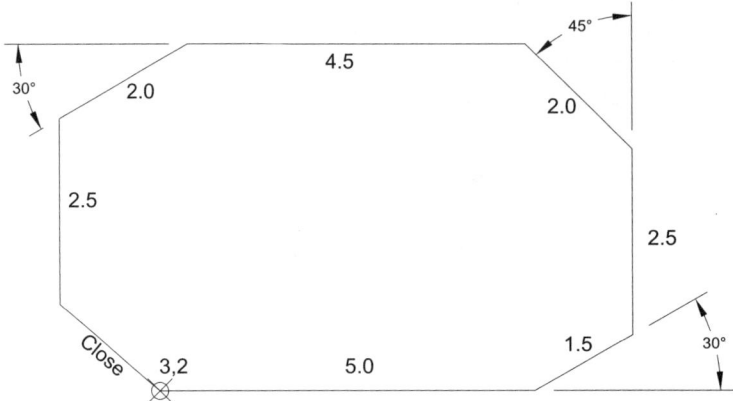

5. Save the file and close it.

ERASE COMMAND

■   The **Erase** command is used to delete any selected object.
■   Make sure you are at the **Home** tab on the **Ribbon**, and using the **Modify** panel, click the **Erase** button. The following prompt will appear:

`Select objects:`

■   Once this prompt appears the cursor will change to a pick box:

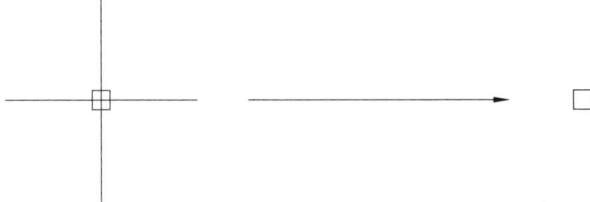

■   Basically you can do three things with the pick box:
    •   Touch an object and click to select it.
    •   Go to an empty place, click and go to the right; this will get you a **Window**.
    •   Go to an empty place, click and go to the left; this will get you a **Crossing**.

- A window is a rectangle specified by two opposite corners. The first corner will be when you click on the empty place. Then you will release your hand, go to a suitable place, and click the second corner.

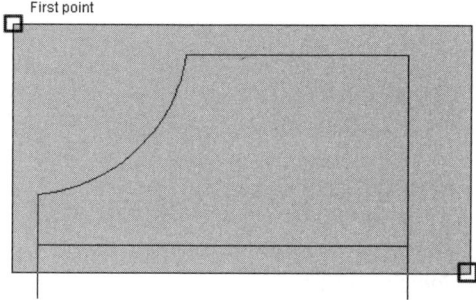

- Whatever is fully inside the rectangle will be selected. If any part (even a small part) is outside the rectangle it will not be selected. See the following:

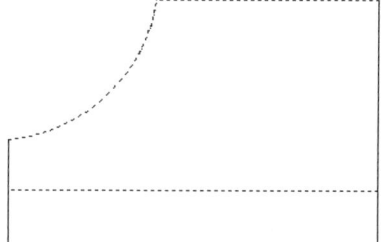

- A crossing is just like a window, except that whatever is inside it will be selected, and whatever it touches as well.

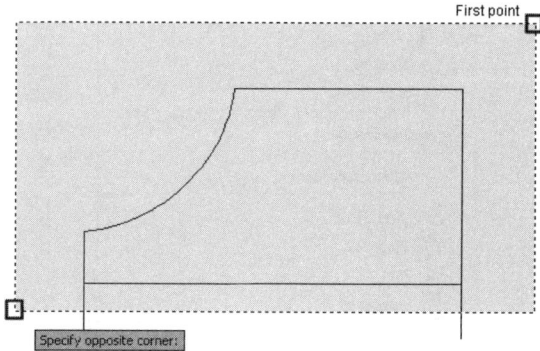

- The result will be:

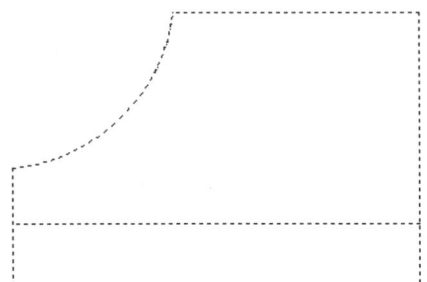

NOTE

- These three methods can be used with almost all the modifying commands, not just the **Erase** command.
- The Select Objects prompt is repetitive. You need to always finish by pressing [Enter], or by right-clicking and using the menu.
- Other ways to erase objects include:
- Without issuing any command, click on the object(s) desired, then press the [Del] key.
- Without issuing any command, click on the object(s) desired, then right-click, and the following shortcut menu will appear. Select **Erase**.

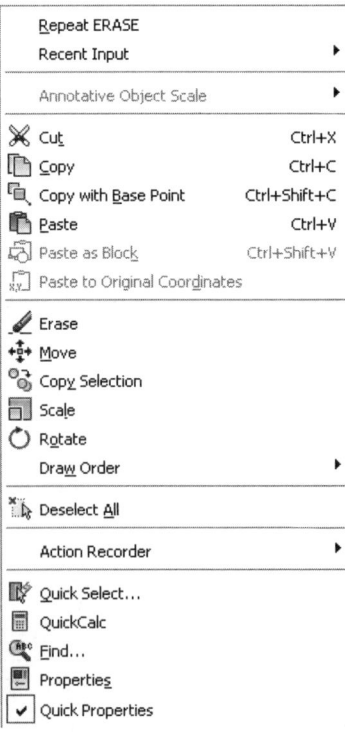

OOPS, UNDO, AND REDO COMMANDS

- This group of commands can help you correct your mistakes.
- They can be used in the current session only (i.e., once you close the file, they will be useless).

Oops

- **Oops** is used to retain the last group of erased objects, but works only with the **Erase** command.
- This command is only available in the Command Window.
- You have to type the full command in the Command Window: **Oops**.
- No prompt will be displayed, except you will see the last group of erased objects back in the drawing.

Undo

- **Undo** is used to undo the last command.
- You can reach this command using one of the following methods:

  - From the Quick Access toolbar, click the **Undo** button.
  - Type u at the Command Window (don't type **undo**, because it has a different meaning).
  - Press Ctrl + Z.
- The last command will be undone.
- You can undo as many commands as you want in the current session.

Redo

- This command is used to undo the undo.
- You can use this command using one of the following methods:
  - From the Quick Access toolbar, click the **Redo** button.
  - Type **redo** at the Command Window.
  - Or press **Ctrl + Y**.
- The last undone command will be redone.
- You can redo as many commands as you want in the current session.

REDRAW & REGEN COMMANDS

- There are many times you will need to refresh the screen for one reason or another.
- Or you will need AutoCAD to regenerate the whole drawing to show the arcs and circles as smooth curves.
- Neither command has a toolbar button.

Redraw

- From the Menu Browser select **View/Redraw**, or type r at the Command Window.
- The screen will be refreshed.

Regen

- From the Menu Browser select **View/Regen**, or type re at the Command Window.
- See the following example.
- This is how a drawing looks before the **Regen** command:

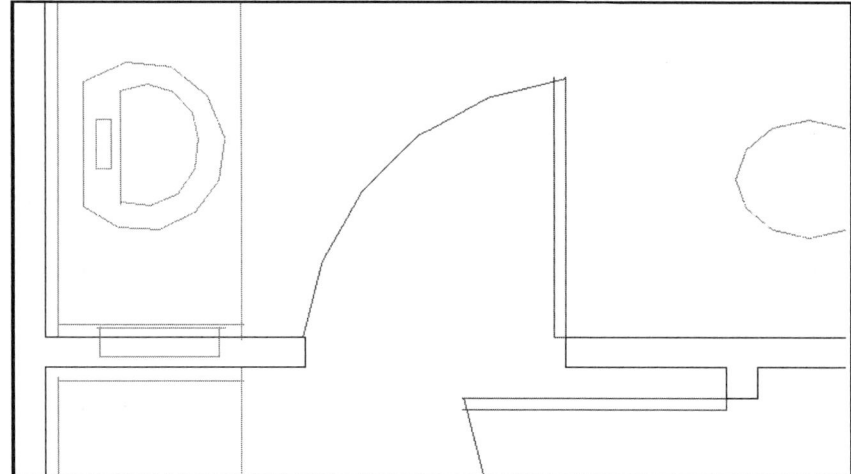

- And this is how it looks after the **Regen** command:

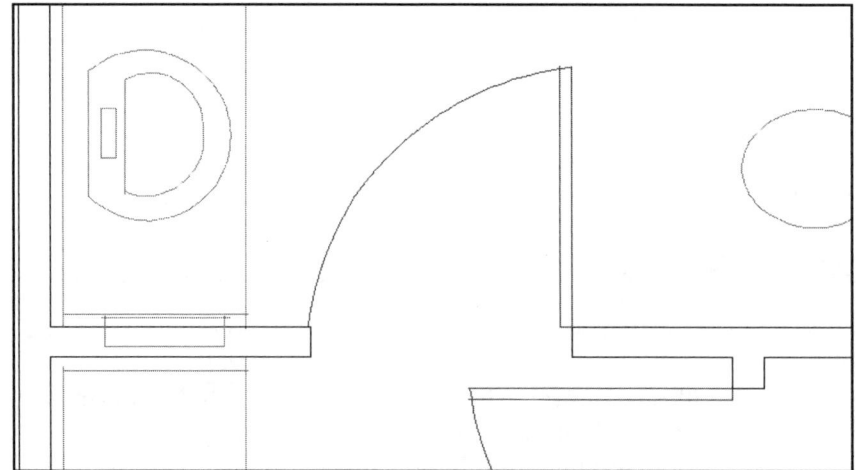

ERASE, OOPS, UNDO, AND REDO

 Exercise 11

1. Start AutoCAD 2009.
2. Open the **Exercise_11.dwg** file.
3. Using the **Erase** command with Window or Crossing and perform the following steps:
   a. Using Window, try to erase all the rectangles in the middle. Press [Enter], then use the **Oops** command to retain the objects.
   b. Using Crossing try to erase the circles at the right of the shape, press [Enter], and then **Undo**. Try **Redo** also to see the effect.
   c. Using the pick box try to erase the lines of the frame, press [Enter], and then use **Undo** to undo the erasing.
4. Close the file without saving.

CHAPTER REVIEW

1. Which of the following statements are true:
   a. Snap will help us control the mouse whereas **Grid** is complementary to **Snap**.
   b. **ORTHO** and **Direct Distance Entry** will help us draw exact orthogonal lines.
   c. **Direct Distance Entry** can be used with **DYN**, **ORTHO**, and **POLAR**.
   d. All of the above.
2. The **Arc** command in AutoCAD will draw a _____ arc.
3. Using **OTRACK**, you can:
   a. Specify a point using two existing points.
   b. Specify the radius of an arc.
   c. Specify the end of an existing line.
   d. None of the above.
4. **OTRACK** doesn't need **OSNAP** to work:
   a. True.
   b. False.
5. In Polar, if the increment angle didn't fulfill all your needs:
   a. **ORTHO** will help.
   b. Set the additional angles.

    c. The command **POLARNEWANGLES** will help.

    d. None of the above.

6. There are _____ ways to draw a circle in AutoCAD.

CHAPTER REVIEW ANSWERS

1. d
2. Circular
3. a
4. b
5. b
6. 6 (six)

Chapter 3

SETTING UP YOUR DRAWINGS

In This Chapter
◊ Things you need to consider before setting up your drawings
◊ Setting up drawing units
◊ Setting up limits
◊ Creating and controlling layers
◊ Quick Properties, Properties, and Match Properties

THINGS YOU NEED TO CONSIDER BEFORE SETTING UP YOUR DRAWING

- There are lots of things you need to think about while setting up your drawing file. Of course we can't cover them all in this chapter, but we will mention the most important things.

Drawing Units
- As a first step define the drawing distance and angle units, along with their precision.

Drawing Limits
- Try to figure out what size (area) workspace will be sufficient to accommodate your drawing.

Layers
- Layers are an effective way to organize your drawings so we will learn what they are, how to create them, and how to control them.
- In Appendix A we will discuss how to create templates in AutoCAD, which are more applicable for establishments than for individuals.

STEP 1: DRAWING UNITS

- From the Menu Browser select **Format/Units**. The following dialog box will appear:

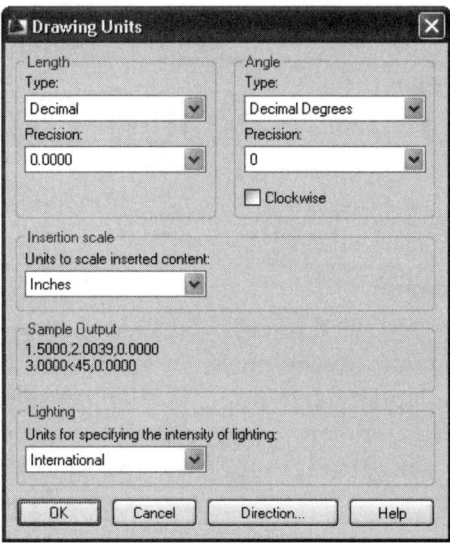

- Under **Length**, set up the desired **Type**. You will have five choices:
    - Architectural (example: 1'-5 3/16")
    - Decimal (example: 20.4708)
    - Engineering (example: 1'-4.9877")
    - Fractional (example: 17 1/16)
    - Scientific (example: 1.6531E+01)
- Under **Angle**, set up the desired **Type**. Again, you will have five choices:
    - Decimal Degrees (example: 45.5)
    - Deg/Min/Sec (example: 45d30'30")
    - Grads (example: 50.6g)
    - Radians (example: 0.8r)
    - Surveyor's Units (example: N 45d30'30" E)
- For the desired Length and Angle select the **Precision**, for example:
- Architectural precision can be 0'-0 1/16," 0'-0 1/32," etc.
- Decimal precision can be 0.00, 0.000, etc.
- Deg/Min/Sec precision can be 0d00'00," 0d00'00.0," etc.
- By default AutoCAD deals with the positive angles CounterClockWise. If you want it the other way around, check the **Clockwise** box.
- Under **Insertion scale**, specify **Units to scale inserted content**, which is your drawing's scale against the scale of any object (a block, for instance) coming to your drawing, which will help AutoCAD to make the suitable conversion.

- Click the **Direction** button to see the following dialog box:

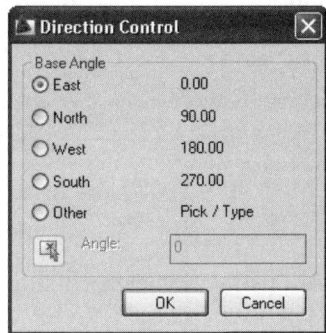

- As we discussed in Chapter 1, AutoCAD always starts the zero angle measuring from the East. If you want to change it, select the desired angle to be considered as the new zero.

STEP 2: DRAWING LIMITS

- In Chapter 1, we learned that AutoCAD offers us an unlimited drawing sheet, which extends in all directions. But we will not use it all; instead we will specify an area, which will be our limits.
- Drawing limits can be specified using two points: lower left corner and upper right corner.
- Since we will draw in Model Space and print from Paper Space, we don't need to think about drawing scale at this point.
- To know the needed limits exactly, make sure you know the following information:
- What is the longest dimension in your sketch in both X and Y?
- What AutoCAD unit have you selected (e.g., m, cm, mm, inch, foot, etc.)?
- Accordingly you will know the limit of your drawing.

Example

- Assume we have the following case:
  - We want to draw an architectural plan, which extends in X for 50 m and in Y for 30 m.
  - Also, assume that AutoCAD unit = 1 m.
- Since an AutoCAD unit = 1 m, 50 m is equal to 50 AutoCAD units. The same thing applies for the 30 m.
- Note that 0,0 is always the favorite lower left corner, so there is no need to change it. The upper right corner will be 50,30.

- From the Menu Browser, select **Format/Drawing Limits**, or type **limits** in the Command Window. The following prompt will appear:

```
Specify lower left corner or [ON/OFF] <0,0>: (press [Enter]
to accept the default value)
Specify upper right corner <12,9>: (type in the coordinate
of the upper right corner)
```

ON/OFF

- To keep yourself from using any area outside this limit, turn the limits on.

UNITS & DRAWING LIMITS

 Exercise 12

1. Start AutoCAD 2009.
2. Open the **Exercise_12.dwg** file.
3. Note the current units (look at the lower left corner of the screen and you will see the coordinates of the drawing).
4. From the Menu Browser select **Format/Units**. Change the units to:
   - Length Type = Architectural
   - Length Precession = 0'-0 1/32"
   - Angle Type = Deg/Min/Sec
   - Angle Precision = 0d00'00"
5. Check the coordinates again and see how the numbers changed to the new units.
6. From the Menu Browser select **Format/Drawing Limits** and do the following:
   - Accept the default point for the lower left corner.
   - For the upper right corner type 30',20'.
   - Switch Grid on, and double-click the mouse wheel.
7. You will see your current settings.
8. Save and close the file.

STEP 3: LAYERS

What are layers?

- Let's assume that we have a huge number of transparent papers, along with 256 colored pens.

- Taking care that we don't draw except on the paper at the top, we take the red pen and we draw the border of the drawing.
- Then we move the second paper to the top, and we draw an architectural wall plan using the yellow pen.
- Next, we move the third paper to the top and we draw the doors using the green pen. Doing the same procedure we draw windows, furniture, electrical outlets, hatching, text, dimensions, etc.
- Then we took all the papers, and look at them at the same time. What do we see? A full architectural plan!
- In AutoCAD we call each paper a layer.
- Each layer should have a name, color, linetype, lineweight, and other information.
- There will be a layer, which will be in all of AutoCAD's drawings. This layer is 0 (zero). You can't delete it or rename it.
- In order to draw on a layer, make it **current** first. There will be only one current layer.
- The objects drawn on a layer will automatically inherit the properties (color, linetype, lineweight, etc.) of the current layer. Hence, a line in a red layer, with a dashdot linetype and 0.3 lineweight will have the exact same properties.
- The setting of the object's color is by default = BYLAYER.
- The setting of the object's linetype is by default = BYLAYER.
- The setting of the object's lineweight is by default = BYLAYER.

- It is highly recommended that you keep these settings intact, as changing them may lead to creating objects with non-standard properties.

- On the **Ribbon** make sure you are at the **Home** tab, and using the **Layers** panel click the **Layer Properties** button. The following dialog box will appear:

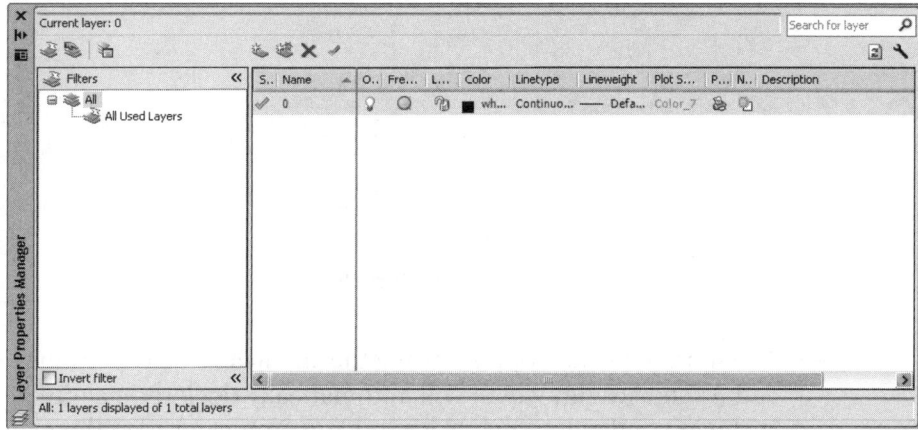

- The Layer Properties is not a normal dialog box, it is a palette, which can be docked, resized, and hidden:
- Drag the title to the right, left, top, or bottom of the screen, and you will see the Layer Properties palette change its size and dock at the place you select.
- You can hide the entire palette and show only the title bar by clicking the Auto-hide button as shown below. Whenever you want to see the palette again, simply go back to the title and the palette will appear.

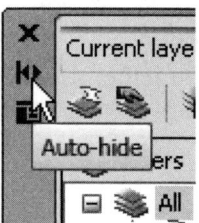

- You can show the Properties menu to control the palette. Click the Properties button as shown below:

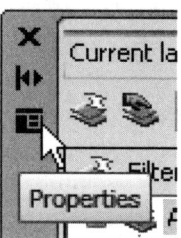

- The following menu will appear:

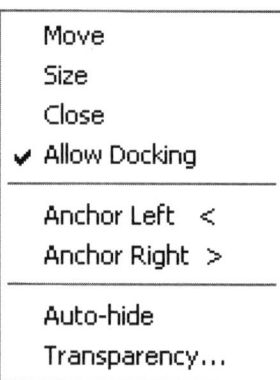

- The most important options using this menu are the two options Anchor Left and Anchor Right, which will automatically dock the palette at the right or at the left and will switch Auto-hide on. You can resize the palette to larger or smaller sizes. Go to the lower right corner of the palette and the cursor will change to the following:

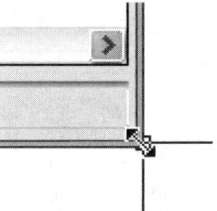

- Click and drag to the right to make it bigger, and to the left to make it smaller.

Create a New Layer

- To create a new layer in the drawing, you have to prepare all the necessary information of the new layer.
- Click the **New Layer** button.
- AutoCAD will add a new layer with the temporary name *Layer1*. The **Name** field will be highlighted. Type the desired name of the layer (you can use up to 255 characters, spaces are allowed). Use ONLY the following:
- Letters (a, b, c, ..., z) lower or uppercase doesn't matter.
- Number (0, 1, 2, ..., 9).
- (-) hyphen, (_) underscore, and ($) dollar sign.
- It is a common practice to use good layer naming, using a name that gives an idea of the contents of the layer. For example, a layer that contains the walls of a building would be named WALL.

Setting a color for a layer

- After you create a layer, you set its color.
- AutoCAD uses 256 colors for the layers (as a matter of fact, they are only 255 if we exclude the color of the Graphical Area).
- The first seven colors can be called by their names or numbers:
  - Red (1)
  - Yellow (2)
  - Green (3)
  - Cyan (4)
  - Blue (5)
  - Magenta (6)
  - Black/White (7)
- The rest of the colors can be called only by their numbers.
- You can have the same color for more than one layer.

- Select the desired layer, under the field **Color**, and click either the name of the color, or the icon. The following dialog box will appear:

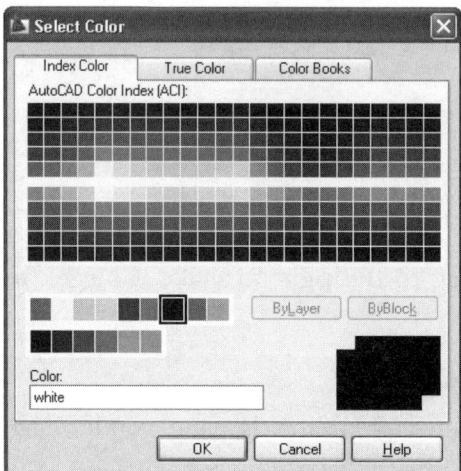

- Move to the desired color (or type in the name/number) of the color, and then click OK.

Setting a linetype for a layer

- AutoCAD comes with a good number of generic pre-defined linetypes saved in a file called *acad.lin*.
- You can also buy other linetypes from third-parties, which can be located on the Internet. Just go to any search engine (such as Yahoo, Google, etc.) and search for "autocad linetype," and you will find lots of linetype files, some free of charge and some you can buy for few dollars.
- Not all linetypes are loaded in the drawing files; you may need to load the desired linetype first before you use it.
- Select the desired layer, under the field **Linetype**, and click the name of the linetype. The following dialog box will appear:

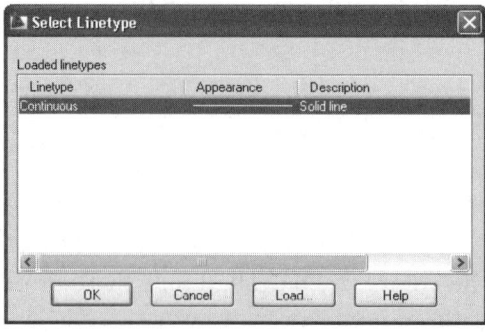

- By default only **Continuous** is loaded.
- To load another linetype, click the **Load** button. The following dialog box will appear:

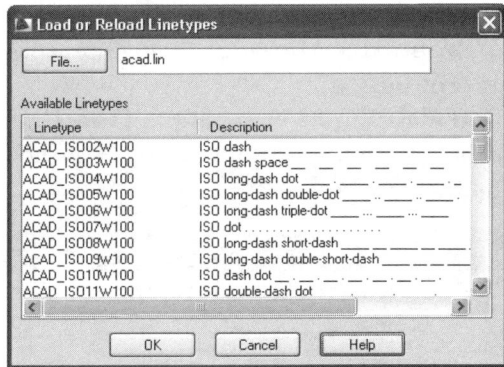

- Select the desired linetype to be loaded, and click OK. Now the linetype is loaded. Next, it will appear in the Select Linetype dialog box. Select it and click OK.

Setting a lineweight for a layer

- Select the desired layer, under the field **Lineweight**, and click either the number or the shape of the lineweight. The following dialog box will appear:

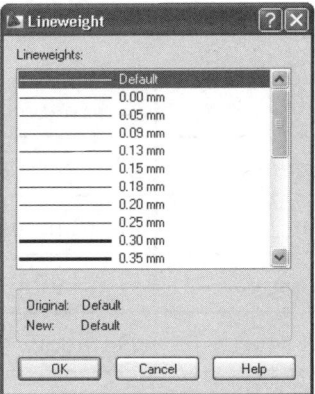

- Select the desired Lineweight, and click OK.
- Using the Status Bar, click the **Show/Hide Lineweight** button if you want to view the lineweight of any layer on the screen.
- We prefer to see the lineweight using Plot Style (discussed in the last chapter) that will affect the hardcopy.

How do you make a layer the current layer?

- There are three ways to make a certain layer is the current layer. They are:
- In the **Layer Properties Manager** dialog box, double-click on the name, or the status of the desired layer.
- In the **Layer Properties Manager** dialog box, select the desired layer and click **Set Current** button.
- On the **Ribbon** make sure you are at the **Home** tab, and using the **Layers** panel, there is a pop-up list for the layers, select the desired layer name, and it will become the current layer:

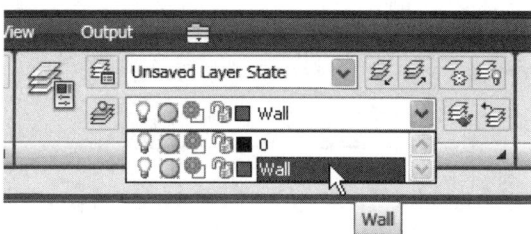

LAYER NAMES, COLORS, LINETYPES, AND LINEWEIGHTS

Exercise 13

1. Start AutoCAD 2009.
2. Open the **Exercise_13.dwg** file.
3. Create the following layers:

Layer Name	Color	Linetype	Lineweight
Shaft	Magenta	Continuous	0.3
Body	Cyan	Continuous	0.3
Base	Green	Continuous	0.3
Centerlines	9	Dashdot2	0.5

4. Make **Centerlines** current (make sure that **DYN** is off).
5. Draw a line from 6,7.5 to 6,4.5, AND draw another line from 8,6 to 4,6.
6. Save the file and close it.

LAYER FUNCTIONS

Adding more layers

- The easiest way to add more layers is while you are in the **Layer Properties Manager** click on the name of any layer and then press [Enter].
- Or, you can use the **New Layer** button.
 - By default AutoCAD will always sort the layers according to their names.

How do you select layers?

- All of the methods discussed will be done in the **Layer Properties Manager** dialog box.
- There are several ways to select layers:
- To select a single layer, simply click on it.
- To select multiple nonconsecutive layers, select the first layer, then hold the [Ctrl] key, and click on the other layers.
- To select multiple consecutive layers, select the first layer, then hold the [Shift] button, and click on the last layer you wish to select.
- To select multiple layers in one step, click on an empty area and hold the mouse. Move to the right or to the left and a rectangle will appear. Cover the layer that you wish to select and release the mouse.
- To select all layers, press Ctrl+A.
- To unselect a selected layer, hold the Ctrl key and click it.
- One of the most important advantages of selecting multiple layers is to set the color, linetype, or lineweight for a group of layers in one step.

Deleting a layer

- First, you can't delete a layer that contains objects, so the first step is to remove the objects from the layer.
- Using the **Layer Properties Manager** palette select the desired layer (or layers) to be deleted, and do one of the following:
- Press the [Del] key on the keyboard.
 - Click the **Delete Layer** button.

What happens when you right-click?

- Right-clicking here is done in the **Layer Properties Manager** dialog box.
- If you select any layer and right-click the following shortcut menu will appear:

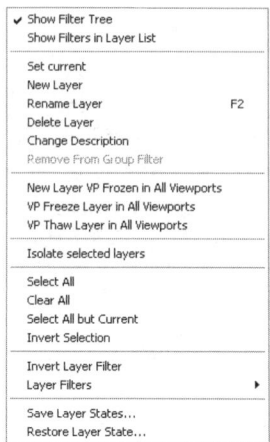

- Through this shortcut menu you can do many of things we discussed earlier such as:
  - Set the current layer
  - Create a new layer
  - Delete a layer
  - Select All layers
  - Clear the selection
  - Select All but Current
  - Invert Selection (make the selected unselected, and vice versa)
- The first two choices in this shortcut menu are:
- Show Filter Tree (turned on by default)
- Show Filters in Layer List (turned off by default)
- By turning off the **Show Filter Tree**, the dialog box will have more space, just like the following:

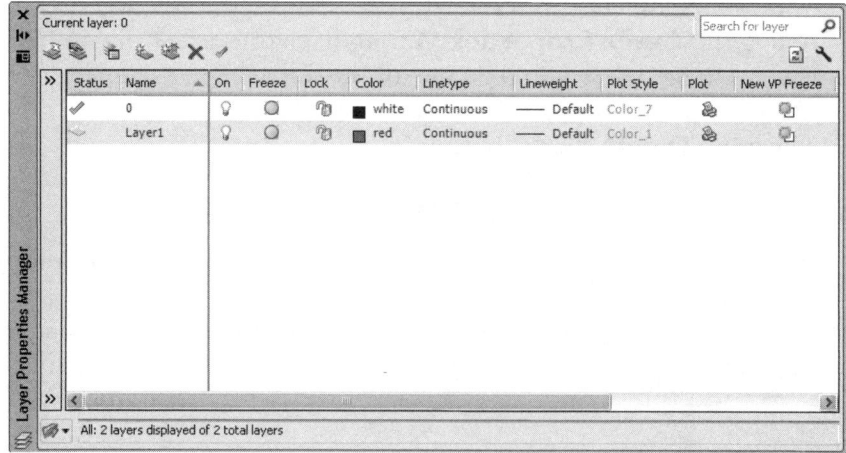

How do you change an object's layer?

- Each object should exist in a layer.
- The fastest method to change an object's layer is the following:
  - Without issuing any command, select the object (by clicking it).
  - In the **Layers** toolbar, the object's layer will be displayed. To change it, click the layer's pop-up list and select the new layer.
  - Press [Esc] one time.

- There are other methods to change an object's layer, which will be discussed in later sections.

How do you make an object's layer current?

- This function is very useful when there are too many layers in your drawing.
- You see an object in your drawing, but you don't know which layer this object resides in.
- What you want to do is make this object's layer the current layer. To do that follow these steps:

- Make sure you are at the **Home** tab on the **Ribbon** and using the **Layers** panel, click the **Make Object's Layer Current** button.
- The following prompt will be shown:

```
Select object whose layer will become current: (click on the
desired object)
Walls is now the current layer.
```

- Now the current layer is the object's layer.

What are the four switches of a layer?

- Each layer has four switches, which determine its state.
- You can see these switches in both the **Layer Properties Manager** palette and layer pop-up list from the **Layer** panel.
- These switches are:
  - On/Off switch
  - Thaw/Freeze switch
  - Unlock/Lock switch
  - Plot/No Plot switch
- These four switches are independent of each other.
- By default, the layers are On, Thaw, Unlock, Plot.
- When you turn a layer off, then the objects in it will not be shown on the screen, and if you plot the drawing, they will not be plotted. But the objects

in this layer will be counted in the total count of the drawing; hence, the drawing size will not change.

- When you freeze a layer, then the objects in it will not be shown on the screen, and if you plot the drawing, they will not be plotted. Also, the objects in this layer will NOT be counted in the total count of the drawing; hence, the drawing size will be less.
- When you lock a layer, none of the objects in it are modifiable.
- When you turn on the No Plot switch in a layer you can see the objects on the screen, but when you use the **Plot** command, these objects will not be plotted.
- Three of these switches can be changed using both the **Layer Properties Manager** palette and the layer pop-up list from the **Layer** panel; the fourth (i.e., Plot/No Plot) can be changed only from the **Layer Properties Manager** palette.
- To change the switch, simply click it.
 - You can't freeze the current layer, but you can turn it off. See the following dialog box:

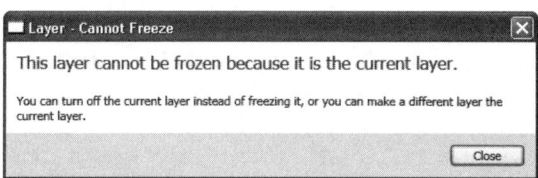

- You should be careful when you turning the current layer off because each and every time you draw a new object it will disappear.

What is Layer Previous?

- While you are working in AutoCAD, you will change the state of layers often so you need a tool to help you get back to the previous state quickly. **Layer Previous** helps you do that.
 - Make sure you are at the **Home** tab on the **Ribbon** and using the **Layers** panel, click the **Previous** button.
- AutoCAD will give you the following message:

```
Restored previous layer status
```

- While you are in the Layer Properties Manager palette, or layer pop-up list from the **Layer** toolbar, and you made several changes on several switches for several layers, AutoCAD will consider them all as one action and will restore them in one previous command.

What is Layer Match?

- In order to convert objects from one layer to another, you can use the **Layer Match** tool which will help you unify objects belonging to different layers.
- Make sure you are at the **Home** tab on the **Ribbon** and using the **Layers** panel, click the **Match** button.
- The following prompt will appear:

```
Select objects to be changed: (Select the desired objects and
once you are done, press [Enter])
Select object on destination layer or [Name]:
```

- Once the command is complete, something like the following message will appear:

```
8 objects changed to layer "Layer1" (the current layer)
```

LAYER FUNCTIONS

Exercise 14

1. Start AutoCAD 2009.
2. Open the **Exercise_14.dwg** file.
3. Change the object's layer as follows:
   - Change the layer of the two circles from 0 to Shaft.
   - Change the layer of the two arcs from 0 to Body.
   - Change the layer of the lines from 0 to Base.
4. Using the **Status Bar**, switch on Show/Hide Lineweight to see the objects displaying the assigned lineweight.
5. Lock the layer Shaft. Then try to erase the objects in it. What message do you receive from AutoCAD?
6. Unlock the layer Shaft.
7. Using the Make Layer Object's Current button select one of the centerlines. Which layer becomes current?
8. Click the Layer Previous button twice. What happened?
9. Try to freeze the current layer. What message do you receive from AutoCAD?
10. Try to rename layer 0. What message do you receive from AutoCAD?
11. Rename layer **Centerlines** as **Center_lines**.
12. Try to delete the layer Shaft. What message do you receive from AutoCAD? Why?
13. Save the file and close it.

QUICK PROPERTIES, PROPERTIES, AND MATCH PROPERTIES

- Earlier in this chapter, we said that each object will inherit the properties of the layer that it resides in. By default the settings of the current color, linetype, and lineweight is BYLAYER, which means that the object follows the layer it resides in.
- This makes controlling the drawing easier because it is easier to control a handful of layers than it is to control hundreds of thousands of objects. So, we recommend not changing these settings. However, sometimes we may need to change some of the properties, so to do that we can use three commands. They are:
  - Quick Properties
  - Properties
  - Match Properties

Quick Properties

- Quick Properties is an automatic function that pops up when you select any object.
- From the Status Bar, click the **Quick Properties** button.
- Click any object and the following small panel will appear:

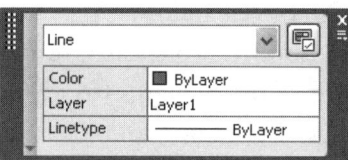

- In this panel you can change the Color, Layer, and Linetype.

Properties

- The easiest way to initiate this command is to select the desired object(s), and then right-click. When the shortcut menu appears, select **Properties**. There are two possibilities:
- The selection set you made consists of different object types (lines, arcs, circles, etc.). Here, you can change only the **General** properties of these objects. The following will appear:

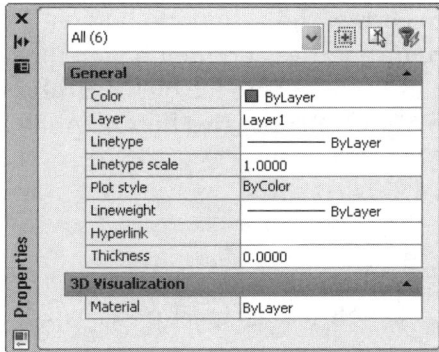

- The selection set you made consists of a single object type. In this case you can change the **General** properties and object-specific properties. The following will appear:

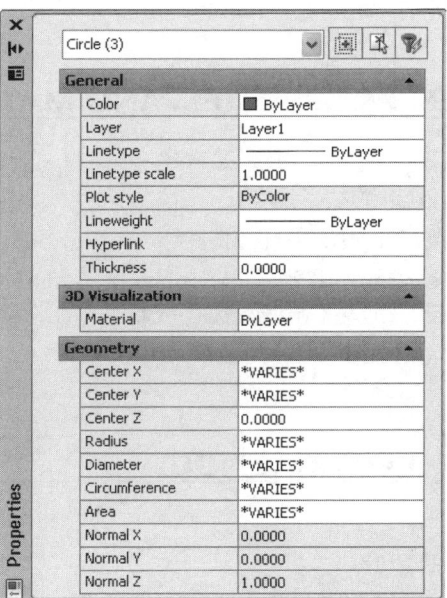

 - Properties is a palette, so all the things we learned about the Layer palette are applicable here.

Match Properties

- Match Properties is useful when you open a drawing and find that the creator of the drawing didn't use the BYLAYER.
- For example, you found that a green line resides in a red layer, and a dashdot circle is in a layer with continuous linetype.

- The best way to correct this is to try to find one object in each layer that has the correct right properties and then match the other objects to it.
- Make sure you are at the **Home** tab on the **Ribbon** and using the **Properties** panel, click the **Match Properties** button. AutoCAD will give the following prompt:

```
Select source object:
```

- Click on the object that holds the right properties.
- The mouse pointer will change to a brush shape, and AutoCAD will give this prompt:

```
Select destination object(s):
```

- Click on the objects whose properties you want to correct. Once you are done, press [Enter].

QUICK PROPERTIES, PROPERTIES, AND MATCH PROPERTIES

Exercise 15
1. Start AutoCAD 2009.
2. Open the **Exercise_15.dwg** file.
3. Mistakenly we draw all objects in layer 0. Using all the commands you learned put each object in its correct layer.
4. Close the file and save it.

CREATING OUR PROJECT (METRIC)

Workshop 1-A
1. Start AutoCAD 2009.
2. Close any opened file.
3. Create a new file based on the acad.dwt template.
4. Double-click on the mouse wheel to zoom extents.
5. Select **Format/Units**, and make the following changes:
   - Length Type = Decimal, Precision = 0
   - Angle Type = Decimal Degrees, Precision = 0
   - Unit to scale inserted content = Millimeters
6. Assume that an AutoCAD unit = 1 mm, and you have a 30 x 20 m plan you want to draw, therefore, your limits will be:

- Lower left corner = 0,0
- Upper right corner = 30000,200000

7. Select **Format/Drawing Limits**, and set the limits accordingly.

8. Double-click on the mouse wheel to zoom extents to the new limits.

9. Create the following layers:

Layer Name	Color	Linetype	Special Remarks
Frame	Magenta	Continuous	
Walls	Red	Continuous	
Doors	Yellow	Continuous	
Door_Swing	Yellow	Dashed	
Windows	150	Continuous	
Centerlines	Green	Dashdot	
Bubbles	Green	Continuous	
Furniture	41	Continuous	
Staircase	140	Continuous	
Text	Cyan	Continuous	
Hatch	White	Continuous	
Dimension	Blue	Continuous	
Viewports	8	Continuous	No Plot

10. Save the file in the **Metric** folder (in the copied folder from the DVD) as **Workshop_01.dwg**.

CREATING OUR PROJECT (IMPERIAL)

 Workshop 1-B

1. Start AutoCAD 2009.

2. Close any open files.
3. Create a new file based on the acad.dwt template.
4. Double-click on the mouse wheel to zoom extents.
5. Select **Format/Units**, and make the following changes:
   - Length Type = Architectural, Precision = 0'-0"
   - Angle Type = Decimal Degrees, Precision = 0
   - Unit to scale inserted content = Inches
6. Assume that the AutoCAD unit = 1 inch, and you have a 70' x 60' m plan you want draw, therefore, your limits will be:
   - Lower left corner = 0,0
   - Upper right corner = 70',60'
7. Select **Format/Drawing Limits**, and set the limits accordingly.
8. Double-click on the mouse wheel to zoom extents to the new limits.
9. Create the following layers:

Layer Name	Color	Linetype	Special Remarks
Frame	Magenta	Continuous	
Walls	Red	Continuous	
Doors	Yellow	Continuous	
Door_Swing	Yellow	Dashed	
Windows	150	Continuous	
Centerlines	Green	Dashdot	
Bubbles	Green	Continuous	
Furniture	41	Continuous	
Staircase	140	Continuous	
Text	Cyan	Continuous	
Hatch	White	Continuous	
Dimension	Blue	Continuous	
Viewports	8	Continuous	No Plot

10. Save the file in the **Imperial** folder (in the copied folder from the DVD) as **Workshop_01.dwg**.

CHAPTER REVIEW

1. Layer names can:
   a. Have up to 255 characters.
   b. Include spaces in the name.
   c. Have letters, numbers, hyphens, underscores, and dollar signs in the name.
   d. All of the above.
2. There are _____ different length units in AutoCAD.
3. What do you need to know to set up limits in a certain file:
   a. The size paper you will print on.
   b. The longest dimension of your sketch in both X and Y.
   c. The measure of each AutoCAD unit.
   d. B & C.
4. Only the first seven colors can be called by name and number:
   a. True.
   b. False.
5. What is true about linetypes in AutoCAD?
   a. They are stored in **acad.lin**.
   b. They are loaded in all AutoCAD drawings.
   c. If you need to use a linetype you have to load it first.
   d. A & C.
6. If I assign a lineweight to a layer, and on this layer I draw lines, I need to click _____ on the **Status Bar** to see this lineweight on the screen.
7. I can change only the _____ properties of non-similar objects using the **Properties** command.

CHAPTER REVIEW ANSWERS

1. d
2. 5 (five)
3. d
4. a
5. d
6. Show/Hide Lineweight button
7. General

4

A Few good Construction Commands

In This Chapter

◇ Creating a parallel duplicate using the Offset command
◇ Creating neat intersections using the Fillet and Chamfer commands
◇ Trimming and Extending objects
◇ Lengthening objects

INTRODUCTION

- So far we have learned four drawing commands: line, arc, circle, and polyline.
- These alone can help you accomplish only 20% of your drawing.
- Also, if you think that each and every line (or arc, or circle) should be drawn by you, you are wrong!
- In this chapter, we will discuss six commands:
  - The **Offset** command, which creates parallel copies of your original objects.
  - The **Fillet** command, which allows you to close unclosed shapes either by extending the two ends to an intersecting point, or by an arc.
  - The **Chamfer** command, which is exactly the same as the Fillet command, except it will create a slanting edge.
  - The **Trim** command, which allows some objects to act as cutting edges for other objects to be trimmed.
  - The **Extend** command, which allows you to extend objects to a boundary.
  - The **Lengthen** command, which allows you to extend or trim length from an existing line.

OFFSET COMMAND

- The Offset command will create a new object parallel to the selected object.
- The new object (by default) will have the same properties of the original object, and will reside in the same layer.
- There are two methods to offset:
    - Using offset distance.
    - Using a through point.
- Make sure you on the **Home** tab on the **Ribbon** and using the **Modify** panel, click the **Offset** button. The following prompt will appear:

```
Current settings: Erase source=No  Layer=Source
OFFSETGAPTYPE=0
Specify offset distance or [Through/Erase/Layer] <Through>:
```

Offset Distance

- If you want to use this method, you should know the distance between the original object and the parallel duplicate (i.e., the offset distance).
- Then select the object that will be offset.
- Finally, specify the side of the offset by clicking (to the right, left, up, or down).
- The prompts will be as follows:

```
Specify offset distance or [Through/Erase/Layer] <Through>:
(type in the desired distance)
Select object to offset or [Exit/Undo] <Exit>: (select a
single object)
Specify point on side to offset or [Exit/Multiple/ Undo]
<Exit>: (click in the desired side)
```

- The command will repeat the last two prompts for further offsetting.
- To end the command press [Enter], or right-click.
- Here is an example:

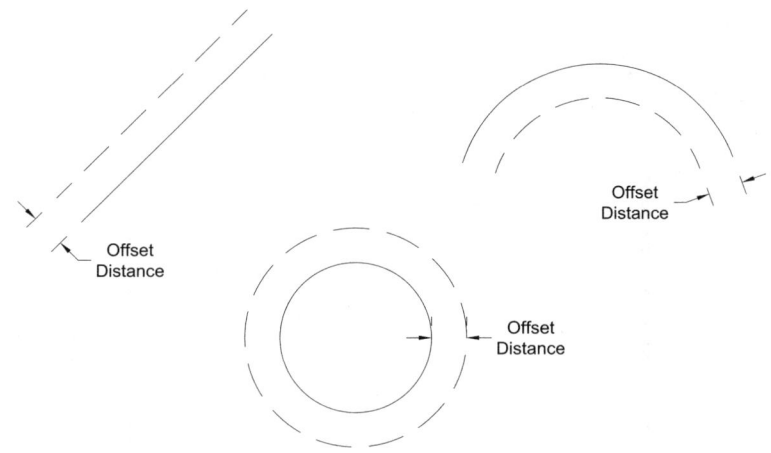

Through Point

- With this method, there is no need to know the distance but you should know any point that the new parallel image will pass through.
- The prompt will be as follows:

```
Specify offset distance or [Through/Erase/Layer] <Through>:
(type t and press [Enter])
Select object to offset or [Exit/Undo] <Exit>: (Select a
single object)
Specify through point or [Exit/Multiple/Undo] <Exit>:
(Specify the point that the new image will pass through)
```

- The command will repeat the last two prompts for further offsetting.
- To end the command press [Enter], or right-click.
- Here is an example:

Before   After

Multiple

- With both methods, you can use the **Multiple** option, if you have the following:

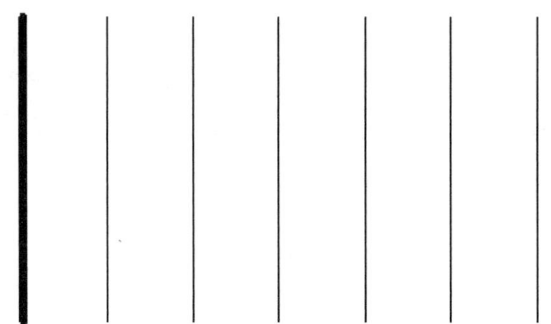

- The original object is the thick one, and the rest are offset objects. As you can see the distance between all objects is the same; hence, instead of selecting the object and specifying the side, the **Multiple** option will allow you only to specify the side of the offset.
- The prompt will be as follows:

```
Specify offset distance or [Through/Erase/Layer] <Through>:
(Select either method)
Select object to offset or [Exit/Undo] <Exit>: (Select a
single object)
Specify through point or [Exit/Multiple/Undo] <Exit>: (Type
m and press [Enter])
Specify point on side to offset or [Exit/Undo] <next
object>: (simply click on the desired side, and you can keep
doing the same, once you are done, press [Enter])
```

Undo

- At any time you can use the **Undo** option to undo the last offsetting action.
- AutoCAD will recall the last Offset distance, so there is no need to keep typing it, unless you want to use another value.
- The **Offset** command will produce a bigger or smaller arc, circle, or polyline.
- You can right-click to show shortcut menus displaying the different options of the Command Window.
- In the **Offset** command you can use only one offset distance. If you want another offset distance, end the current command and issue a new **Offset**

command. *(We hope to see in the next versions of AutoCAD an **Offset** command that will allow the user to use more than one offset distance per command.)*

OFFSETTING OBJECTS

Exercise 16

1. Start AutoCAD 2009.
2. Open the **Exercise_16.dwg** file.
3. Offset the walls (magenta) to the inside using the distance = 1'.
4. Offset the stairs using distance = **1'-6"** and using the **Multiple** option to create 8 lines represnting 8 steps.
5. Explode the inner polyline.
6. Offset the right vertical line to the left using the **Through** option and the left endpoint of the upper right horizontal line.
7. Offset the new line to the right using distance = **6"**.
8. The new shape of the plan should look like the following:

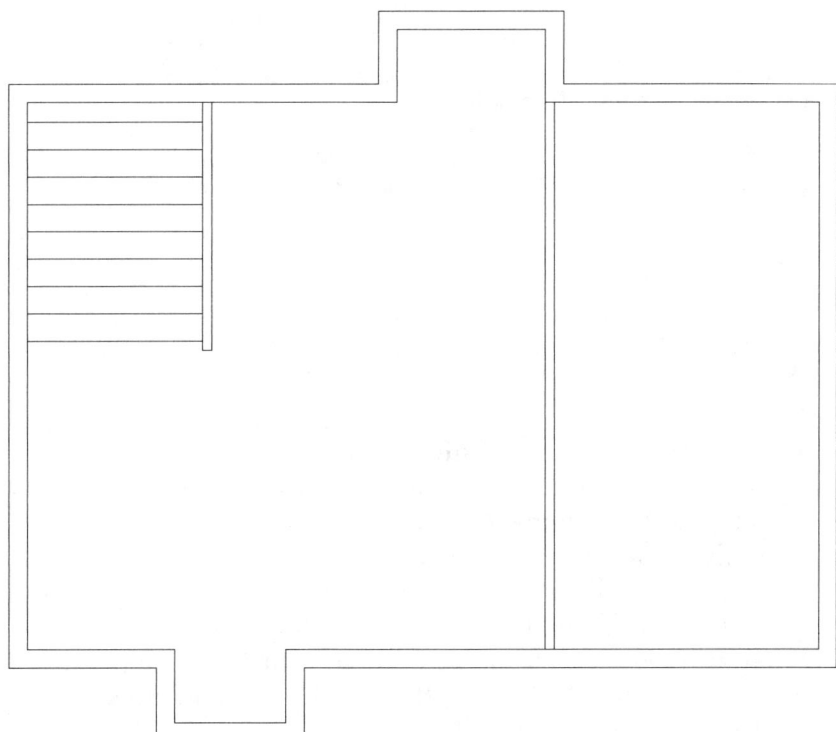

FILLET COMMAND

- If you have the following:

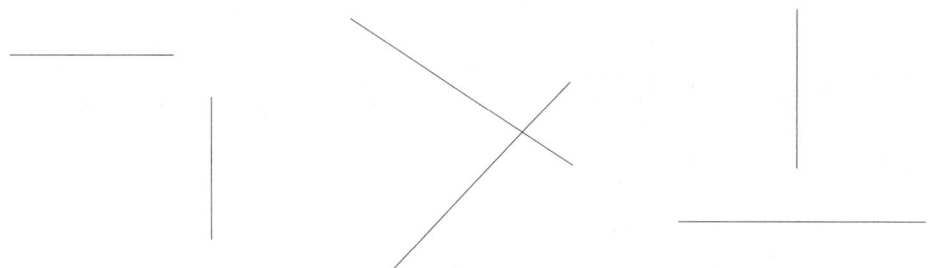

- And you want them to look like this:

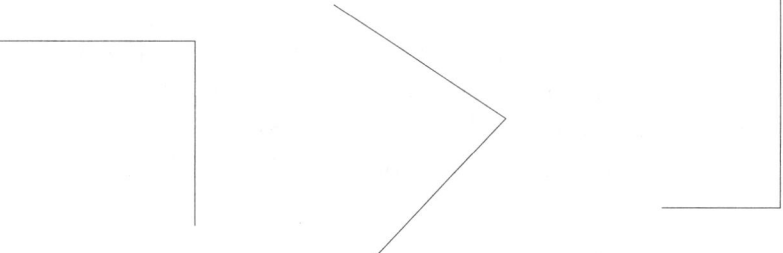

- Or, you want them to look like this:

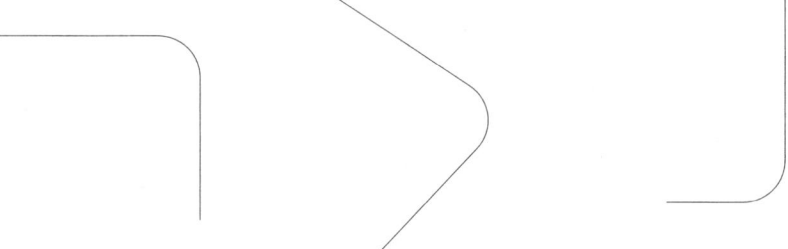

- Then you need to use the **Fillet** command.
- To issue the **Fillet** command, first select the object and then the second object. It is a very simple AutoCAD command.
- The **Fillet** command works with two different settings:
  - Radius = 0 will create a neat intersection.
  - Radius > 0 will do the same except using an arc.
- When you close the shape with an arc, what will happen to the original objects? To resolve this issue, the **Fillet** command works in two different modes:

- In **Trim** mode, the arc will be produced, and the original objects will be trimmed accordingly.
- In **No trim** mode, the arc will be produced, but the original objects will stay intact.
- Here is an example:

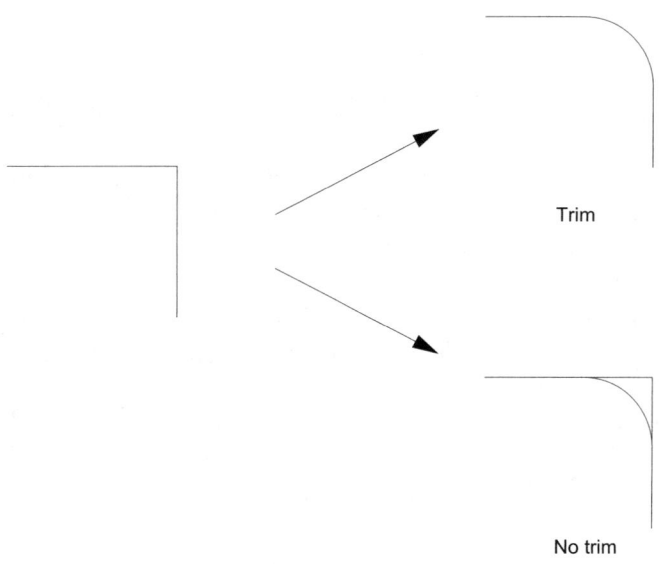

Trim

No trim

- Make sure you are at the **Home** tab on the **Ribbon** and using the **Modify** panel, click the **Fillet** button.
- The following prompt will appear:

```
Current settings: Mode = TRIM, Radius = 0.0000
Select first object or [Undo/Polyline/Radius/Trim/Multiple]:
```

- The first line reports the current value of Mode and Radius.
- Choose between the different options:

Radius

- To set a new value for the Radius, the following prompt will appear:

```
Specify fillet radius <0.0000>: (type in the new radius)
```

Trim

- To change the mode from Trim to No trim, or vice versa, the following prompt will appear:

```
Enter Trim mode option [Trim/No trim] <Trim>:(type t, or n)
```

Multiple

- By default you can perform a single fillet per command by selecting the first object and then the second object.
- If you want to perform multiple fillets in a single command, you have to select this mode first.

Undo

- At any moment while you are filleting you can use the **Undo** option to undo the last filleting action.

- When you fillet with a radius, the radius will be created in the current layer so make sure that you are in the right layer.
- When you use the **Multiple** option, to end the command press [Enter] or right-click.
- Even if R > 0, you can still fillet with R = 0. To do so, simply hold the [Shift] key and click on the desired objects. Regardless of the current value of R, you will fillet with R = 0.
- You can use the **Fillet** command to fillet two parallel lines with an arc. AutoCAD will calculate the distance between the two lines, and take the Radius to be one-half of this length.

FILLETING OBJECTS

Exercise 17
1. Start AutoCAD 2009.
2. Open the **Exercise_17.dwg** file.
3. Using the **Fillet** command do the following:
   a. Set the radius = 0.5
   b. Mode = Trim
4. Fillet the four edges to make the shape look like the following:

5. Using the **Fillet** command do the following:
   a. Mode = No Trim
   b. Set Fillet to be Multiple
6. Fillet the lines to get the following shape:

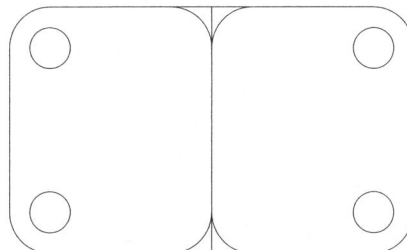

7. Save the file and close it.

CHAMFER COMMAND

- The **Chamfer** command is identical to the **Fillet** command in many ways, except it creates a slanting edge rather than an arc.
- To create the sloped edge, we will use one of two methods:
  - Two distances
  - Length and Angle

Two Distances

- There are three different examples of this method:
- (Dist1 = Dist2) = 0.0, as in the following example:

Before   After

- (Dist1=Dist2) > 0.0, as in the following example:

Before   After

- (Dist1#Dist2) > 0.0, as in the following example (whichever will be selected first, Dist1 will be used):

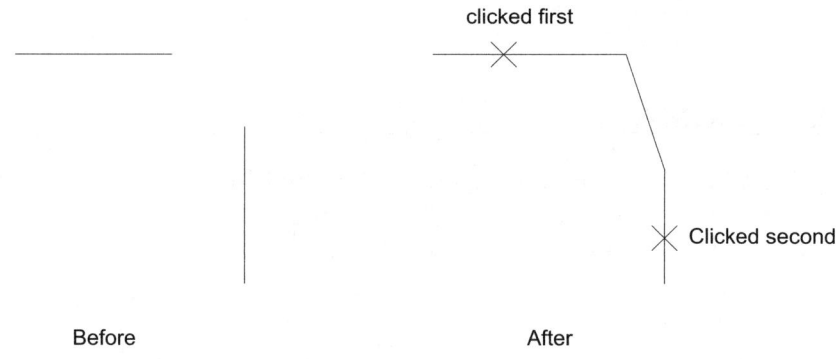

Before   After

Length and Angle

- To use this method specify a length (which will be removed from the first object) and an angle, just like the following example:

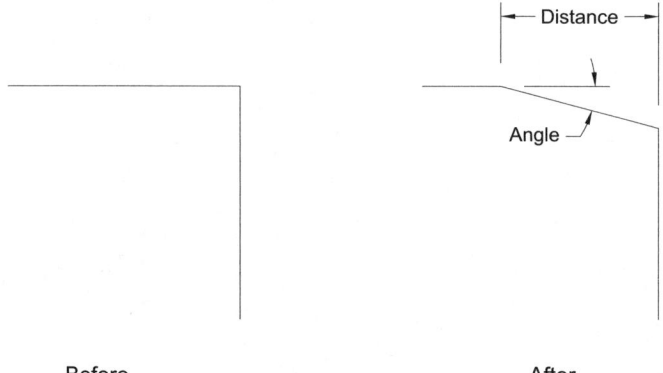

Before   After

- Make sure you are at the **Home** tab on the **Ribbon** and using the **Modify** panel, click the Chamfer button (Fillet and **Chamfer** are the same button).
- The following prompt will appear:

```
(TRIM mode) Current chamfer Dist1 = 0.0000, Dist2 = 0.0000
Select first line or [Undo/Polyline/Distance/Angle /Trim/
mEthod/Multiple]:
```

- The first line reports the current Mode and the Distances (or Length and Angle).
- Choose between the different options:

Distances

- To set a new value for the **Distances**, the following prompt will appear:

```
Specify first chamfer distance <0.0000>: (input the first
distance)
Specify second chamfer distance <0.0000>: (input the second
distance)
```

Angle

- To set the new values for both length and angle, the following prompt will appear:

```
Specify chamfer length on the first line <0.0000>: (input the
length on first line)
Specify chamfer angle from the first line <0>: (input the
angle)
```

Trim

- To change the mode from Trim to No trim, or vice versa, the following prompt will appear:

```
Enter Trim mode option [Trim/No trim] <Trim>: (type t, or n)
```

Method

- To specify the default method to be used with the **Chamfer** command, the following prompt will appear:

```
Enter trim method [Distance/Angle] <Distance>: (type d, or a)
```

■ By default you can perform a single chamfer per command by selecting the first object and the second object. If you want to perform multiple chamfers in a single command, you have to select this mode first.

 ■ When you chamfer, the sloped line will be created in the current layer so make sure that you are in the right layer.

■ When you use the **Multiple** option, to end the command press [Enter] or right-click.

CHAMFERING OBJECTS

Exercise 18

1.   Start AutoCAD 2009.
2.   Open the **Exercise_18.dwg** file.
3.   Using the **Chamfer** command do the following:
     • Set Dist1 = 1.0
     • Set Dist2 = 0.4
     • Mode = Trim
4.   Set Chamfer to Multiple.
5.   Chamfer the four edges by selecting the proper line for the proper chamfering distance to make the shape look like the following:

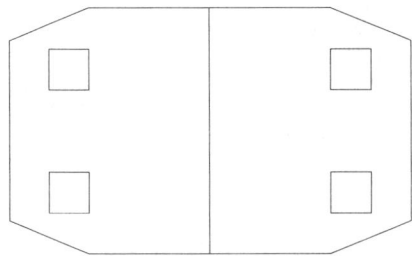

6.   Using the **Chamfer** command do the following:
     • Distance = 0.5
     • Angle = 30
     • Mode = No trim
     • Set the Chamfer to Multiple
7.   Chamfer the inner line to make the shape look like the following (Hint: The distance will be cut from the horizontal line and the angle will be cut from the vertical line):

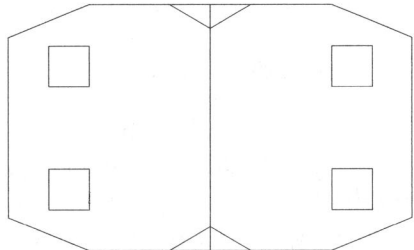

8. Save the file and close it.

TRIM COMMAND

- Trimming means we want to remove part of an object by cutting edge(s).
- The Trim command is a two-step command:
  - The first step is to select the edge(s) to be cut. It can be one object or as many as you wish.
  - The second step is to select the objects to be trimmed.
- The following example illustrates the trimming process:

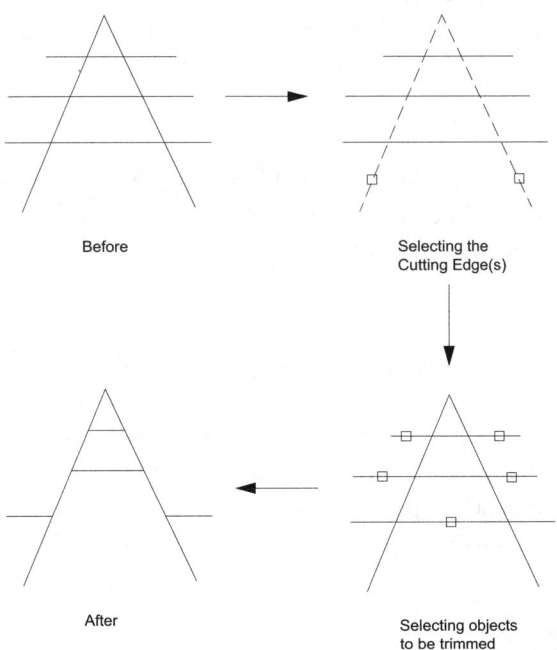

- Make sure you are at the Home tab on the Ribbon and using the Modify panel, click the Trim button. The following prompt will appear:

```
Current settings: Projection=UCS, Edge=Extend
Select cutting edges ...
Select objects or <select all>:
```

- The first line displays the current settings.
- The second line is telling you to select the cutting edges.
- Use any of the methods we learned in the **Erase** command. Once you are done press [Enter] or right-click and the use the menu.
- You can also use the fastest way, the select all option, which will **select all** the objects.
- The following prompt will appear:

```
Select object to trim or shift-select to extend or
[Fence/Crossing/Project/Edge/eRase/Undo]:
```

- Now click on the parts you want to trim, one-by-one.
- If you make a mistake, simply right-click to bring on the shortcut menu and select **Undo**, or type **u**.

Fence

- You can use the **Fence** option to speed up the process of selecting the objects to be trimmed. This can be done by specifying two points or more. A dotted line will be created, and whatever objects are touched will be trimmed.

Crossing

- The same thing applies for the **Crossing** option, but this can be done by specifying two opposite corners. A crossing window will appear and any object touched by crossing will be trimmed.

eRase

- Sometimes, as a result of trimming, there will be unwanted objects created. So, instead of finishing the command, and using the **Erase** command, AutoCAD allows you to erase objects while you are still in **Trim** command.
- Type **r**, and AutoCAD will ask you to select the objects you want to erase. When you are done, press [Enter]. The prompts will appear again to allow you to select another option.

TRIMMING OBJECTS

Exercise 19
1. Start AutoCAD 2009.

2. Open the **Exercise_19.dwg** file.

3. Using the Trim command, create the following two shapes (Hint: If you get a residual object you can use the **eRase** option in **Trim** command to get rid of it):

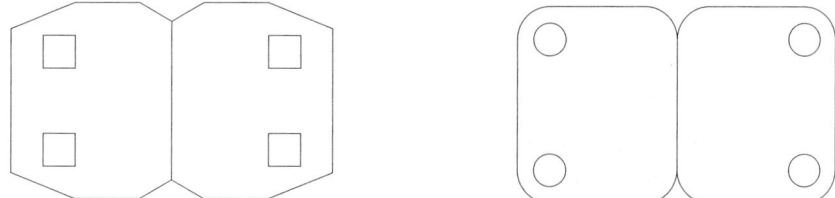

4. Save the file and close it.

EXTEND COMMAND

- The **Extend** command is the opposite of the **Trim** command.
- When you use the **Extend** command you will extend selected objects to boundary edge(s).
- To use the **Extend** command, you will follow two steps:
  - The first step is to select the boundary edge(s). It can be one object, or as many as you wish.
  - The second step is to select the objects to be extended.
- The following example will illustrate the process of extending:

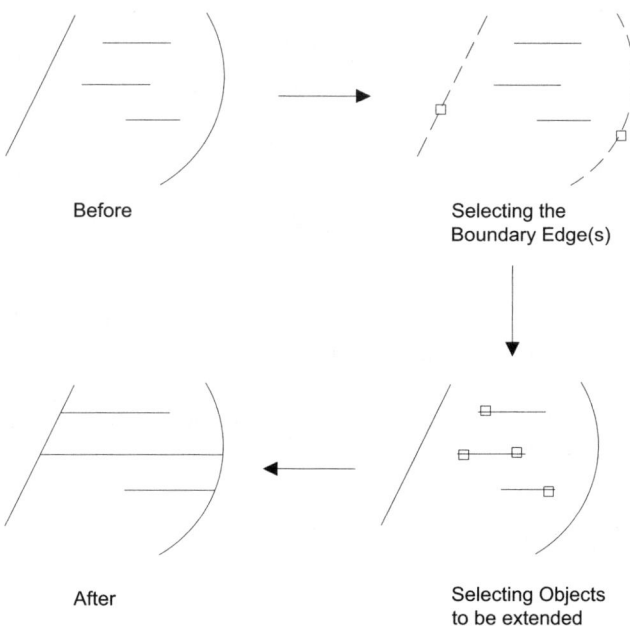

Before

Selecting the
Boundary Edge(s)

After

Selecting Objects
to be extended

- Make sure you are at the **Home** tab on the **Ribbon** and using the **Modify** panel, click the **Extend** button.
- The following prompt will appear:

```
Current settings: Projection=UCS, Edge=Extend
Select boundary edges ...
Select objects or <select all>:
```

- The first linerrent displays the current settings.
- The second line is telling you to select the boundary edges.
- Use any of the methods you know. Once you are done press [Enter] or right-click.
- The following prompt will appear:

```
Select object to extend or shift-select to trim or
[Fence/Crossing/Project/Edge/Undo]:
```

- Now click on the parts you want to extend, one-by-one.
- If you made a mistake, simply either right-click to open the shortcut menu and select **Undo**, or type **u**.
- The rest of the options are just like the **Trim** command.
- While you are using the **Trim** command, and while you are clicking on the objects to be trimmed, if you hold the [Shift] key and click, you will extend the objects and not trim them.
- See the following example.
- Assume you have the following case:

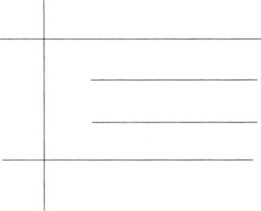

- Start the **Trim** command and select the vertical line as the cutting edge, then press [Enter].
- Click the left part of both the upper and lower horizontal lines.
- The result will be as follows:

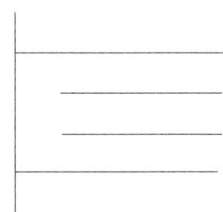

- While still in the **Trim** command, hold the [Shift] key and click the two intermediate horizontal lines. They will extend, even though you are in the **Trim** command. You will have the following picture:

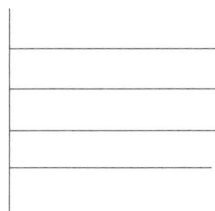

EXTENDING OBJECTS

Exercise 20
1. Start AutoCAD 2009.
2. Open the **Exercise_20.dwg** file.
3. Using the Extend and Trim commands, try to create the following shape:

4. Save the file and close it.

LENGTHEN COMMAND

- With the Extend command, we needed an object to serve as a boundary in order to extend the rest of the objects to it.
- The **Lengthen** command (or shorten, as it serves both purposes) will do this without a boundary.
- Make sure you are at the Home tab on the Ribbon and using the Modify panel and extending it, select the Lengthen button.
- The following prompt will appear:

```
Select an object or [DElta/Percent/Total/DYnamic]:
```

- If you click on any object, AutoCAD will give you the current length.
- The **Lengthen** command will do the lengthening (or shortening) using the following methods:

DElta

- This command is used if you want to add (remove) an extra length to (from) the current length.
- If you input a negative value, the **Lengthen** command will shorten the line.
- The following prompt will appear:

```
Enter delta length or [Angle] <0.0000>: (input the extra
length to be added)
```

Percent

- If you want to add (remove) to (from) the length, you can do this by specifying a percentage of the current length.
- The number should be positive and a non-zero number. If it was > 100, it will lengthen. If it was < 100, it will shorten.
- The following prompt will appear:

```
Enter percentage length <100.0000>: (input the new percentage)
```

Total

- Use Total if you want the new total length of the line to be equal to the number you will input.
- If the new number > the current length, the line will lengthen. If the new number < the current length, the line will shorten.
- The following prompt will appear:

```
Specify total length or [Angle] <1.0000)>: (input the new
total length)
```

- This option is used to specify a new length of the object, using the dynamic move of the mouse.
- The following prompt will appear:

```
Select an object to change or [Undo]: (select the desired
object)
Specify new endpoint: (move the mouse, up until you reach to
the desired length)
```

 ■ You can use only one method per command.

LENGTHENING OBJECTS

Exercise 21
1. Start AutoCAD 2009.
2. Open the **Exercise_21.dwg** file.
3. Using the **Lengthen** command and the **Delta** option, shorten the two vertical lines by 1 unit.
4. Using the **Lengthen** command and the **Total** option, make the two horizontal lines total length = 5.
5. As you can see the lower line didn't come to the end like the upper line.
6. Using the **Lengthen** command and the **Percent** option, make Percent = **104**, and select the end of the line.
7. The output should look like the following:

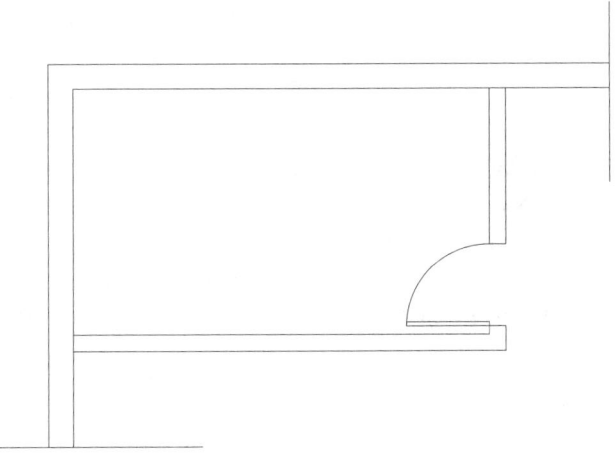

8. Save and close the file.

DRAWING THE PLAN (METRIC)

Workshop 2-A
1. Start AutoCAD 2009.
2. Open the **Workshop_02.dwg** file.
3. Make layer **Walls** current.
4. Using the **Polyline** command, draw first the lines (without the dimension) starting from point 8000,3000 using all the methods you learned in Chapter 2.

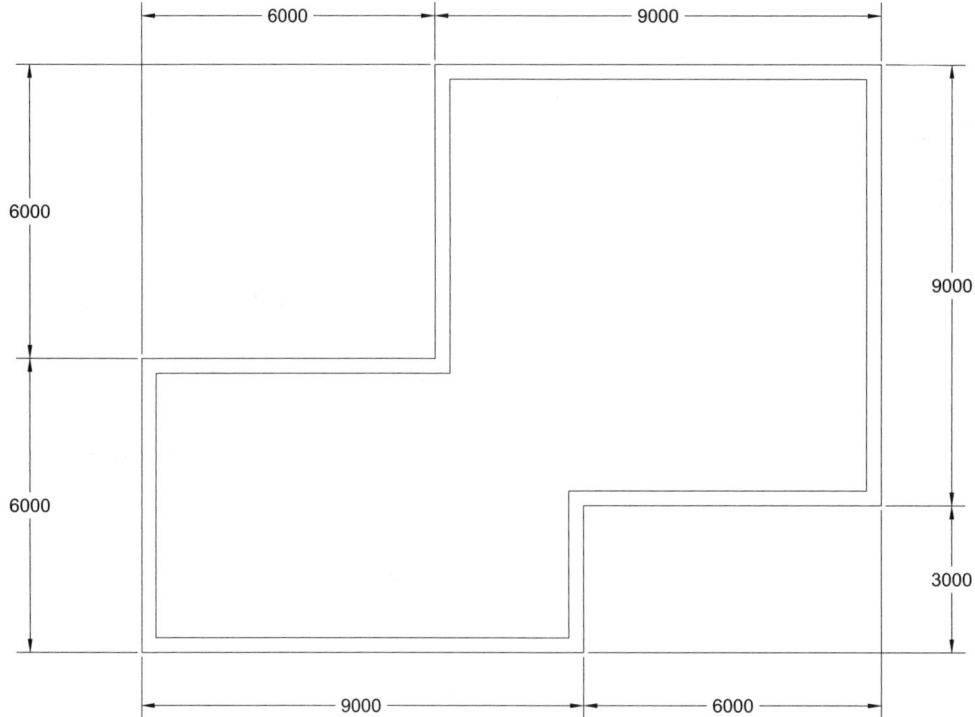

5. Using the **Offset** command offset the polyline to the inside with an offset distance = **300**.
6. Explode the inner polyline.
7. Using the Offset, Fillet, Chamfer, Trim, Extend, Lengthen, and Zoom commands try to create the interior walls using the following dimensions:

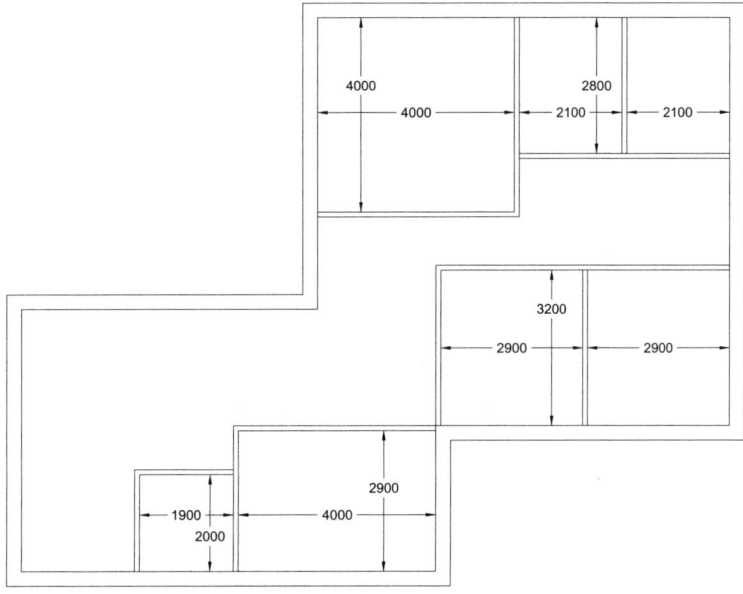

NOTE ■ The thickness of all inner walls is = 100.

8. Make the door openings as follows, taking into consideration the following:

   a. All door openings are 900.

   b. Always take 100 clear distances from the walls for the door openings (except for the outside door take 500).

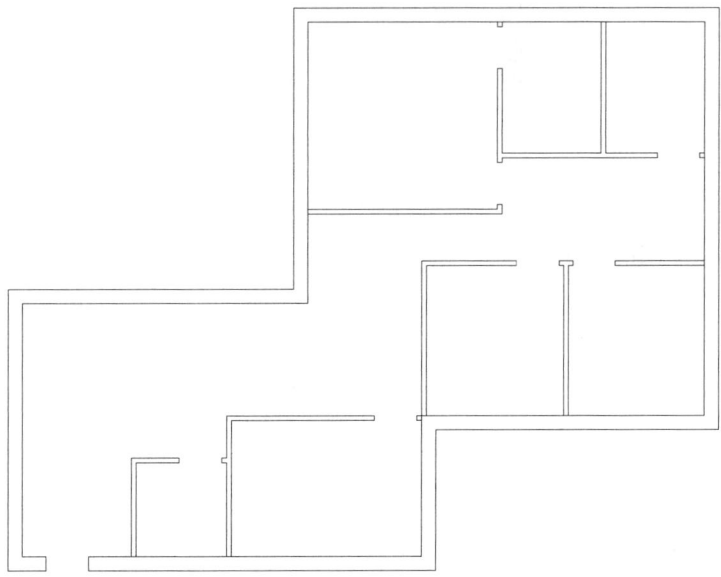

▪ To make the door openings, use the following technique:

       • Offset an existing wall (say 100 for internal doors).

       • Offset the new line (say 900 for room doors).

▪ You will have the following shape:

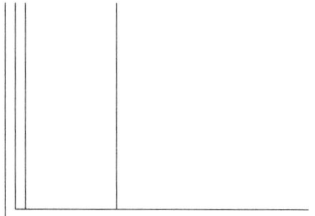

▪ Extend the two vertical lines to the lower horizontal line, just like this:

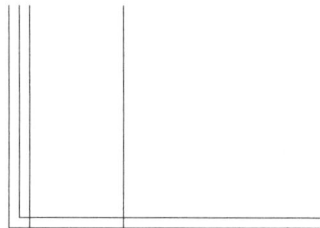

▪ Using the **Trim** command, select all the horizontal lines and vertical lines as cutting edges, then press [Enter].

▪ As for the objects to trim, click the following parts (you can use **Crossing** which is quicker):

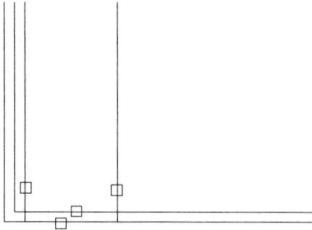

▪ This is what you will get:

9. Save the file and close it.

DRAWING THE PLAN (IMPERIAL)

Workshop 2-B

1. Start AutoCAD 2009.

2. open the **Workshop_02.dwg** file.

3. Make the layer **Walls** current.

4. Using the **Polyline** command, draw the lines (without dimensions) starting from point 16',10' using all the methods you learned in Chapter 2.

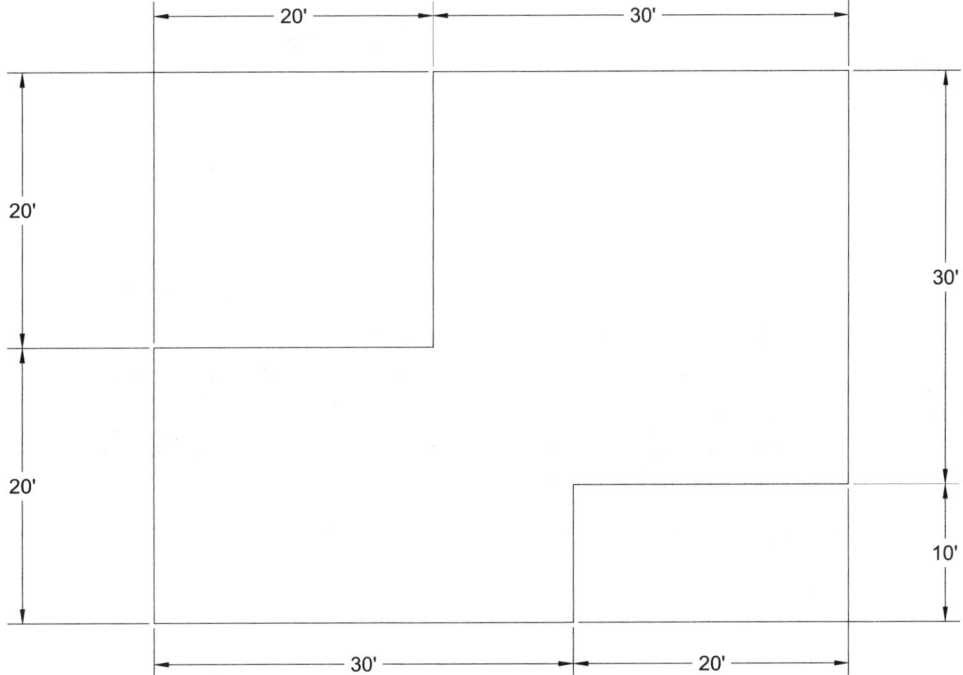

5. Using the **Offset** command offset the polyline to the inside with offset distance = 1'.

6. Explode the inner polyline.

7. Using the Offset, Fillet, Chamfer, Trim, Extend, Lengthen, and Zoom commands try to create the interior walls using the following dimensions:

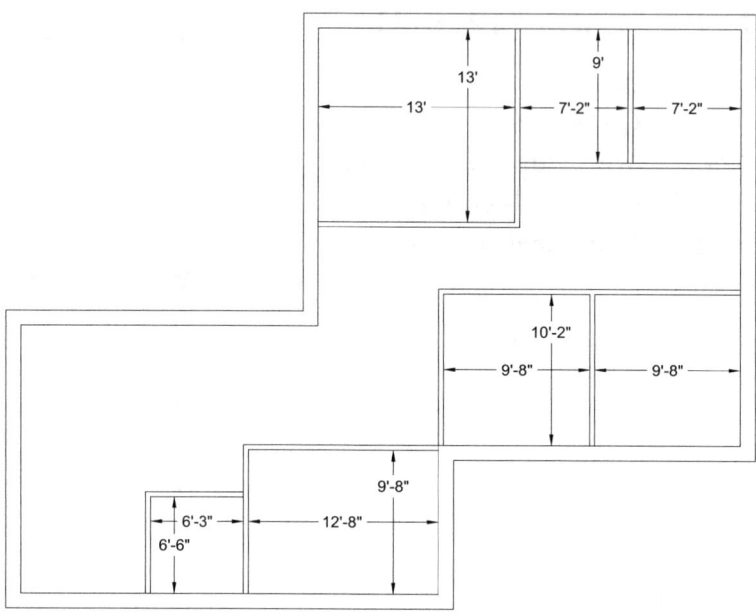

 ▪ The thickness of all inner walls is = 4".

8. Make the door openings as follows taking into consideration the following:

a. All door openings are 3'.

b. Always take 4" clear distance from the walls for the door openings (except for the outside door take 1'6").

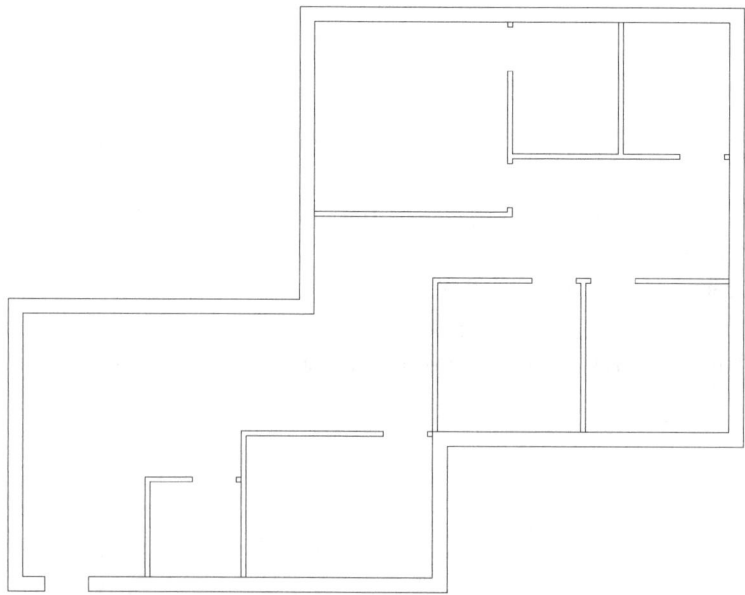

■ To create the door openings, use the following technique:
   • Offset an existing wall (say 4" for internal doors).
   • Offset the new line (say 3' for the room door).
■ You will have the following shape:

■ Extend the two vertical lines to the lower horizontal line, just like this:

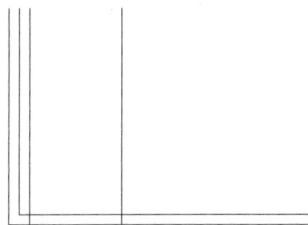

■ Using the **Trim** command, select all the horizontal lines and vertical lines as cutting edges, then press [Enter].
■ As for the objects to trim, click the following parts (you can use Crossing which is quicker):

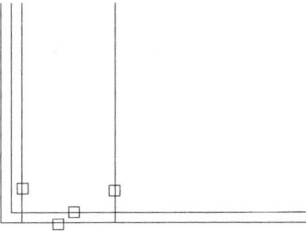

■ This is what you will get:

9. Save the file and close it.

NOTES

CHAPTER REVIEW

1. Using the same **Offset** command I can use more than one offset distance:
   a. True, I can use two offset distances.
   b. True, I can use as many as I wish.
   c. False, only one offset distance can be used.
   d. The only method available in the **Offset** command is the Through point method.

2. In the **Lengthen** command, using the Percent option, 150% should be input as _____.

3. While I am trimming I can extend and vice versa:
   a. True.
   b. False.

4. I can fillet using an arc, but I need to specify:
   a. Distances
   b. Radius
   c. Radius and Distances
   d. Length and Angle

5. There are two methods to chamfer: Distances and Length/Angle.
   a. True.
   b. False.

6. The first step in the **Extend** command is to select _____, and the second step is to select _____.

CHAPTER REVIEW ANSWERS

1. c
2. 150
3. a
4. b
5. a
6. Boundary Edge(s), Objects to extend

Chapter **5** # MODIFYING COMMANDS

In This Chapter

◊ Advanced techniques for selecting objects
◊ Moving and copying objects
◊ Rotating and scaling objects
◊ Creating duplicates using the Array command
◊ Mirroring objects
◊ Stretching objects
◊ Breaking objects
◊ Using Grips to modify objects

INTRODUCTION

- In this chapter we will learn about Modifying commands in AutoCAD.
- We will cover nine commands, which will enable you to make any type of change in a drawing.
- First we will discuss the selection process (more advanced than we discuss in Chapter 2).
- Then we will discuss the following commands:
  - The **Move** command, which is used to move objects from one place to another.
  - The **Copy** command, which is used to copy objects.
  - The **Rotate** command, which is used to rotate objects using rotation angles.
  - The **Scale** command, which is used to create bigger or smaller objects using a scale factor.
  - The **Array** command, which is used to create copies of objects either in a matrix fashion or circular or semi-circular fashion.
  - The **Mirror** command, which is used to create mirror images of selected objects.

- The **Stretch** command, which is used to change the length of objects, increasing or decreasing.
- The **Break** command, which is used to break an object into two pieces.
▪ We will end this chapter with a discussion on using Grips in AutoCAD.

SELECTING OBJECTS

▪ All of the Modifying commands (with some exceptions) will ask you the same question:

```
Select objects:
```

▪ In Chapter 2, we learned some of the methods used to select objects. We will now expand our knowledge in this area.
▪ All the methods we will discuss will involve typing a letter or more at the **Select objects** prompt.

W (Window)

▪ If you type **W**, the **Window** mode will be available whether you went to the right or to the left.

C (Crossing)

▪ If you type **C**, the **Crossing** mode will be available whether you went to the right or to the left.

WP (Window Polygon)

▪ Excellent choice when your drawing is based on angles such as 30, 45, 60, etc.
▪ When you type **WP** and press [Enter], the following prompt will appear:

```
First polygon point: (specify the first point of the polygon)
Specify endpoint of line or [Undo]: (specifying the second
point)
Specify endpoint of line or [Undo]: (specify the third
point, etc.)
```

▪ When you are done press [Enter] to end **WP** mode.
▪ Whatever is inside the **WP** FULLY will be selected. If any part (even a very small part) is outside the shape it will not be selected. See this example:

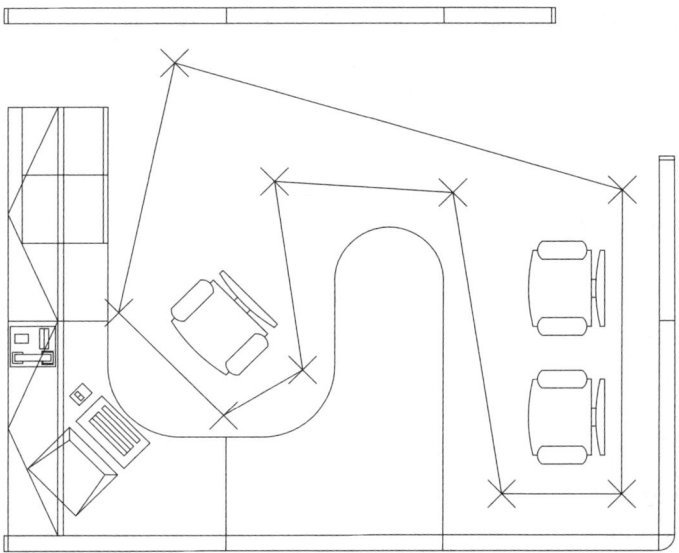

CP (Crossing Polygon)

- **CP** is the same as **WP**, except it has the features of **C**, which means whatever it contains fully, plus any object that touches it will be selected.

F (Fence)

- The main function of this mode is to touch objects.
- Discussed in the sections on Trim and Extend.

L (Last)

- To select the last object drawn.

P (Previous)

- To select the last selection set used.

All

- To select all objects in the current file.

Deselect

- If you select a group of objects, you may discover that one or two of the selected objects were selected by mistake. How do you deselect them?
- Simply hold the [Shift] key and click the objects and they will be deselected.

OTHER METHODS FOR SELECTING OBJECTS

- There are other methods to selecting objects, which will make your life easier.
- There is a good technique called **Noun/Verb selection**, which will allow you to select first, then issue the command.
- The cursor looks like the following:

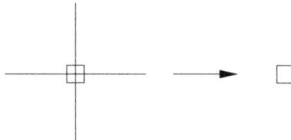

- As you can see there is a pick box inside the cursor, which means, without issuing any command, you can:
- Click on any object to select it.
- Or you can find an empty space, then click, and go to the right to start **Window** mode.
- Or you can find an empty space, then click, and go to the left to start **Crossing** mode.
- Once you select the desired objects, you can right-click, and you will get the following shortcut menu:

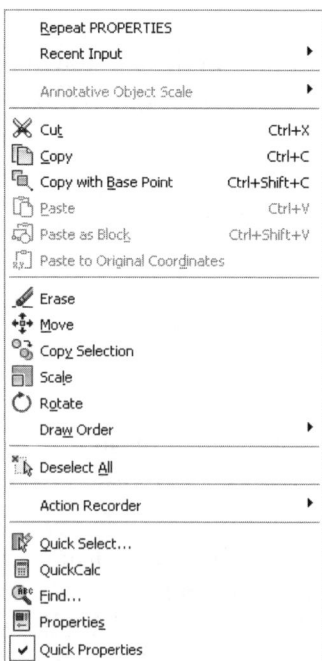

- From this shortcut menu, you can select from five modifying commands, which you can access without typing a single letter on the keyboard or using the toolbar. These commands are: **Erase**, **Move**, **Copy Selection**, **Scale**, and, **Rotate**.

- Make sure that the **Noun/Verb** technique is turned on using the Menu Browser by selecting **Tools/Options**, then the **Selection** tab, and under **Selection Modes**, click the **Noun/Verb selection** checkbox to turn it on (that is, if it was off).

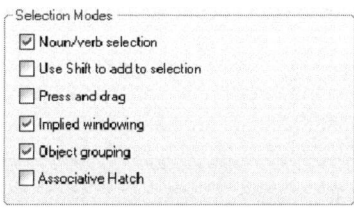

  - This technique will not work with the **Offset**, **Fillet**, **Chamfer**, **Trim**, **Extend**, and **Lengthen** commands.

MOVE COMMAND

- The **Move** command is used to move objects from one place to another.
- Make sure you are at the **Home** tab on the **Ribbon** and using the **Modify** panel, select the **Move** button.
- This command involves three steps:
  - The first step is:

```
Select objects:
```

  - Once you are done press [Enter], or right-click.
  - The next prompt will ask you to:

```
Specify base point or [Displacement] <Displacement>:
```
(Specify the base point)

- The ***Base point*** concept will be repeated in four other commands, so let's take a moment to define it.
- The simplest definition of Base point is to call it a *Handle* point.
  There no golden rule that defines a right point as a base point; instead, you have to take it case by case, so it may sometimes be the center of group of objects, and in another situation it will be the upper left corner.
- This is also true for commands such as **Move**, **Copy**, and **Stretch**. But for a command such as **Rotate**, a Base point is the point which the whole shape will rotate around. In the **Scale** command, it will be the point that the whole shape will shrink, or enlarge relative to it.

- The third prompt will be:

```
Specify second point or <use first point as displacement>:
(Specify the second point)
```

- The command will end automatically.
- See the following example:

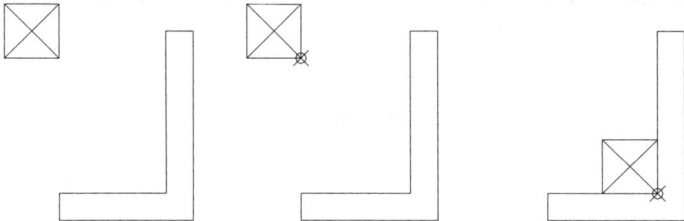

MOVING OBJECTS

Exercise 22

1. Start AutoCAD 2009.
2. Open the **Exercise_22.dwg** file.
3. Move the four objects (Bath tub, Toilet, Sink, and Door to their respective places to make the bathroom look like the following):

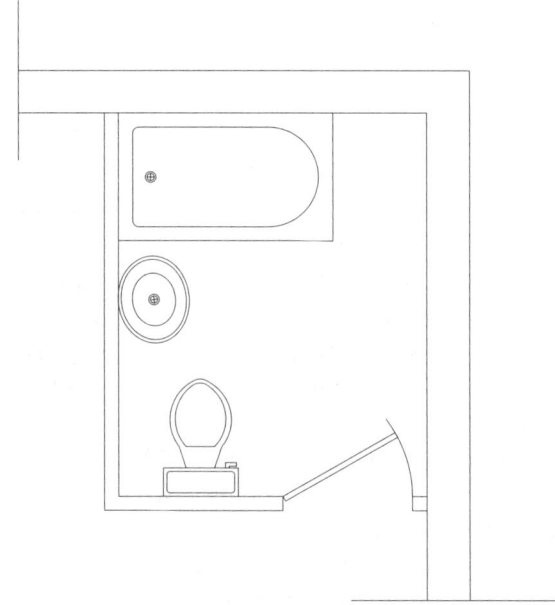

- Once you are done press [Enter], or right-click.
- The next prompt will ask you to:

```
Specify base point: (Specify the base point)
```

- The third prompt will be:

```
Specify scale factor or [Copy/Reference] <1.0000>: (specify
the scale factor, the number should be non-zero positive
number)
```

- You can use the **Copy** option if you want to scale a copy of the objects selected keeping the original intact.
- The command will end automatically.
- See the following example:

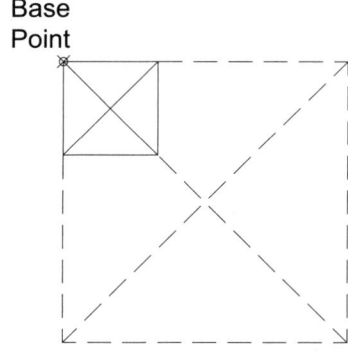

Base Point

Scale factor = 3

SCALING OBJECTS

Exercise 25

1. Start AutoCAD 2009.
2. Open the **Exercise_25.dwg** file.
3. Using scale factor = 0.8 to scale the bathtub using the upper left corner as the Base point.
4. Using scale factor = 1.2 scale the sink using the quadrant of the left side as the Base point.

5. The room should look like the following:

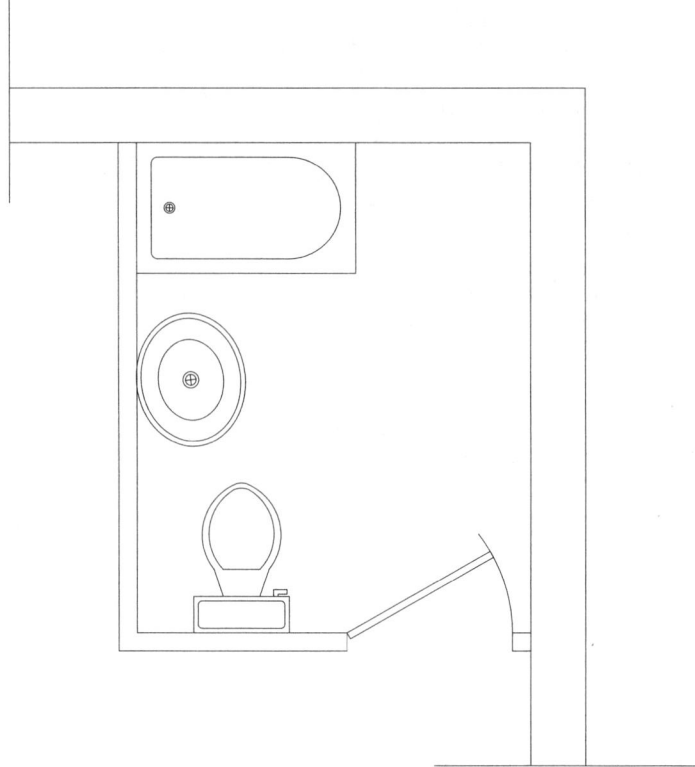

6. Save the file and close it.

ARRAY COMMAND

- This command is used to create duplicates of objects using two methods:
- Rectangular array (matrix shape).
- Polar array (circular or semi-circular shape).
- Make sure you are at the **Home** tab on the **Ribbon** and using the **Modify** panel, select the **Array** button.

Rectangular

- If you want to create a duplication of certain objects simulating the matrix shape, you want to use the rectangular array.

- The following dialog box will appear:

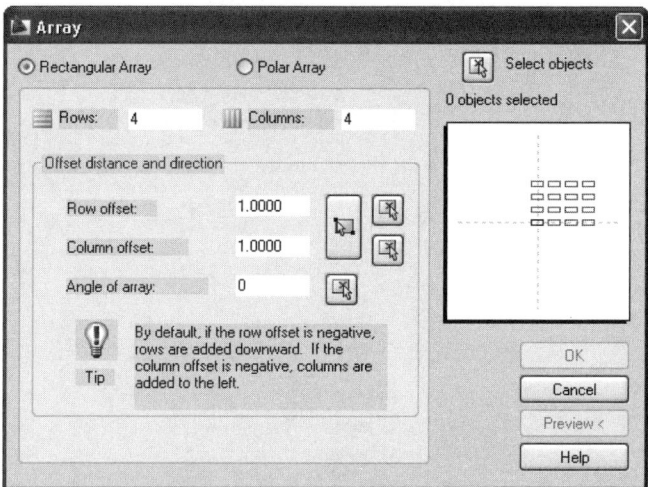

- First, click the **Select Objects** button to select the desired objects. Once you are done press [Enter], or right-click.
- Then, specify the number of **Rows** and the number of **Columns** (original object is inclusive).
- Specify the **Row offset** (which is the distance between rows) and specify the **Column offset** (which is the distance between columns). While you are doing this keep two things in mind:
  - You have to be consistent. Measure the distance from the same reference (e.g., it is either from top-to-top, or from bottom-to-bottom, or from center-to-center, etc.).
  - You have to take care of the direction of copying. If you input a positive number, it will be either to the right, or up. If you input a negative number, it will be either to the left, or down.
- Specify the **Angle of the array**. By default it will be repeating the objects using the orthogonal angles.
- Click the **Preview** button to see the result of your inputs.
- AutoCAD will display the result, and the following prompt will appear:

```
Pick or press Esc to return to dialog or <Right-click to
accept array>:
```

- If you like the results, press [Enter], or right-click.
- If not, press [Esc].

■ See the following example:

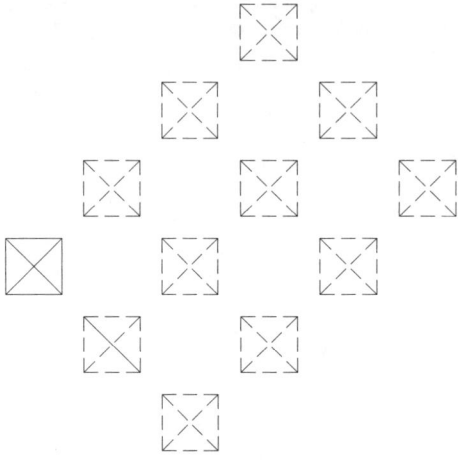

Dashed objects are duplicates
# of rows = 3, # of columns = 4
row offset=-ve, column offset=+ve
Angle of arrary = 45

RECTANGULAR ARRAY

Exercise 26

1. Start AutoCAD 2009.
2. Open the **Exercise_26.dwg** file.
3. Using rectangular array, array the chair to look like the following:

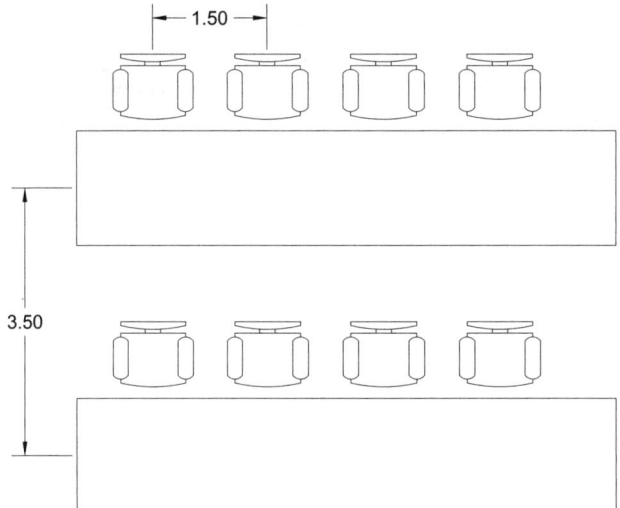

4. Save the file and close it.

Polar

- If you want to create duplications of certain objects simulating circular or semi-circular shapes, you want to use the Polar array.
- The following dialog box will appear:

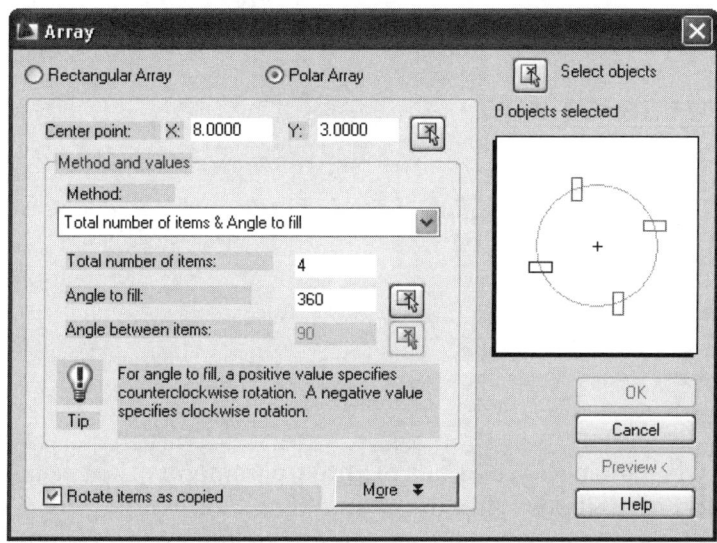

- First, click the **Select Objects** button to select the desired objects. Once you are done press [Enter], or rig ht-click.
- Then, specify the **Center point** of the array, either by inputting the coordinates in X and Y, or by clicking the **Pick Center Point** button and specifying the point with the mouse.
- You have three pieces of data to input and AutoCAD will only take two of these. These are:
  - Total number of items
  - Angle to fill
  - Angle between items

- The following diagram will illustrate the relationship between the three parameters:

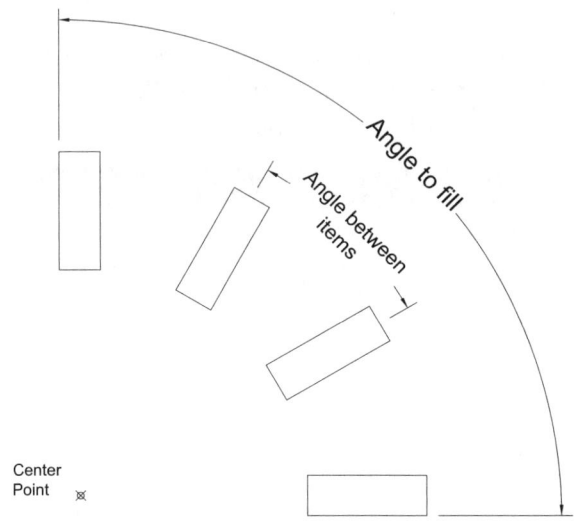

Total number of items = 4

- So you can specify two out of three parameters, which make them three different methods. They are:
  - Method 1: Specify the Total number of items & Angle to fill and AutoCAD will figure out the angles between items.
  - Method 2: Specify the Total number of items & Angle between items and AutoCAD will know the Angle to fill.
  - Method 3: Specify the Angle to fill & Angle between items and AutoCAD will calculate the Total number of items.
- Under **Methods and values**, select the proper method and input the corresponding values.
- Specify whether or not you want to **Rotate items as copied**. See the following example:

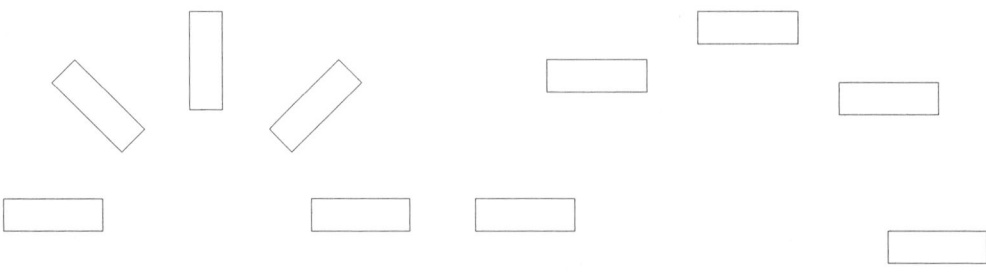

Rotate items as copied = ON   Rotate items as copied = OFF

POLAR ARRAY

Exercise 27

1. Start AutoCAD 2009.
2. Open the **Exercise_27.dwg file**.
3. Using the Polar array, array the square so you will get the following result:

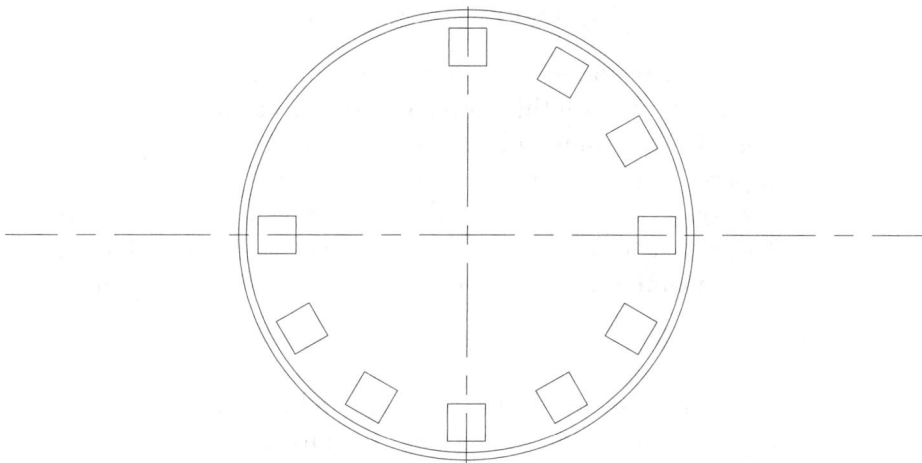

4. Save the file and close it.

MIRROR COMMAND

- The **Mirror** command is used to create a mirror image of selected objects.
- Make sure you are at the **Home** tab on the **Ribbon** and using the **Modify** panel, select the **Array** button.
- The first step is to:

```
Select objects:
```

- Once you are done press [Enter], or right-click.
- Now you need to specify the mirror line by specifying two points:

```
Specify first point of mirror line: (specify the first point
of the mirror line)
Specify second point of mirror line: (specify the second
point of the mirror line)
```

- The following applies to the mirror line:
  - There is no need to draw a line to act as a mirror line; two points will do the job.
  - The length of the mirror is not important, but the location and angle of the mirror line will affect the final result.
- The last prompt will be:

```
Erase source objects? [Yes/No] <N>: (type N, or Y)
```

- The **Mirror** command will produce an image in all cases, but what should AutoCAD do with the source objects? You can keep them or erase them.
- The **Mirror** command ends automatically.
- If part of the objects to be mirrored is text, you have to control whether or not you want to treat it as other objects and mirror it, or just copy it.
- To do that, prior to issuing the **Mirror** command, type at the Command Window **mirrtext**, and the following prompt will appear:

```
Enter new value for MIRRTEXT <0>:
```

- If you input 0 (zero) then the text will be copied.
- If you input 1, then the text will be mirrored.
- See the following example:

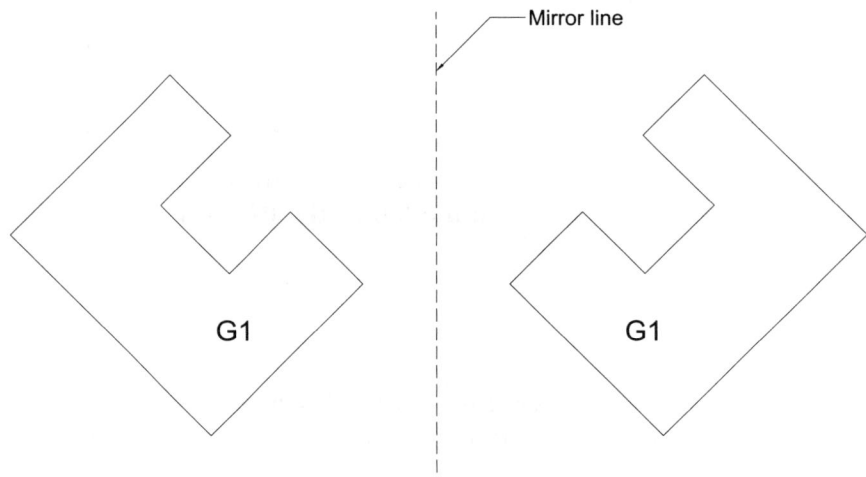

Mirrtext = 0 & Delete source objects = No

MIRRORING OBJECTS

 Exercise 28
1. Start AutoCAD 2009.
2. Open the **Exercise_28.dwg** file.
3. Using the **Mirror** command create the following shape:

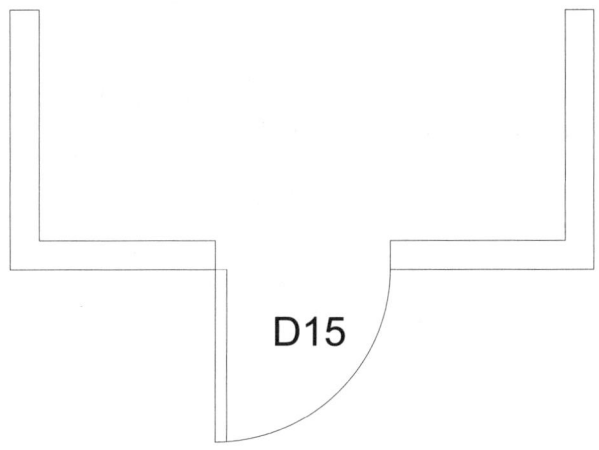

D15

4. Save the file and close it.

STRETCH COMMAND

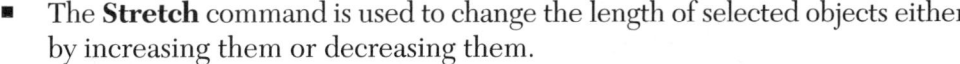

- The **Stretch** command is used to change the length of selected objects either by increasing them or decreasing them.
- Make sure you are at the **Home** tab on the **Ribbon** and using the **Modify** panel, select the **Stretch** button.
- The first step is to:

```
Select objects to stretch by crossing-window or crossing-
polygon...
```

- The **Stretch** command is one of few commands that insist on a certain method of selecting.
- The **Stretch** command asks you to select using either C or CP.
- As we discussed previously C and CP will select any object contained inside and any object will be touched (crossed) by C or CP lines.
- The **Stretch** command will utilize both facilities by setting the following rules:

- Any object contained FULLY inside C or CP will be moved.
- Any object crossed by C or CP will be stretched.
- Once you are done press [Enter], or right-click.
- The second prompt will be:

```
Specify base point or [Displacement] <Displacement>:
(specify Base point)
```

- The third prompt will be:

```
Specify second point or <use first point as displacement>:
(specify the destination point)
```

- The **Stretch** command ends automatically.
- See the following example:

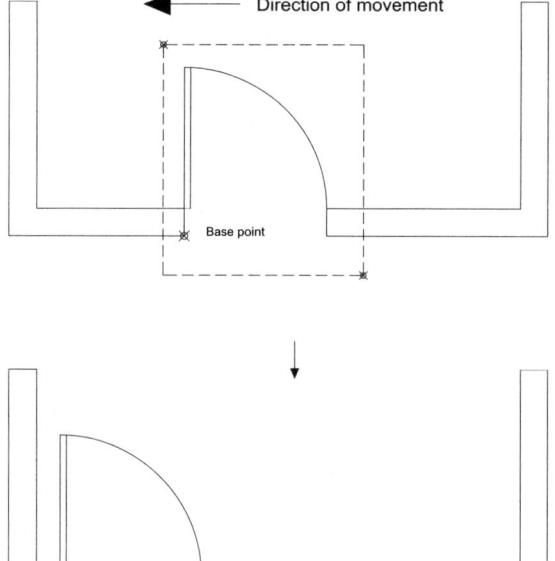

STRETCHING OBJECTS

Exercise 29

1. Start AutoCAD 2009.
2. Open the **Exercise_29.dwg** file.

3. Using the **Stretch** command, stretch the door 2 units to the left so it will look like the following:

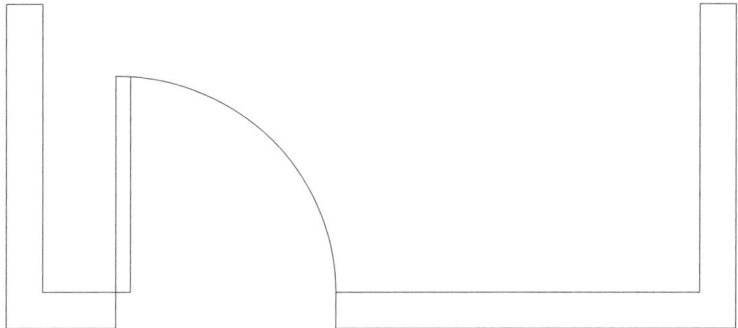

4. Save and close the file.

BREAK COMMAND

- The **Break** command is used to break an object into two pieces.
- Make sure you are at the **Home** tab on the **Ribbon** and using the **Modify** panel, select the **Break** button.
- The first step is to:

```
Select object:
```

- You can break one object at a time. When you select this object, AutoCAD will give you the following prompt:

```
Specify second break point or [First point]:
```

- To understand this prompt, note the following points:
  - In order to break an object you have to specify two points on it.
  - The selection you made can be considered a selection and also a first point, or can be considered a selection only. If you consider the selection as a selection and first point, respond to this prompt by specifying the second point.
- On the other hand, if you want the selection to be only the selection, type the letter F and AutoCAD will respond by the following prompt:

```
Specify first break point: (specify first breaking point)
Specify second break point: (specify second breaking point)
```

 ■ When you want to break a circle, take care to specify the two points CCW.

- See the following example:

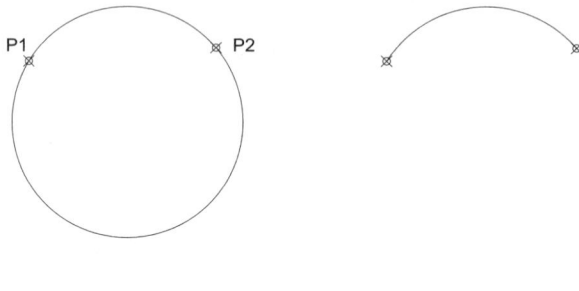

Before   After

- Make sure you are at the **Home** tab on the **Ribbon** and on the **Modify** panel, there is another tool called **Break at Point**, which is similar to the **Break** command except for the following differences:
- You will be asked to select only one point.
- AutoCAD will assume that the first point and the second point are in the same place.
- The object will be broken into two objects but connected.

BREAKING OBJECTS

Exercise 30
1. Start AutoCAD 2009.
2. Open the **Exercise_30.dwg** file.
3. Using the **Break** command, break the two circles to look something like this:

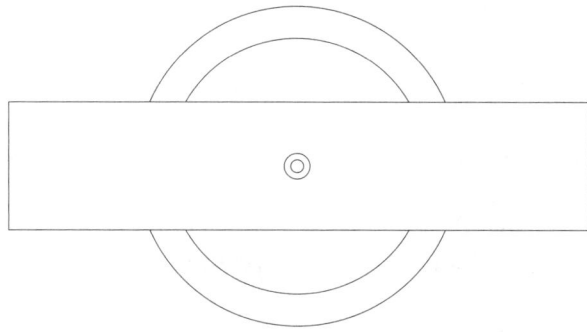

4. Save the file and close it.

GRIPS: INTRODUCTION

- Grips is a method of modifying your objects in an easy and quick fashion.
- Grips is done with a simple click on object(s) without issuing any command.
- Grips will do two things for you:
  - It will select the objects, and they will be ready for any Modifying commands to be issued, as they will act as a selection set.
  - A blue (default color) square will appear at certain places depending on an object's type. Here are some examples:

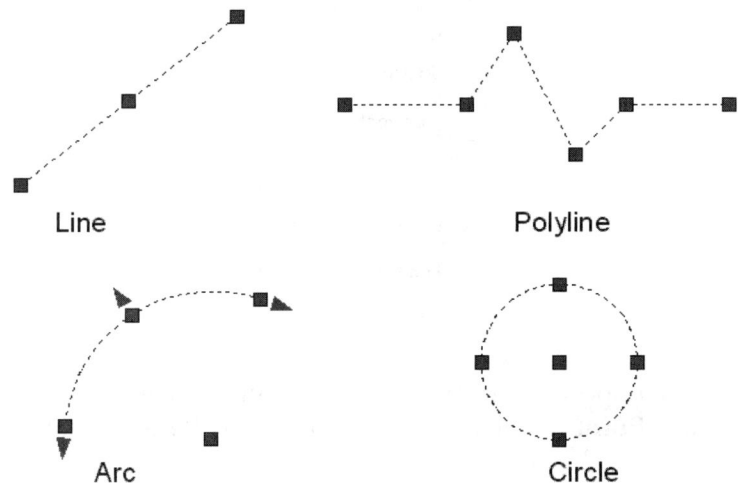

- These squares are the grips.
- There is a magnet relationship between these squares and the pick box of the cross hairs. So if you hover over them, the blue will turn to green to indicate that this is the current grip.
- If you click on one of these blue squares, you will:
  - Make it hot, turning it to red.
  - Make this grip a base point.
  - Start a group of five Modify commands (using the right-click menu).

GRIPS: THE FIVE COMMANDS

- Once you make one of the blue squares hot (by clicking on it), this grip will become the Base point for the five commands. They are:
  - Move
  - Mirror

- Rotate
- Scale
- Stretch

■ To see these commands, right-click, and the following shortcut menu will appear:

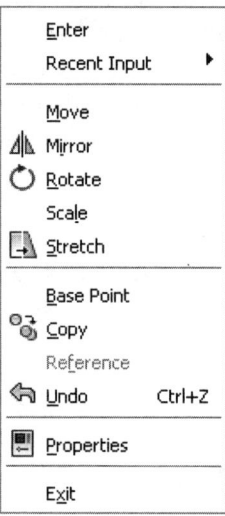

<u>E</u>nter
<u>R</u>ecent Input ▸
<u>M</u>ove
Mi<u>r</u>ror
<u>R</u>otate
Sca<u>l</u>e
<u>S</u>tretch
<u>B</u>ase Point
<u>C</u>opy
Re<u>f</u>erence
<u>U</u>ndo   Ctrl+Z
<u>P</u>roperties
E<u>x</u>it

■ The other options available in the shortcut menu are:
- **Base Point**, which is used to define a new Base point other than the one you started with.
- **Copy** is a mode rather than a command. Copy mode works with the other five commands mentioned above, and hence, will give you the ability to Rotate with Copy, Scale with Copy, etc.

GRIPS: STEPS & NOTES

■ The steps required to use Grips are as follows:
- Select the object(s) desired (direct clicking, window mode, or crossing mode).
- Select one of the grips to be your Base point, click it, and it will become hot (by default red).
- Right-click, and select from the short-cut menu the desired command, meanwhile you can specify another Base point, and/or you can select the Copy mode.
- Perform the steps of the desired command.
- Once you are done, press [Esc] once.

■ You can use **OSNAP** with Grips with no limitations. Also you can use **Polar** and **OTRACK**, so the modification will be done with accuracy.

■ **Mirror** is the only command that doesn't ask explicitly for the Base point. Why is it listed with the other four commands? The answer is that AutoCAD considers the first point of the mirror line to be the Base point.

■ Using Grips, to keep both the original and the mirrored image, you have to select Copy mode after you select the **Mirror** command.

■ You can *deselect* certain objects from the Grips by holding [Shift] and clicking on the object, avoiding the squares.

GRIPS & DYNAMIC INPUT

■ Dynamic Input can give you information about the objects with their grips appearing on the screen.

■ If you hover over an end grip of a line, Dynamic Input tells the length and the angle of that line.

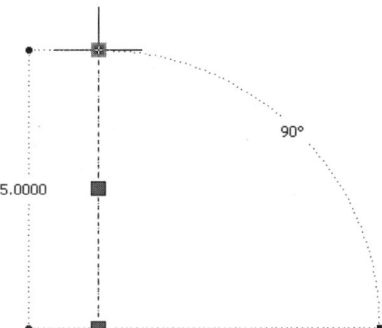

■ If you hover over an end grip shared between two lines, Dynamic Input tells you the length and angle of both lines:

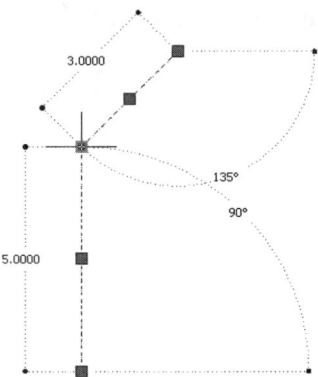

■ If you hover over the middle grip of an arc, Dynamic Input tells you the Radius and the Included Angle of the arc:

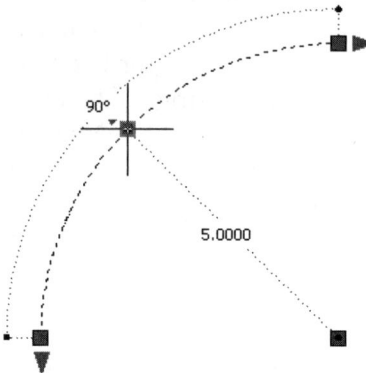

■ If you hover over the quadrant grip of a circle, Dynamic Input tells you the radius of the circle:

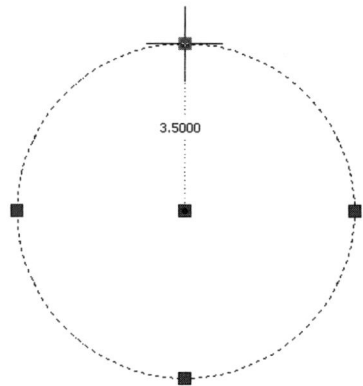

■ If you hover over an intermediate grip of a polyline, Dynamic Input tells you the lengths of the line segments (without the angles):

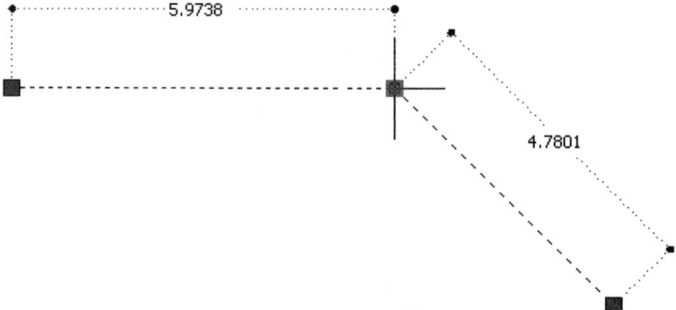

USING GRIPS

Exercise 31

1. Start AutoCAD 2009.

2. Open the **Exercise_31.dwg** file.

3. Without issuing any command, select the upper circle. Make the center hot, then right-click, select **Scale**, then right-click again, and select **Copy**. For the **Scale factor** prompt type **0.5** and press [Esc] twice.

4. In the right part of the base, without issuing any command, select the rectangle. Make one of the blue grips hot, by clicking it, right-click, select **Rotate**, then right-click again, and select **Base Point**, so you can specify a new base point, which is the center of the rectangle (using **OSNAP** and **OTRACK**) and using **Rotation angle** = 90. Press [Esc] twice.

5. Select the rotated rectangle at the right part of the base, select any grip to make it hot, then right-click and select **Mirror**, then right-click again, and select **Copy**, and right-click for the thrid time and select **Base Point**, and specify one of the two endpoints of the vertical lines separating the two parts of the base, then specify the other endpoint. Press [Esc] twice. The shape will end up like this:

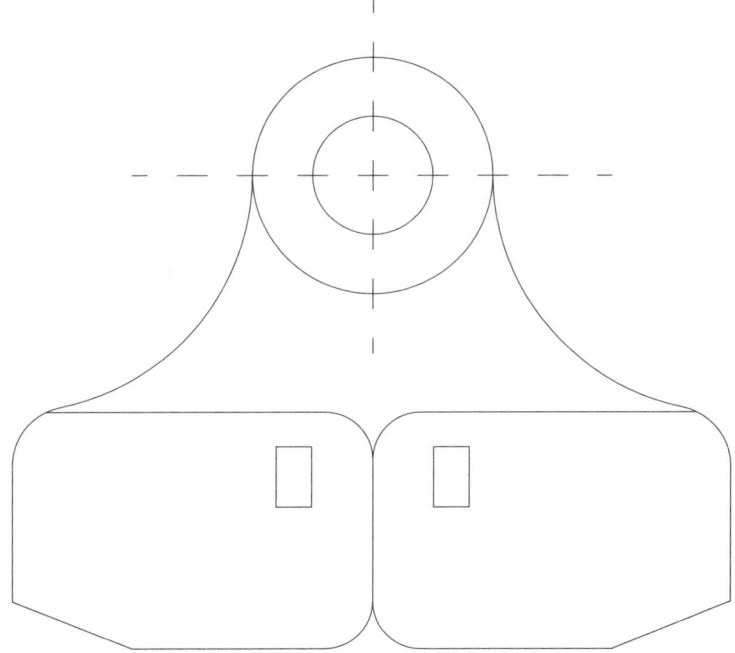

6. Save the file and close it.

NOTES

CHAPTER REVIEW

1. What is common between the Move, Copy, Rotate, Scale, Stretch commands?
   a. They are all Modifying commands.
   b. They all use Base points.
   c. They all change the length of an object.
   d. A & B.

2. In the **Stretch** command, you have to use _____ or _____ while selecting objects.

3. Mirrtext is used to control whether to copy or to mirror the text in the **Mirror** command:
   a. True.
   b. False.

4. If you break a circle, take care to specify the two points:
   a. CCW.
   b. CW.
   c. Doesn't matter.
   d. You can't break a circle.

5. I can scale using Scale factor = -1.
   a. True.
   b. False.

6. Using the Array command and the Rectangular option, the Row offset must be _____ if you want to repeat the objects downward.

CHAPTER REVIEW ANSWERS

1. d
2. C or CP
3. a
4. a
5. b
6. negative

6 DEALING WITH BLOCKS

In This Chapter
◊ What are blocks?
◊ Creating and inserting blocks
◊ Exploding blocks
◊ Design Center and Tool Palettes and their effect on blocks
◊ Editing blocks

WHAT ARE BLOCKS?

- A Block in AutoCAD is any shape that is repeated in one or more drawings more than once.
- So, instead of drawing it each and every time you need it, use the following steps:
  - Draw it once.
  - Store it as a block.
  - Insert it as many times as you wish.
- Blocks in AutoCAD have changed in the past five years, which has made some of the old procedures obsolete.
- In our discussion we will discuss the old methods, but we will concentrate more on the new methods for using blocks.

CREATING BLOCKS

- The first step in creating blocks in AutoCAD is to draw the desired shape.
- While drawing the shape, consider the following three guidelines:
- Draw the shape in Layer 0 (zero).

- Draw the shape in certain units.
- Draw the shape in the right dimensions.

Why layer 0?

- Layer 0 is different from any other layer in AutoCAD because it will allow the block to be transparent both in color and in linetype.
- If you draw the shape, which will be a block while layer 0 is current, then insert it in another layer with the red color and dashdot linetype.

Why certain units?

- If you want AutoCAD to automatically re-scale your block to fit into the current drawing units, you have to specify the units of the block.

What are right dimensions?

- Right dimensions are either:
- The real dimension of the shape.
- Or, values such as 1, 10, 100, 1000 for the distances, so it will be easy for you to scale the block once you insert it.
- Let's assume we draw the following shape:

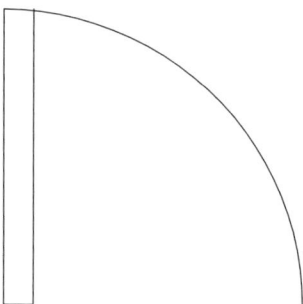

- The next step would be to think about a point that will act as the Base point (the handle for this block).
- Also, think of a good name for this block.
- If all of these things are ready in your mind, now issue the command.
- Make sure you are at the **Home** tab on the **Ribbon** and using the **Block** panel, select the **Create** button.

- The following dialog box will appear:

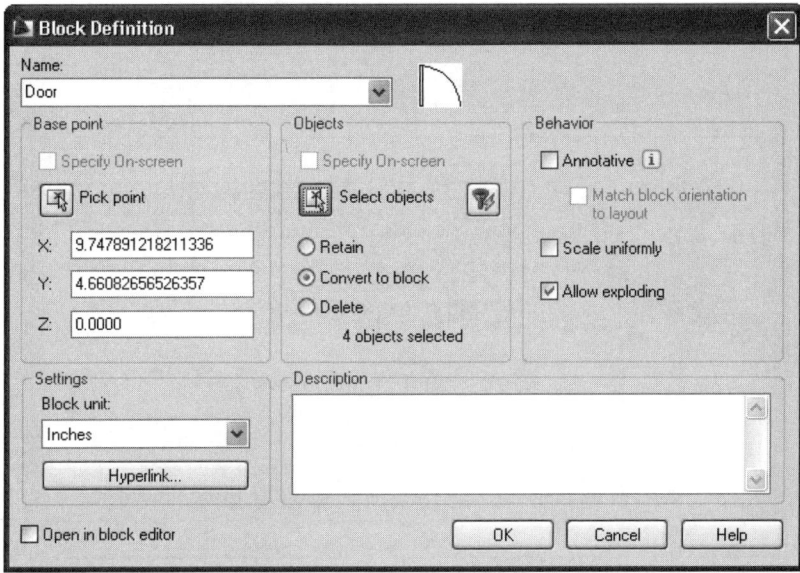

- Type the name of the block (should not exceed 255 characters, similar to the layer naming conditions).
- Under **Base point**, click the **Pick point** button to input the base point of the block. Once you are done press [Enter], or right-click. Or, you can click the checkbox **Specify On-screen** to specify the Base point after the dialog box closes.
- Under **Objects**, click the **Select objects** button to select the objects. Once you are done press [Enter], or right-click. Or, you can click the checkbox **Specify On-screen** to specify the Base point after the dialog box closes.
- Now select one of three choices of what to do with the objects you draw to create this block:
  - **Retain** them as objects.
  - **Convert** them to blocks.
  - **Delete** them.
- Leave **Annotative** off (this is an advanced feature).
- Select whether the block should be always be **Scaled uniformly** (X scale = Y scale).
- Select whether the block can be exploded in the future.
- Under **Block unit**, select the unit by which you draw the shape. This will help AutoCAD in the Automatic scaling feature.

- Click the **Hyperlink** button. The following dialog box will appear:

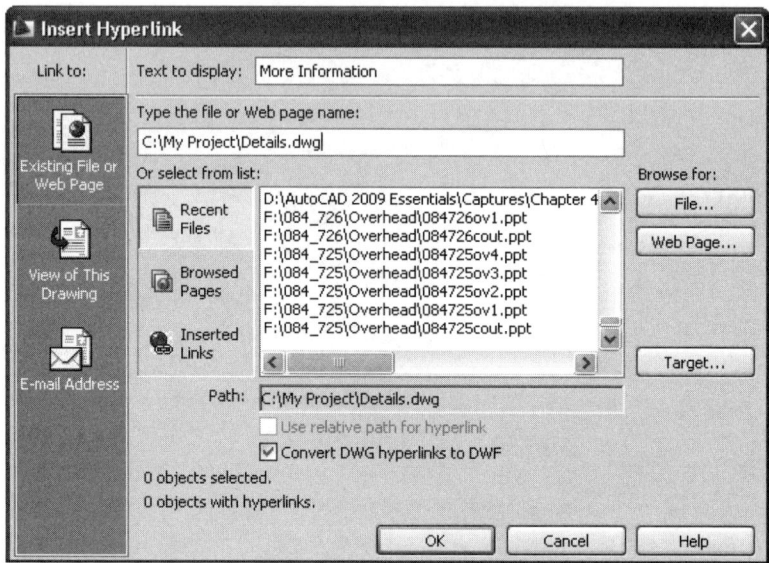

- This dialog box will allow the user to insert a hyperlink inside the block to take the user to a web site, a drawing file with more detail, MS Word file, Excel file for calculation, etc.
- After you finish, when you get close to the block, you will see something like the following:

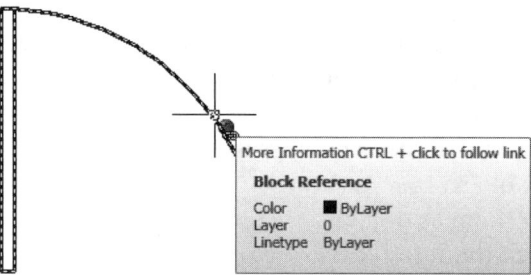

- As you can see the shape of the hyperlink will be displayed, and a help message will appear telling you to hold [Ctrl] + click the block to open the desired link.
- Write a description for your block.
- Select whether to allow this block to be opened in the block editor (block editor is an advanced feature used to create dynamic blocks) or keep it off for the time being.
- When you are done, click **OK**.

- At this moment, let's imagine that our drawing has a cabinet, the door of the cabinet will be opened, and the defined block will be put inside it. This block will be intact. Even when you insert it, you will insert a copy of it.
- You can define as many blocks as you wish.

CREATING A BLOCK (METRIC)

 Workshop 3-A

1. Start AutoCAD 2009.
2. Open the **Workshop_03.dwg** file.
3. Make layer 0 current.
4. Choose an empty space and draw the following shape (without dimensions):

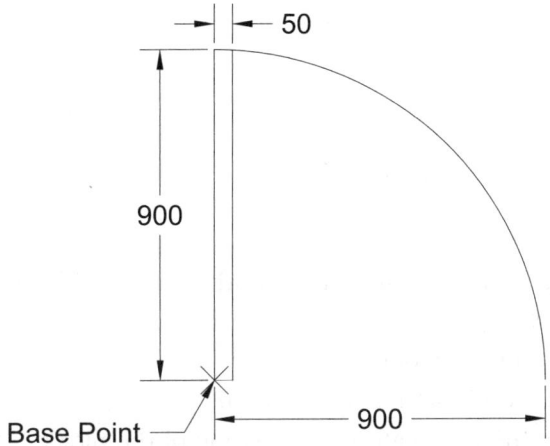

5. Using the **Make Block** command, create a block using the following information:
   a. Block name = Door.
   b. Specify the designated Base point.
   c. Delete the shape after the creation of the block.
   d. Block unit = Millimeters.
   e. Scale uniformly = off, Allow exploding = on.
   f. Description = Door to be used inside the building. Refer to the door table.
   g. Open in block editor = off.
6. Save the file and close it.

CREATING A BLOCK (IMPERIAL)

Workshop 3-B

1. Start AutoCAD 2009.
2. Open the **Workshop_03.dwg** file.
3. Make layer 0 current.
4. Choose an empty space and draw the following shape (without dimensions):

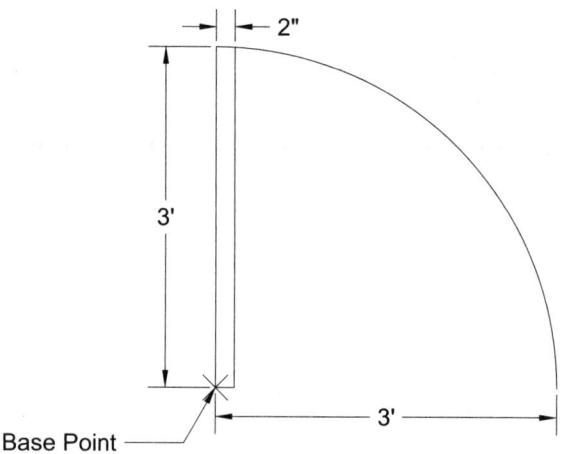

5. Using the **Make Block** command, create a block using the following information:
   a. Block name = Door.
   b. Specify the designated Base point.
   c. Delete the shape after the creation of the block.
   d. Block unit = Inches.
   e. Scale uniformly = off, Allow exploding = on.
   f. Description = Door to be used inside the building. Refer to the door table.
   g. Open in block editor = off.
6. Save the file and close it.

INSERTING BLOCKS

■   Once you create a block, you can use it in your drawing as many times as you wish.

- When inserting the block in your drawing, consider the following guidelines:
- Set the desired layer to be current.
- You have to make the drawing ready to accommodate the block (e.g., finish the door openings before inserting the door block).
- After you consider all of these things, now issue the command.

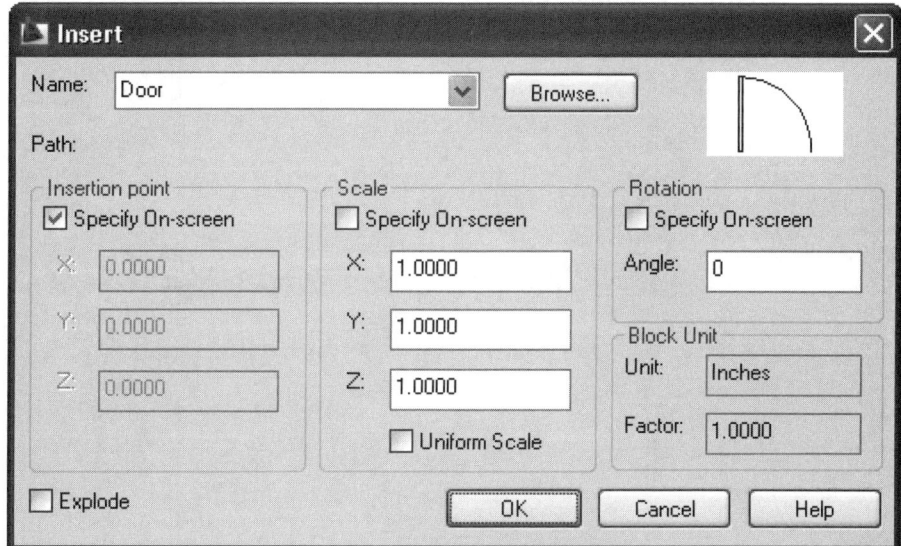

- Make sure you are at the **Home** tab on the **Ribbon** and using the **Block** panel, select the **Insert** button.
- The following dialog box will appear:

- Select the name of the desired block from the list.
- Specify the **Insertion point**, using one of two methods:
- Click the **Specify On-screen** checkbox, which means you will specify the insertion point using the mouse (this is easier than the next method).
- Type the coordinates of the insertion point.
- Specify the **Scale** of the block by using one of the following methods:
- Click the **Specify On-screen** checkbox, which means you will specify the scale using the mouse.
- Type the scale factor in all three directions of the insertion point, which means you can set the X scale factor not equal to the Y scale factor.
- Another way to do scaling is to click the **Uniform Scale** checkbox, which will allow you to input only one scale, the others will follow.
- Specify the **Rotation** of the block by using one of the following methods:
- Click the **Specify On-screen** checkbox, which means you will specify the rotation angle using the mouse.

- Type the rotation angle.
- The **Block unit** part will be read-only, and hence will show you the unit that you specified when you created this block. Also, it will show the **Factor,** which is based on the Block unit and the drawing unit (which is defined in the **Format/Units** dialog box). According to this factor AutoCAD will automatically scale the block to suit the current drawing.
- Click **OK** to end th e command.
- Using the Scale of the block you can use negative values to insert mirrored images of your block.
- See the following example:

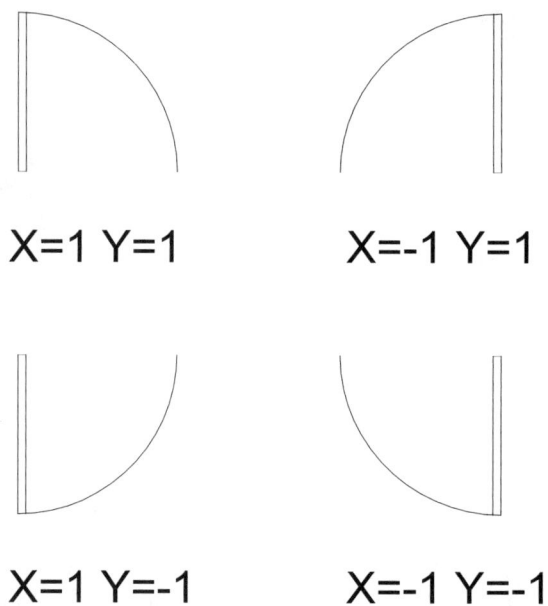

INSERTING BLOCKS (METRIC)

Workshop 4-A

1. Start AutoCAD 2009.
2. Open the **Workshop_04.dwg** file.

3. Make layer **Doors** current.

4. Using the **Insert** command, insert block **Door** in the proper places as shown below:

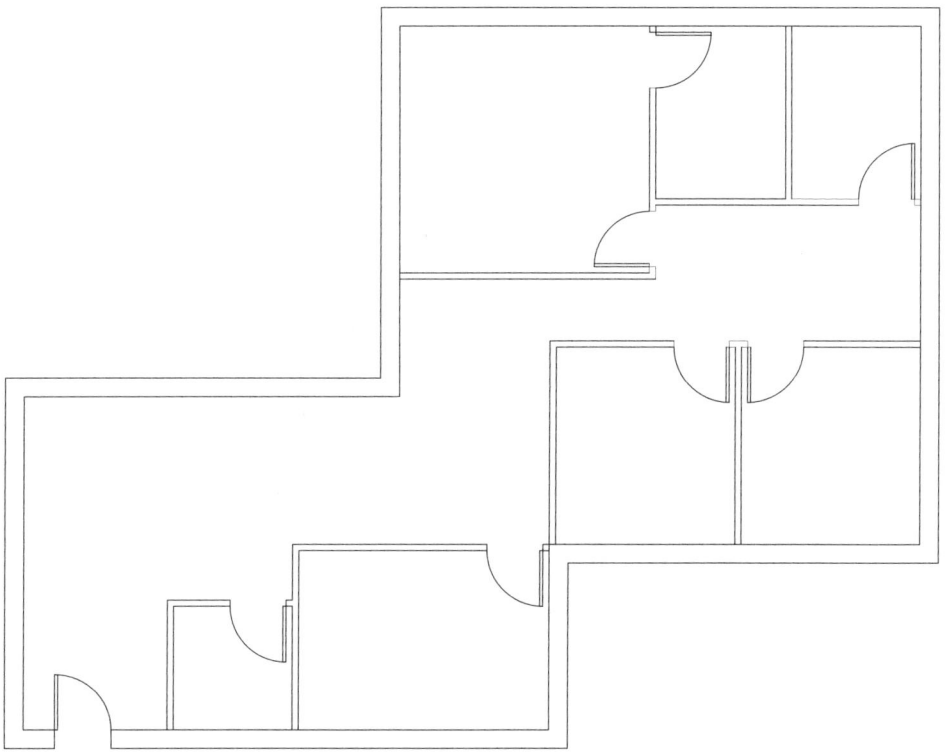

5. Save the file and close it.

INSERTING BLOCKS (IMPERIAL)

Workshop 4-B

1. Start AutoCAD 2009.

2. Open the **Workshop_04.dwg** file.

3. Make layer **Doors** current.

4. Using the **Insert** command, insert block **Door** in the proper places as shown below:

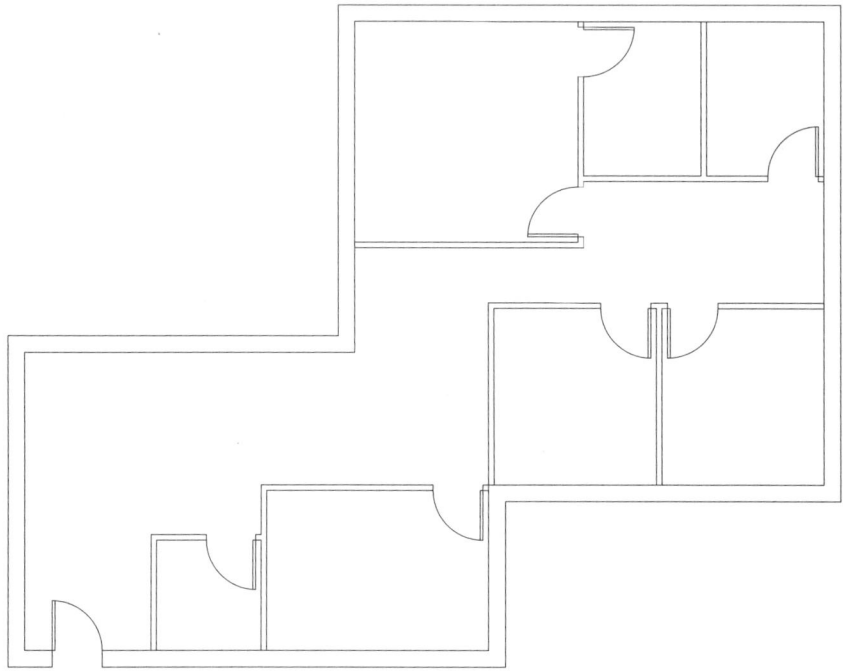

5. Save the file and close it.

EXPLODING BLOCKS

- By default when you insert incidences of blocks, keep them as blocks, and don't try to change their nature. But, in some (rare) cases, you may want to explode the block (which is one object) to the objects forming it.
- To do this, you have to use the **Explode** command.

- Make sure you are at the **Home** tab on the **Ribbon** and using the **Modify** panel, select the **Explode** button.
- AutoCAD will prompt you to:

```
Select objects:
```

- Once you are done, press [Enter], or right-click. Once you explode a block, it will go back to its original layer (the layer the block was created in).

- Don't use this command unless you really need it.

- In older versions of AutoCAD, a block can't be defined as a cutting edge or boundary edge in the Trim and Extend commands, but starting with AutoCAD 2005, you can select blocks as cutting edges and boundary edges. So, no need to explode the block for this purpose.
- You can use this command to explode **Pline** to lines and arcs.

SHARING DATA BETWEEN AUTOCAD FILES USING DESIGN CENTER (BLOCKS)

- AutoCAD has a very handy tool called **Design Center**, which allows you to share blocks, layers, and other things between different files.
- We will concentrate on blocks in this section.
- The file you want to take the blocks from could be anywhere:
- It can be on your computer.
- It can be on your colleague's computer, which is hooked up on the local area network of your company.
- It can be on a web site on the Internet.
- To start the **Design Center** command make sure you are at the **View** tab on the **Ribbon** and using the **Palettes** panel, select the **Design Center** button.
- The following will appear on the screen:

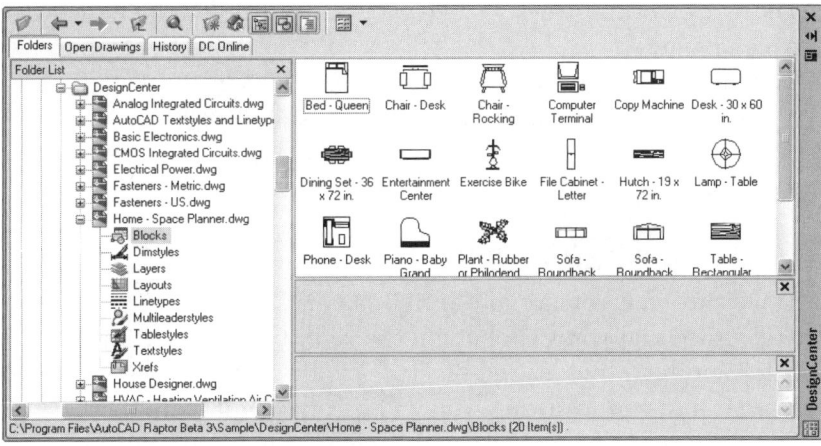

- As you can see the Design Center palette is split into two parts.
- At the left, you will see the hierarchy of your computer, including all your hard disks and network places (just like **My Computer** in Windows).

- Select (by double-clicking) the desired hard disk, folder, drawing, and you will see something like the following:

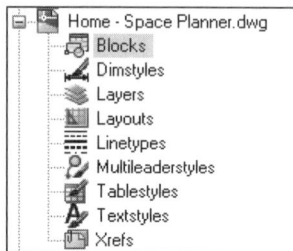

- As you can see you can take from this drawing the following:
  - Blocks
  - Dimstyles
  - Layers
  - Layouts
  - Linetypes
  - Tablestyles
  - Textstyles
  - Xrefs
- Once you click (you don't need to double-click) the word Blocks, look at the right part of Design Center and you will see the blocks available in this drawing.
- There are several ways to take blocks from this drawing to your drawing, which include:
  - Drag-and-Drop (using the left mouse button)
  - Drag-and-Drop (using the right mouse button)
  - Double-click
  - Right-click

Drag-and-Drop using the left mouse button

- Make sure that you are in the right layer.
- Make sure that you switched on the right **OSNAP** settings.
- Click and hold the desired block.
- Drag it into your drawing; you will be holding it from the Base point.
- Once the right **OSNAP** is caught release the mouse button.

Drag-and-Drop using the right mouse button

- Make sure that you are in the right layer.
- Make sure that you switched on the right **OSNAP** settings.
- Right-click and hold the desired block.

- Drag it into your drawing.
- Release the mouse button, and the following shortcut menu will appear:

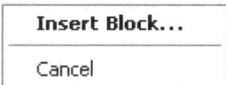

- It is the same as the **Insert** command discussed earlier.
- Follow the sam e steps.

Double-click

- If you double-click any block in Design Center, the **Insert** dialog box will appear and you can perform the same steps.

Right-click

- Select the desired block, and right-click. The following shortcut menu will appear:

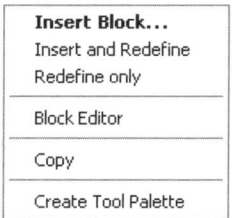

- If you select **Insert Block**, the Insert dialog box will appear as discussed before.
- We will be discussing redefining in the following pages.
- Select the **Block Editor** option if you want to open this block in the Block Editor in order to add Dynamic features to it.
- If you select **Copy**, that means you will copy to the clipboard of Windows, and hence you can use it in AutoCAD or other programs. To use it select **Edit/Paste**, or **Ctrl+V**.
- In the following sections we will discuss **Tool Palette**, the last option in this shortcut menu.

BLOCK AUTOMATIC SCALING

- If you are using the Design Center to pull blocks from other drawings and find that the block is either too big, or too small, you will know that there is something wrong with the Automatic Scaling.
- To control the Automatic Scaling you take the following two steps:

- While you are creating the block make sure you set the right **Block unit**.
- Before you bring the block from Design Center, set the **Units to scale inserted contents** in **Format/Units**.

Block unit

- When y ou are creating a block, the following dialog box will appear:

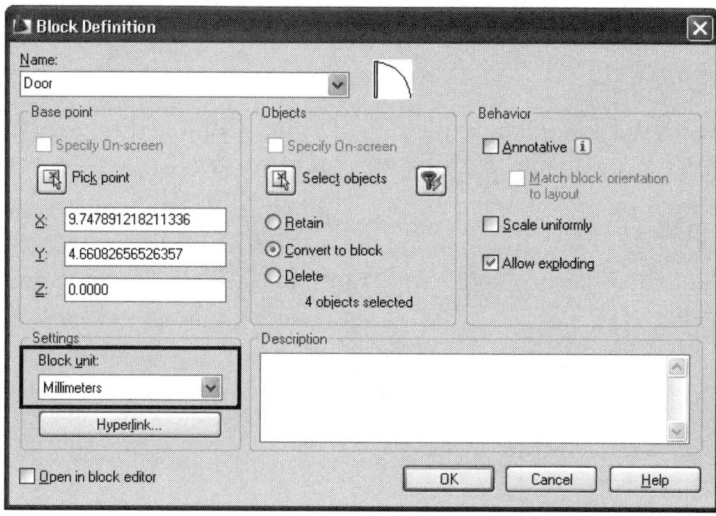

- Under the part labeled **Block unit**, select the desired unit.

Units to scale inserted contents

- Before using any block from the Design Center, select **Format/Units**. The following dialog box will appear:

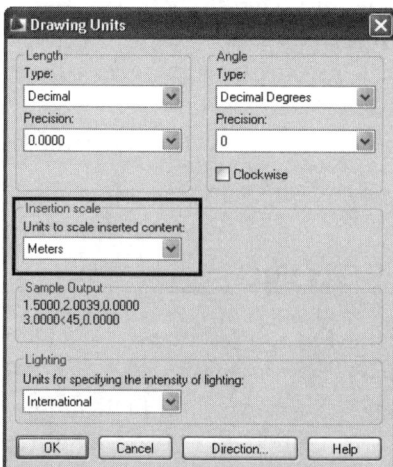

- Under the part labeled **Units to scale inserted contents**, set the desired scale used in your drawing.
- Using the two scales AutoCAD will calculate the proper scale the Block should appear with.

USING DESIGN CENTER (METRIC)

Workshop 5-A

1. Start AutoCAD 2009.
2. Open the **Workshop_05.dwg** file.
3. Make layer **Furniture** current.
4. Select **Format/Units**, and make sure that **Units to scale inserted content** is **Millimeters**.
5. Open the Design Center. From the left part of the Design Center pallette double-click the Drive containing the AutoCAD 2009 folder.
6. Select **AutoCAD 2009/Sample/Design Center**.
7. Using **Home Space Planner.dwg**, **House Designer.dwg**, and **Kitchens. dwg** while **OSNAP** is off drag-and-drop the following blocks as shown:

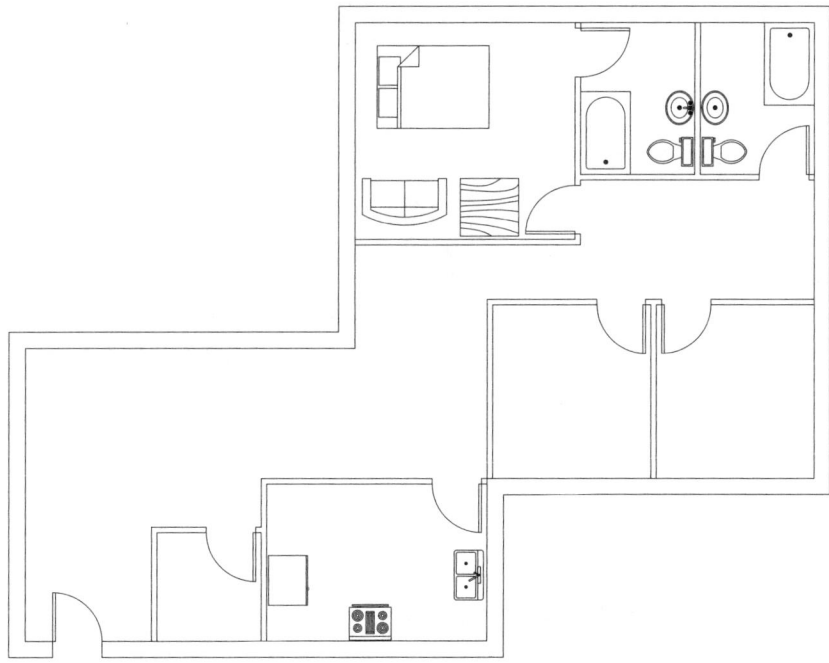

8. Save the file and close it.

USING DESIGN CENTER (IMPERIAL)

Workshop 5-B

1. Start AutoCAD 2009.
2. Open the **Workshop_05.dwg** file.
3. Make layer **Furniture** current .
4. Select **Format/Units**, and make sure that **Units to scale inserted content** is **Inches.**
5. Open the Design Center. From the left part of the Design Center Pallette double-click the drive containing the AutoCAD 2009 folder.
6. Select **AutoCAD 2009/Sample/Design Center.**
7. Using **Home Space Planner.dwg**, **House Designer.dwg**, and **Kitchens. dwg** while **OSNAP** is off drag-and-drop the following blocks as shown:

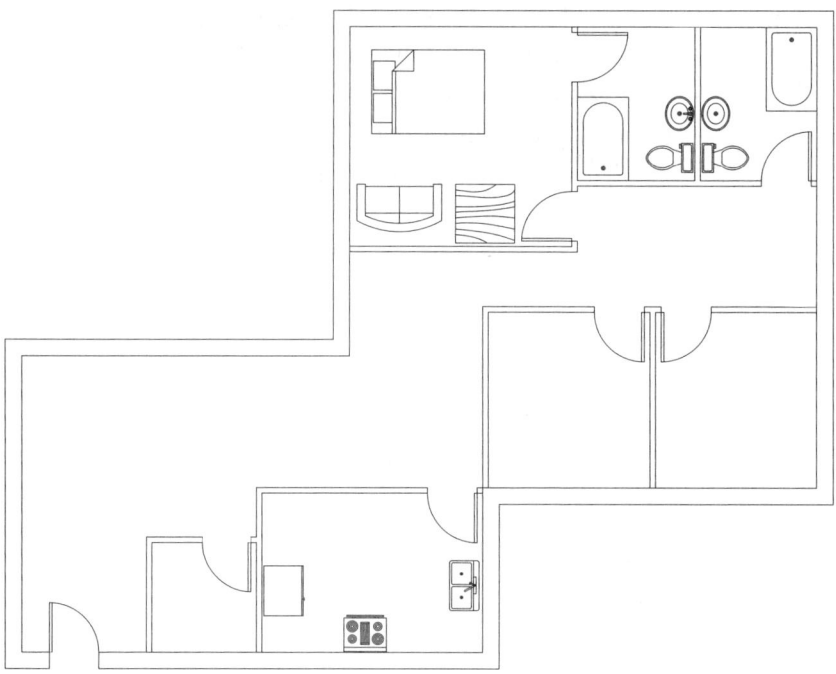

8. Save the file and close it.

TOOL PALETTE: INTRODUCTION

- Design Center gives us the ability to share data from other files. But for blocks you have to do all the labor work such as make sure you are at the right layer, specify the rotation angle, scale factor, etc. Also, you need to search for the desired content each and every time you need it.

- Tool Palette solves all of these problems.
- Tool Palette will keep Blocks, Hatch, and other items available for you regardless of which drawing you are using. You can keep most anything inside the Tool Palette.
- The Tool Palette works with the same Drag-and-Drop method we learned in Design Center, but in Tool Palette the method will be done in one of two ways: from the Tool Palette, and to the Tool Palette, as will be discussed in the following sections.
- The Tool Palette is unique per computer, and not per drawing, hence if you create (customize) a Tool Palette it will be available for all your drawings.
- To start the **Tool Palette** command, make sure you are at the **View** tab on the **Ribbon** and using the **Palettes** panel, select the **Tool Palettes** button:
- The following will appear on the screen:

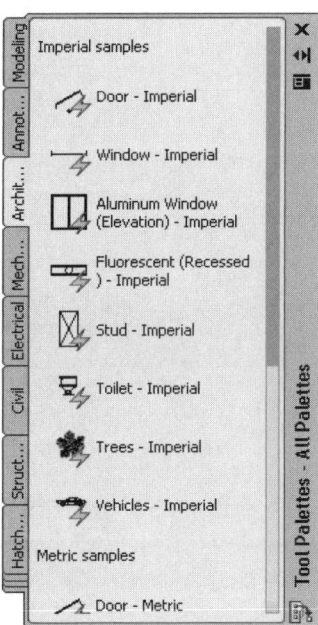

- You will see several premade Tool Palettes by Autodesk for your immediate use.
- You can create your own Tool Palette, using different methods, depending on the source.
- You can copy, cut, and paste Tools inside each Tool Palette.
- You can customize the Tools inside each Tool Palette.

CREATING A TOOL PALETTE FROM SCRATCH

- Right-click over the name of any existing Tool Palette, and the following shortcut menu will appear:

- Select the **New Palette** option and a new Tool Palette will be added. Type in the name of the new Tool Palette:

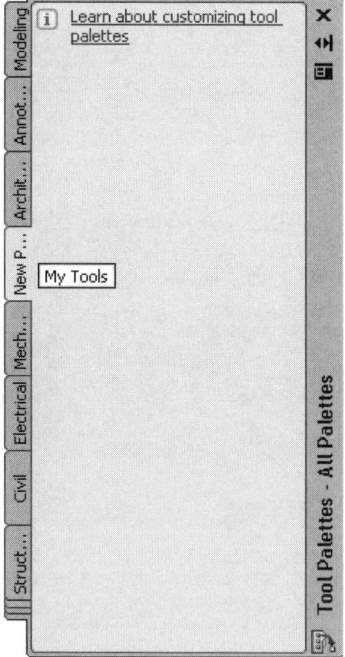

- A new empty Tool Palette will be added.
- To fill this Tool Palette use the drag-and-drop method from the graphical screen or from Design Center.
- By default the local blocks of the current drawing are *NOT* available automatically in your Tool Palettes.

Example

- Assume we have the following drawing in front of us. This drawing contains a polyline, hatch, and dimension:

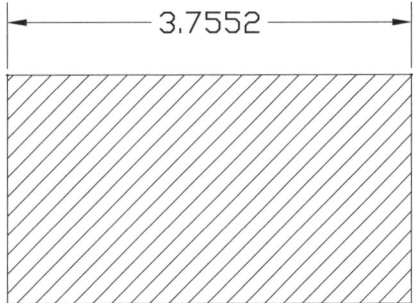

- Without issuing any command, click on the polyline then hold (avoid the blue rectangles) and drag it into the empty Tool Palette. Do the same thing for the hatch and the linear dimension. Your Tool Palette will look like this:

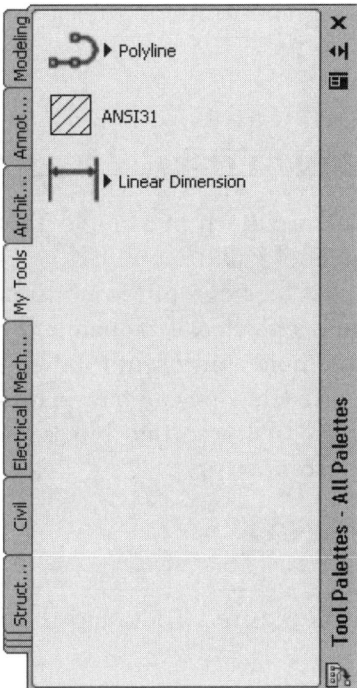

CREATING A TOOL PALETTE USING DESIGN CENTER

- You can copy all blocks in one drawing using Design Center and create a Tool Palette from them, holding the name of the drawing.
- To do that, follow these steps:
  - Start Design Center.
  - Go to the desired folder, then to the desired file.
  - Right-click on the **Blocks** icon, and the following shortcut menu will appear:

- Select the **Create Tool Palette** option and a new Tool Palette will be added with the name of the file you chose and all the blocks.

- You can also drag-and-drop any block from the Design Center to any desired Tool Palette.

CUSTOMIZING TOOL PALETTES

- Blocks and the Hatch pattern in a single Tool Palette can be copied, then pasted in the same Tool Palette.
- The purpose of this is to assign different properties to each tool.
- For example, there is a block called chair and you want to make three copies of it, and each would hold a different rotation angle. The same thing applies to hatch patterns, as each copy can have a different scale factor.
- Also, you can specify that a certain block (or hatch) go to a certain layer regardless of the current layer.

How to copy and paste a tool

- Follow these steps:
  - Right-click on the desired Tool, and the following shortcut menu will appear:

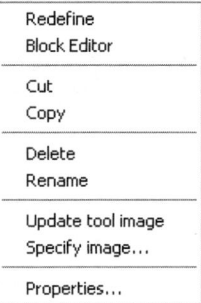

- Select the **Copy** option.
- In the same Tool Palette right-click and the following shortcut menu will appear:

- Select the **Paste** option. The copied tool will reside at the bottom of the Tool Palette and will have the same name.

How to customize a Tool

- Follow these steps:
  - Right-click on the copied tool, and the following shortcut menu will appear:

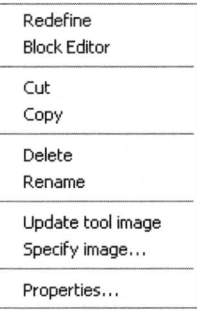

- Select the **Properties** option, and the following dialog box will appear:

Tool Properties

Image:
Name:
Chair - Desk
Description:
DesignCenter Home-Space Planner example

Insert	
Name	Chair - Desk
Source file	C:\Program Files\AutoCAD Raptor B...
Scale	1.0000
Auxiliary scale	None
Rotation	0
Prompt for rot...	No
Explode	No

General	
Color	-- use current
Layer	-- use current
Linetype	-- use current
Plot style	-- use current
Lineweight	-- use current

OK   Cancel   Help

- You can change the **Name** and **Description** of the tool.
- There are two types of properties:
  - Insert properties: Block properties are different from Hatch properties.
  - General properties such as Color, Layer, Linetype, Plot style, and Lineweight.
- By default, the General properties are all **use current**, which means use the current settings.
- Both Insert properties and General properties are all changeable.
- In the **Tool Properties** dialog box, if the image of the block is not clear, you can change it. Take the following steps:
  - Go to the image, right-click, and the following shortcut menu will appear:

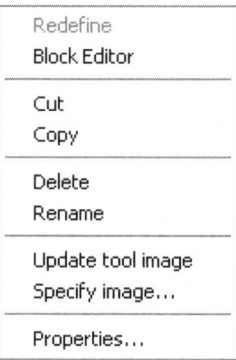

Redefine
Block Editor

Cut
Copy

Delete
Rename

Update tool image
Specify image...

Properties...

• Select **Specify image**, and the following dialog box will appear:

Select Image File			
Look in: 🗁 Images			
Name ▲	Size	Type	Date Mo
ANSI3132	1 KB	PNG Image	26-Feb-C
ANSI3164	1 KB	PNG Image	26-Feb-C
Bed - Queen32	1 KB	PNG Image	26-Feb-C
Bed - Queen64	1 KB	PNG Image	26-Feb-C
Block tool_28989317-FCE4-40...	1 KB	PNG Image	26-Feb-C
Block tool_28989317-FCE4-40...	1 KB	PNG Image	26-Feb-C
Chair - Desk32	1 KB	PNG Image	26-Feb-C
Chair - Desk64	1 KB	PNG Image	26-Feb-C
Chair - Rocking32	1 KB	PNG Image	26-Feb-C
Chair - Rocking64	1 KB	PNG Image	26-Feb-C

File name: _____ **Open**

Files of type: All Image files (*.bmp, *.jpg, *.png, *.gif, *.tif) **Cancel**

• Select the desired folder and the desired file, and click **Open**. Now the new image will appear.

USING AND CUSTOMIZING TOOL PALETTES (METRIC & IMPERIAL)

Workshop 6-A & 6-B

1. Start AutoCAD 2009.
2. Start a new file.
3. Make layer 0 current.
4. Open the Design Center. From the left part of the Design Center Pallette double-click the drive containing the AutoCAD 2009 folder.
5. Select **AutoCAD 2009/Sample/Design Center.**
6. Select the **Home Space Planner.dwg** file.
7. Right-click the Blocks icon, and select **Create Tool Palette**. A new Tool Palette with the name **Home Space Planner** will be added.
8. Select the **House Designer.dwg** file.
9. Show the blocks of this file.
10. Locate **Bath Tub – 26 x 60** in the block and drag-and-drop it into your newly made Tool Palette.
11. Do the same thing for the **Sink Ovel Top** block.
12. Right-click on the name of the Tool Palette and select **Rename**, and change the name to **My Tools.**

13. In the **My Tools** Tool Palette, right-click on the Tool named **Chair – Rocking**, and select **Properties**. In the dialog box, change the **Layer** from **use current** to **Furniture.**

14. Right-click on the same Tool again, and select **Copy**. Select an empty space and **Paste** it <u>three</u> times.

15. Using the same method in step 12, change the Rotation angle of these blocks to be 90, -90, 180.

16. Now you have a Tool Palette that you can use in all of your drawings on this computer.

EDITING BLOCKS

- Assume that after you created a block and inserted it several times in your drawing, you discovered that there is something wrong with it.
- To solve your problem, you need to redefine the original block. We can do this by using the **Edit In-Place** command.
- To start the **Edit In-Place** command, make sure you are at the **Block & References** tab on the **Ribbon** and using the **References** panel, select the **Edit In-Place** button.
- AutoCAD will give you the following prompt:

```
Select reference:
```

- Select any incidence of the block. The following dialog box will appear:

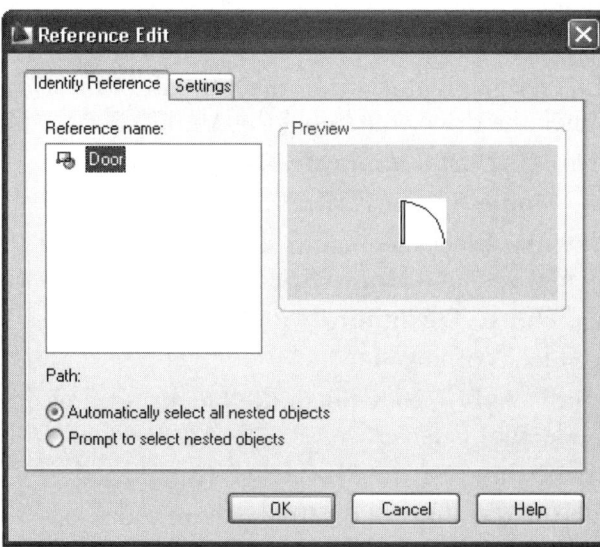

- Click **OK**. Once you do that, the drawing will be dimmed (you can't edit the dimmed objects), except for your block.
- A new panel called Edit Reference will be displayed at the maximum right.
- In this new panel there are four buttons. If for any reason you wanted other objects (normal objects and not blocks) to be available so you can edit the desired block, use one of the following methods:

- Click **Add to Working set** button, and AutoCAD will prompt:

```
Select objects:
```

- Select the desired objects to be added.

- Click the **Remove from Working set** button. AutoCAD will prompt:

```
Select objects:
```

- Select the desired objects to be removed.
- Click the **Close Reference** button. The following dialog box will appear:

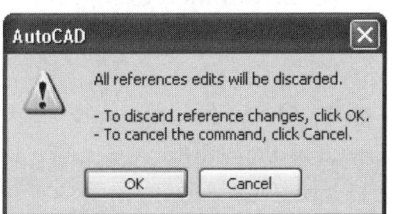

- If you really want to discard all the changes you made to the block, simply click **OK**, otherwise click **Cancel**.
- Click **Save Reference Edits**. The following dialog box will appear:

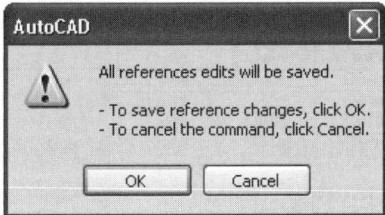

- Click **OK** if you are sure of the changes you made, otherwise click **Cancel**.
- If you issued the command **Save Reference Edits**, and then you clicked **OK**, all incidences of the block would change accordingly.

- Another way to issue the command **Edit In-Place** is to click any incidence of the desired block, then right-click, and in the shortcut menu, select **Edit Block In-Place**.

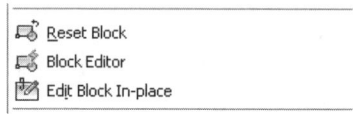

EDITING BLOCKS (METRIC)

Workshop 7-A

1. Start AutoCAD 2009.
2. Open the **Workshop_07.dwg** file.
3. Start the **Refedit** command.
4. Select one of the doors you inserted. Once the dialog box appears click **OK**. All of the drawing will be dimmed except for the selected block.
5. Select the arc representing the swing of the door. Right-click and select **Properties**.
6. Change its layer to be **Door_Swing**.
7. Change the Linetype scale = **200**.
8. Close the Properties palette.
9. Click on **Save back changes to reference**. At the dialog box click **OK**.
10. You will see now that all the doors swings change to dashed linetypes.
11. Save the file and close it.

EDITING BLOCKS (IMPERIAL)

Workshop 7-B

1. Start AutoCAD 2009.
2. Open the **Workshop_07.dwg** file.
3. Start the **Refedit** command.
4. Select one of the doors you inserted. Once the dialog box appears click **OK**. All of the drawing will be dimmed except the selected block.
5. Select the arc representing the swing of the door. Right-click and select **Properties**.
6. Change its layer to be **Door_Swing**.

7. Change the Linetype scale = **10**.
8. Close the Properties palette.
9. Click on **Save back changes to reference**. At the dialog box click **OK**.
10. You will see now that all the doors swings change to dashed linetypes.
11. Save the file and close it.

NOTES

CHAPTER REVIEW

1. You should draw your original shape, which will be a block, in layer 0:
   a. True.
   b. False

2. The Automatic Scaling feature in AutoCAD:
   a. Will change the scale of the block to fit in the current drawing.
   b. Will require two scales to convert the block.
   c. Works for both Blocks and Hatch.
   d. None of the above.

3. By default, when I use the **Edit In-Place** command, all objects in the drawing are available for editing:
   a. True.
   b. False.

4. Which is of the following statements is true about Tool Palettes:
   a. They can be created from blocks coming from Design Center.
   b. You can drag-and-drop from and to a Tool Palette.
   c. You can customize the block inside a Tool Palette.
   d. All of the above.

5. Which of the following commands cannot be used for blocks:
   a. **Explode** command.
   b. **Insert** command.
   c. **Makelocalblock** command.
   d. **Edit In-Place** command.

6. In order to make Design Center and Tool Palettes occupy less space on the graphical screen use _____.

CHAPTER REVIEW ANSWERS

1. a
2. a
3. b
4. d
5. c
6. Auto-hide

Chapter **7** **HATCHING**

In This Chapter

◊ Hatching in AutoCAD
◊ Hatching using the Hatch command
◊ Hatching using Tool Palettes
◊ Gradient command
◊ Editing hatching in AutoCAD

HATCHING IN AUTOCAD

- In order to hatch in AutoCAD you need to draw objects forming a closed area. Beginning with AutoCAD 2005, it became acceptable to hatch an area with a small opening.
- AutoCAD comes with a good number of generic pre-defined hatch patterns saved in a file called *acad.pat*. You can also buy other hatch patterns from third-parties, which can be found on the Internet.
- A Hatch, like any other object, should be placed in a separate layer.
- There are two methods to hatch in AutoCAD, the old method (Hatch command) and the new method (Tool Palette).

HATCH COMMAND: SELECTING THE HATCH PATTERN

- This is the old method of hatching in AutoCAD.

- To start the **Hatch** command, make sure that you are at **Home** tab on the **Ribbon** and using the **Draw** panel, select the **Hatch** button.

■ The following dialog box will appear:

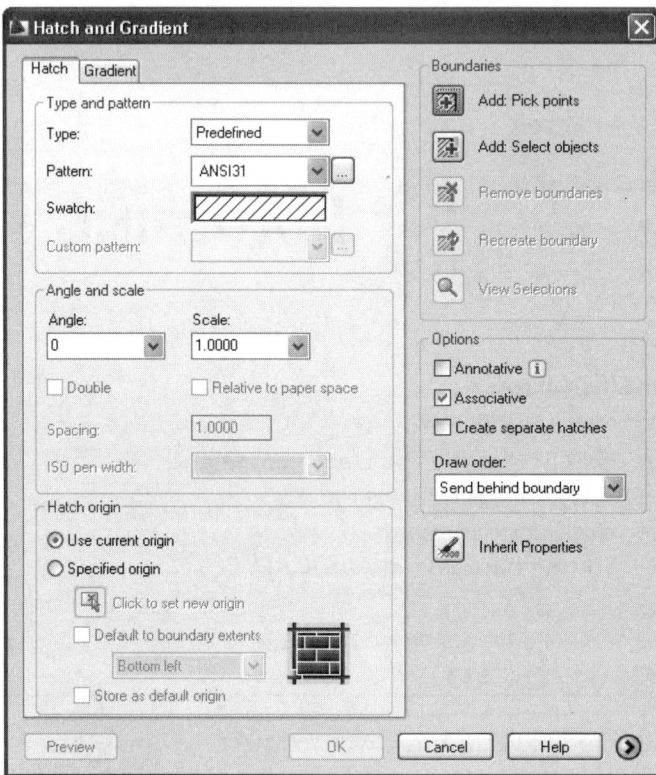

■ Under the **Hatch** tab, select the **Type** pop-up list and you will see the following choices:

User defined

■ The most simple hatch pattern has parallel lines. Once this option is selected the following parameters will be valid:
- **Swatch**: to display a preview of the hatch.
- **Angle**: the angle of the parallel lines.
- **Spacing**: the distance between two parallel lines.
- **Double**: which means, in both ways.

- The following is a **User defined** hatch, using **Angle = 45** and **Double** hatch:

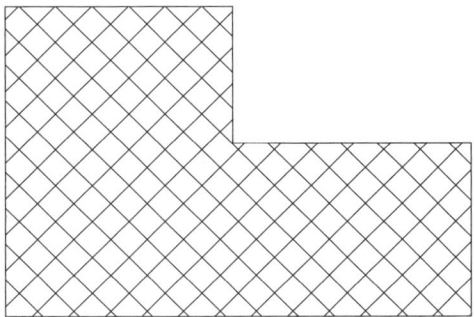

Predefined

- There are a handful of hatch patterns available for use. You will see ANSI hatches, ISO hatches, and commonly used hatches. The following are the parameters to set:
- **Pattern**: whether you select the desired pattern either using the pop-up list, the small button with the three dots, or clicking **Swatch**, the following dialog box will apear showing the **ANSI** hatches:

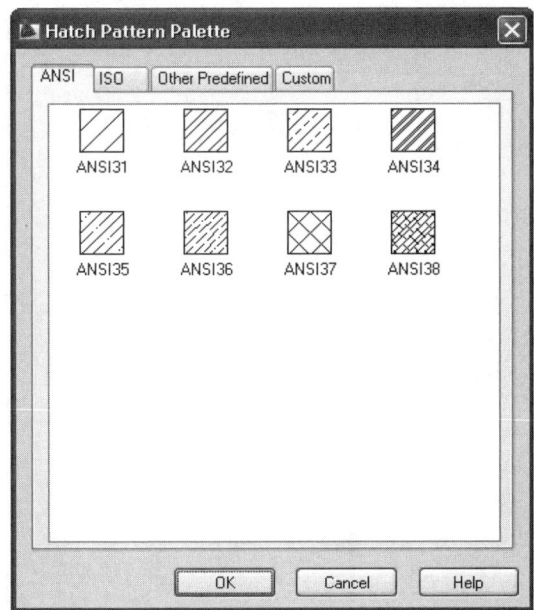

- Or click the **ISO** tab, and you will see:

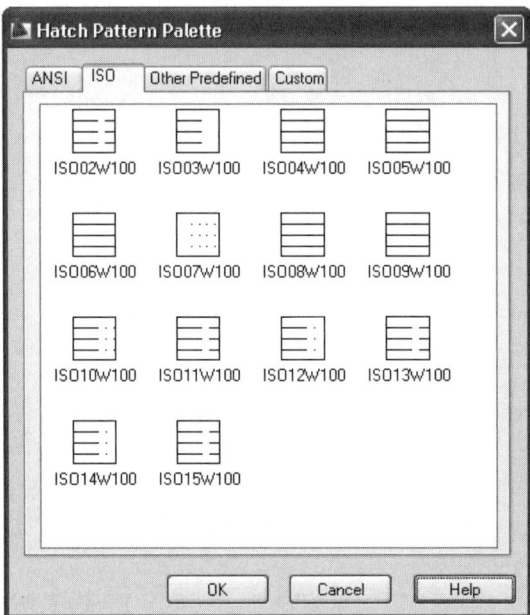

- Or click the **Other Predefined** tab, and you will see:

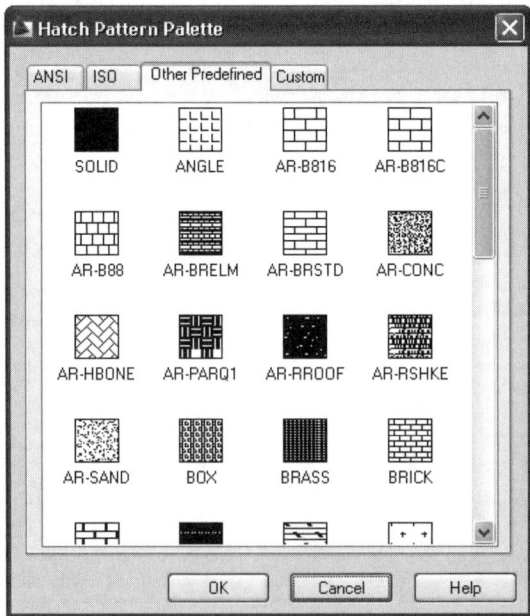

- After you are done selecting the Hatch pattern click **OK**.

- Set up the **Angle**.
- Set up the **Scale** of the hatch pattern.
- If you select the ISO hatches, set up the **ISO pen width**.

Custom

- If you customized a hatch pattern, or if you bought some from a third party, they should be used using the **Custom** command.

HATCH COMMAND: SELECTING THE AREA TO BE HATCHED

- After you've chosen your hatch pattern and set the relative parameters, you need to select the desired area to be hatched.
- You can select more than one area with the same command, but the hatch will be considered either one object or as separate objects.
- There are two ways to select the objects forming the area:
  - Add Pick points.
  - Add Select objects.

Add: Pick points

- This method is very simple, you simply click inside the desired area. AutoCAD will recognize the area automatically.
- This method will also detect any objects (called islands) within the outer area, and select it automatically not to be hatched.
- Islands can be any object type; circle, closed shape, text, etc.

- We will discuss, in detail, island detection shortly.
- Click on the button labeled **Add: Pick points** located at the top-right part of the dialog box.
- The dialog box will disappear temporarily, and the following prompt will appear:

```
Pick internal point or [Select objects/remove Boundaries]:
```

- Click inside the area(s) desired. Once you are done press [Enter], or right-click, then select the **Enter** option. The dialog box will re-appear.

Add: Select objects

- This is the same method used to select any object, as discussed previously.
- Click on the button labeled **Add: Select Objects** located at the top-right part of the dialog box. The dialog box will disappear temporarily, and the following prompt will appear:

```
Select objects or [picK internal point/remove Boundaries]:
```

- Select the desired objects, which form a closed area. Once you are done press [Enter], or right-click, then select the **Enter** option. The dialog box will re-appear.
- After you select, you will be able to do two things:

- **Remove boundaries** from the selection set. Most likely you will need this button when using **Pick Points** because **Pick Points** will select all the inner objects and text as islands, so this button will allow you to remove some of the selected objects as islands.

- **View Selections** is used to view the selection set to make sure that it is the right one.

HATCH COMMAND: PREVIEW THE HATCH

- The data input is complete, you selected the hatch pattern along with its parameters, and you selected the area to be hatched. The next step is to preview the hatch, before you make your final decision to accept the outcome.
- Click the **Preview** button located at the lower left corner of the dialog box.
- The dialog box will disappear temporarily.
- You will see the results of your settings (i.e., hatch pattern, angle, scale, islands, etc.). Accordingly, AutoCAD will prompt you:

```
Pick or press Esc to return to dialog or <Right-click to
accept hatch>:
```

- Which means if you like what you see, right-click or press [Enter], otherwise, press [Esc].
- If you pressed [Esc], the dialog will re-appear, and you can change any of the parameters you think don't fit, and you can preview again, and so on.

HATCHING USING THE HATCH COMMAND (METRIC)

Workshop 8-A
1. Start AutoCAD 2009.
2. Open the **Workshop_08.dwg** file.
3. Make layer **Hatch** current.
4. Start the **Hatch** command, and select the **Type** to be **Predefined**.

5. Click on the **Swatch**, and select the **Other Predefined** tab, and select the **AR-CONC** pattern.

6. Set the Scale = **100**.

7. Click on the **Pick Points** button, and click inside the area representing the outer wall. Press [Enter].

8. Click **Preview** to see the results of the hatching, and then press [Enter] to end the command.

9. Start the **Hatch** command again, and select the **Type** to be **Predefined**.

10. Click on the **Swatch**, and select the **ANSI** tab, and select the **ANSI32** pattern.

11. Set the Scale = **500**.

12. Click on the **Pick Points** button, and click inside the area representing the inner walls. Press [Enter].

13. Click **Preview** to see the results of the hatching, and then press [Enter] to end the command.

14. Save and close the file.

HATCHING USING THE HATCH COMMAND (IMPERIAL)

Workshop 8-B

1. Start AutoCAD 2009.

2. Open the **Workshop_08.dwg** file.

3. Make layer **Hatch** current.

4. Start the **Hatch** command, and select the **Type** to be **Predefined**.

5. Click on the **Swatch**, select the **Other Predefined** tab, and select the **AR-CONC** pattern.

6. Set the Scale = **5**.

7. Click on the **Pick Points** button, and click inside the area representing the outer wall. Press [Enter].

8. Click **Preview** to see the results of the hatching, and then press [Enter] to end the command.

9. Start the **Hatch** command again, and select the **Type** to be **Predefined**.

10. Click on the **Swatch**, select the **ANSI** tab, and select the **ANSI32** pattern.

11. Set the Scale = **20**.

12. Click on the **Pick Points** button, and click inside the area representing the inner walls. Press [Enter].

13. Click **Preview** to see the results of the hatching, and then press [Enter] to end the command.

14. Save and close the file.

HATCH COMMAND: OPTIONS

- There are some options in the **Hatch** command that you should know in order to have full control over the hatching process.
- At the right side of the dialog box, there is a part labeled **Options**:

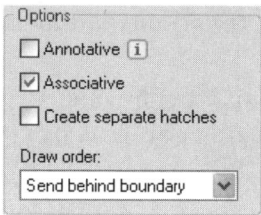

Annotative

- This is an advanced feature, which will be discussed later in this book.

Associative

- Associative means that there is a relationship between the hatch and the boundary. Whenever the boundary changes the hatch changes automatically. It's a good idea to keep this option selected.

Example

- Assume you have the following shape, which you want to hatch:

- You started the **Hatch** command and made sure the **Associative** checkbox is on and hatched the shape. This will be the result:

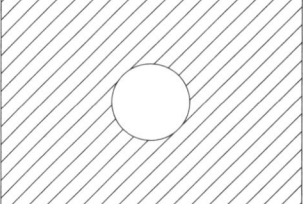

- Now, select the circle and move it to right, and see how the hatch reacts:

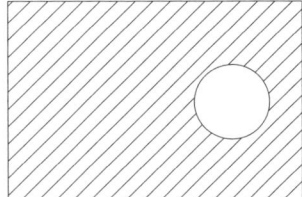

- As you can see the hatch reacted properly to the movement of the circle, which proves that the boundary and the hatch are **Associative**.
- Erase the hatch, then do the same procedure, but this time make sure that **Associative** is off. This is the result of the movement of the circle:

- You can see from above that the hatch didn't react properly to the movement of the circle.

Create separate hatches

- By default when you hatch several areas using the same command, all of the hatches will be considered one object, hence they will move and be erased together.
- Using this option, you can hatch several areas using the same command, and still each hatch would be considered a separate object. To do so, click the **Create separate hatches** checkbox.

Draw order

- In the case of hatched areas intersecting with other hatched areas (specifically hatched with **Solid** hatching) you need to set the Draw order while you are inserting the hatch, so you will ensure the right appearance of each area.
- The four options are:
  - Send to back

- Bring to front (see the following example)

Bring to Front   Send to Back

Before   **After**

- Send behind boundary
- Bring in front of boundary (see the following example)

Send behind
boundary

Bring in front of
boundary

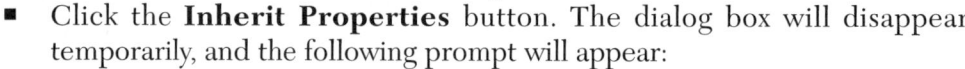

Inherit Properties

- Below the **Options** part, there is a button labeled **Inherit Properties**.
- The purpose of this button is to help the user quickly hatch a new area with the same exact features of an existing hatch.

- Click the **Inherit Properties** button. The dialog box will disappear temporarily, and the following prompt will appear:

```
Select hatch object:
```

- The mouse will change to a painting brush. Click the source hatch pattern.
- The following will happen:
- A new prompt will appear:

```
Inherited Properties: Name <SOLID>, Scale <1.0000>, Angle <0>
Pick internal point or [Select objects/remove Boundaries]:
```

- Meanwhile the mouse cursor will change to a bigger paint brush, with small crosshairs, so you can click inside the new areas you want to hatch.
- Click inside the area(s) desired. Once you are done press [Enter], or right-click, then select the **Enter** option. The dialog box will re-appear, press **OK** to finish the command.

HATCH COMMAND: HATCH ORIGIN

- Each area has something called the "Center of Area."
- By default AutoCAD uses this concept while creating the hatch. So, if you are hatching a circle, AutoCAD will start from the center of the area and go to all directions from there filling the whole area.
- But AutoCAD gives the option for the user to specify a new origin other than the default one.
- At the left lower side of the dialog box you will see a section labeled **Hatch origin**:

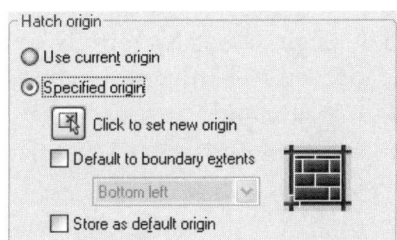

- Click the **Specified origin** radio button.
- When specifying a new origin, you have two options:

- Use the button labeled **Click to set new origin** and select any point you'd like.
- Or click the checkbox labeled **Default to boundary extents**, and select one of the options available: Bottom left, Bottom right, Top left, Top right, and finally Center. You can also use this selection as the default origin.
- See the following example:

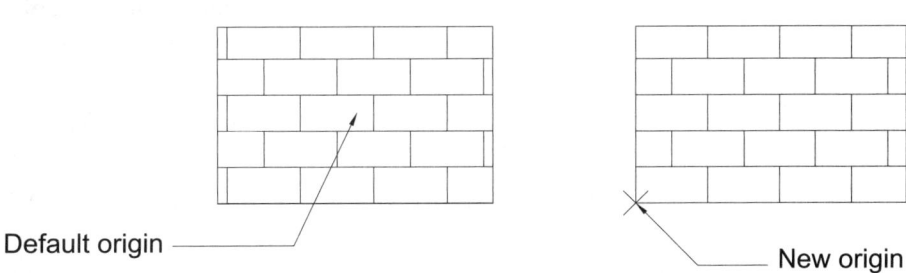

Default origin ————————————　　　　　　　　————— New origin

ASSOCIATIVE HATCHING & HATCH ORIGIN (METRIC)

Workshop 9-A

1. Start AutoCAD 2009.
2. Open the **Workshop_09.dwg** file.

3. Make layer **Hatch** current.

4. Zoom to the kitchen at the lower right of the plan.

5. Start the **Hatch** command, and select the **Type** to be **Predefined**.

6. Click on the Swatch,select the **Other Predefined** tab, and select the **ANGLE** pattern.

7. Set the Scale = **1000** and make sure that Hatch origin = **Use current origin**. Also, make sure that **Associative** is on.

8. Click on the **Pick Points** button, and click inside the area representing the bathroom. Press [Enter].

9. Click **Preview** to see the results of the hatching. Press [Esc] and you will see the dialog box again.Select **Specified origin**, and specify the lower left corner of the kitchen to be the new origin. Click **Preview** again. Press [Enter] to finish the command.

10. Move the oven to the right and notice what happens to the hatch.

11. Save the file and close it.

ASSOCIATIVE HATCHING & HATCH ORIGIN (IMPERIAL)

Workshop 9-B

1. Start AutoCAD 2009.

2. Open the **Workshop_09.dwg** file.

3. Make layer **Hatch** current.

4. Zoom to the kitchen at the lower right of the plan.

5. Start the **Hatch** command and select the **Type** to be **Predefined**.

6. Click on the Swatch,select the **Other Predefined** tab, and select the **ANGLE** pattern.

7. Set the Scale = **50** and make sure that Hatch origin = **Use current origin**. Also, make sure that **Associative** is on.

8. Click on the **Pick Points** button, and click inside the area representing the bathroom. Press [Enter].

9. Click **Preview** to see the results of the hatching. Press [Esc] and you will see the dialog box again. Select **Specified origin** and specify the lower left corner of the kitchen to be the new origin. Click **Preview** again, and notice any changes. Press [Enter] to finish the command.

10. Move the oven to the right and notice whether the hatch responds to this change.

11. Save the file and close it.

HATCH COMMAND: ADVANCED FEATURES

- At the lower right corner of the dialog box you will see a small button with an arrow pointing to the right. Click this button and you will be shown more advanced options for hatching.

Islands

- The first part is the **Islands** option:

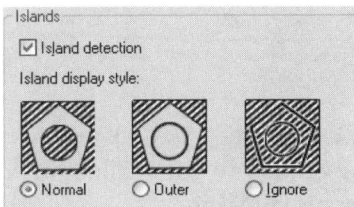

- Islands in AutoCAD are the inner objects inside the outer boundary of an area to be hatched.
- Turn **Islands detection** off if you don't want AutoCAD to recognize the inner objects.
- Turn **Islands detection** on if you want AutoCAD to select the inner objects as boundaries, and hence not hatch them.
- Select one of three styles:
- **Normal** means when there are three objects or more inside each other, AutoCAD will hatch the outer, leave the second, hatch the third, etc.
- **Outer** means when there are three objects or more inside each other, AutoCAD will hatch the outer only, leaving the inner objects intact.
- **Ignore** means when there are three objects or more inside each other, AutoCAD will ignore all the inner objects and hatch the outer area fully.

Boundary retention

- By default, AutoCAD creates a polyline around the detected area, and once the **Hatch** command is finished, AutoCAD will delete this polyline.
- In this section you can tell AutoCAD to keep this temporary polyline.

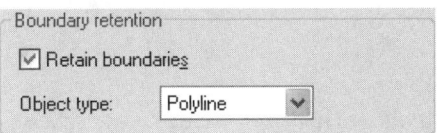

- Click the **Retain boundaries** checkbox, then specify the **Object type** (the other object type is Region).

Boundary set

- When you are using the **Add: Pick points** option to define the boundary to be hatched, by default AutoCAD will analyze all the objects in the current viewport.
- This may take a very long time depending on the complexity of the drawing. To minimize the time, you can provide a selection set for AutoCAD to analyze the boundary from.
- In the **Boundary set**, part of the dialog box will look like the following:

- By default the selected option is **Current viewport**.
- Click the button labeled **New**, the dialog box will disappear temporarily, and the following prompt will appear:

```
Select objects:
```

- Select the desired objects and press [Enter], or right-click, and the dialog box will appear again, but this time the selected option will be **Existing set**, as follows:

- Now when you ask AutoCAD to select a boundary by clicking inside it, AutoCAD will not analyze all objects in the current viewport, but rather will analyze only the objects you select.

Gap tolerance

- AutoCAD will hatch an area with a small gap. The size of the gap is up to you.
- You can set the maximum gap that AutoCAD will ignore.

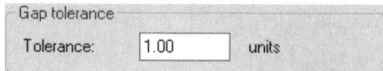

Inherit options

- This section deals with two concepts we discussed in the previous pages, Inherit Properties and Hatch origin.
- When you Inherit Properties from an existing hatch, there are two Hatch origins possible:

- Current origin
- Source hatch origin

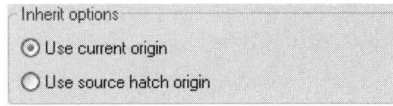

HATCHING USING TOOL PALETTES

- In a previous chapter we introduced Tool Palettes, which included a discussion of both blocks and hatches.
- The main feature of Tool Palettes is the drag-and-drop feature. So we will utilize this feature to speed up the hatching process.
- Take the following steps:
  - Create a new Tool Palette (call it, My Hatches, for example).
  - Use the **Hatch** command to add hatches to different drawings.
  - While you are hatching you are changing the Hatch settings.
- Whenever you want to use a hatch and its setting in other drawings, simply drag-and-drop it in your newly created Tool Palette.
- You can make several copies of your hatch. Then you can use customization to change the different settings of each hatch. Right-click on any hatch in your Tool Palette and select **Properties**, and the following dialog box will appear:

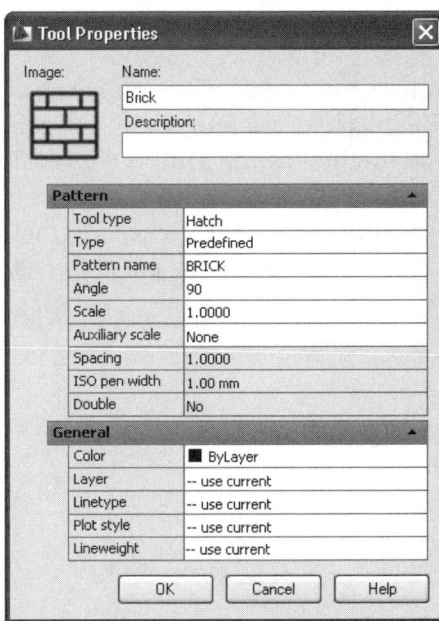

- After several drawings, you will have a large library of hatches.
- Now, use drag-and-drop *from* your Tool Palette to your drawing.
 ■ By default there is a Tool Palette (called **Hatches**) that you can utilize if you don't want to create your own.

HATCHING & TOOL PALETTE (METRIC & IMPERIAL)

 Workshop 10-A & 10-B

1. Start AutoCAD 2009.
2. Open the **Workshop_10.dwg** file.
3. Start Tool Palettes and create a new Tool Palette called **My Hatches**.
4. Drag-and-drop the three hatches we used in our file, which are: AR-CONC, ANSI32, and ANGLE.
5. In the new Tool Palette select any of the three hacthes, right-click, and select **Properties**. Make sure that the Layer is always **Hatch** and not **use current**.
6. Next time you use a hatch from the Tool Palette you will not have to worry about what layer the hatch resides in.
7. Save the file and close it.

GRADIENT COMMAND

- Use the **Gradient** command if you to want to shade a 2D area with one color along with white, black, or something in between, or with two colors.
- It uses the same method as the **Hatch** command, so we don't need to go over the steps again.
 ■ To start the **Gradient** command, make sure that you are at the **Home** tab on the **Ribbon** and using the **Draw** panel, select the **Gradient** button.
- The following dialog box will appear:

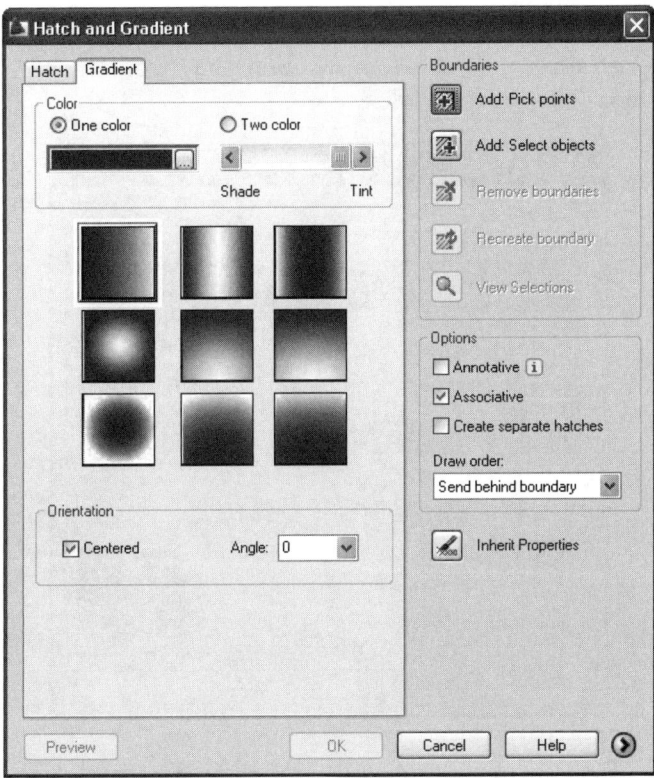

- You start by specifying whether you want to use one color, along with the white color, or if you want to use two colors.

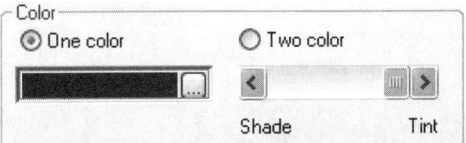

- If you select **One color**, then make the following two adjustments:
- Click the small button (with the three dots in it) to select the desired color.
- Control the slider from **Tint** (total white) to **Shade** (total black) or any color between them.
- If you select **Two color**, the following will appear:

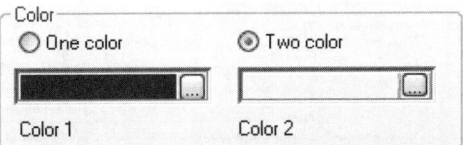

How to select a color

- There are three sets of colors you can select from:
- 255 color called Index Color:

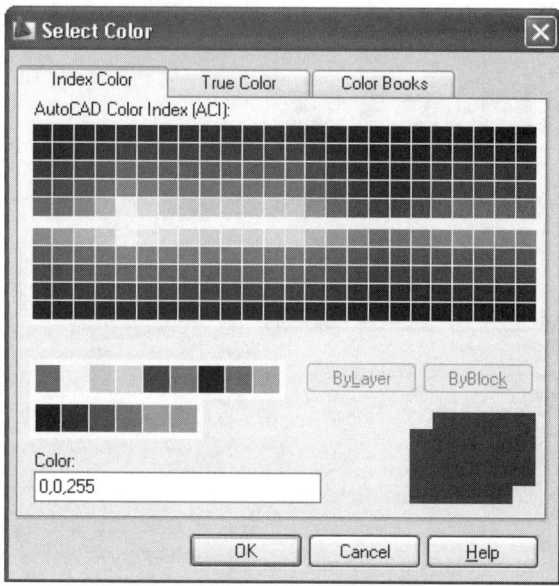

- 24-bit True color, where you can select from two models HSL (Hue, Saturation, and Luminance):

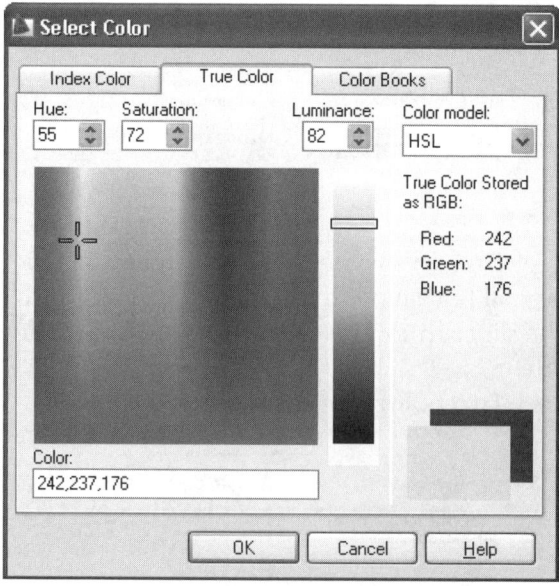

- Or RGB (Red, Green, and Blue):

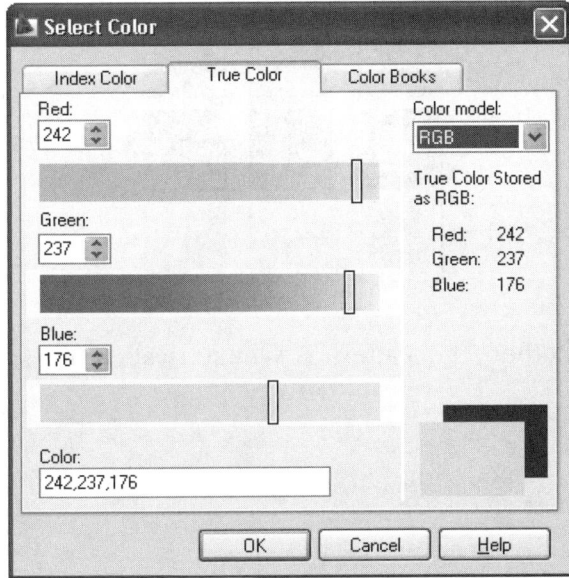

- Or, finally select a color from one of 11 color books available:

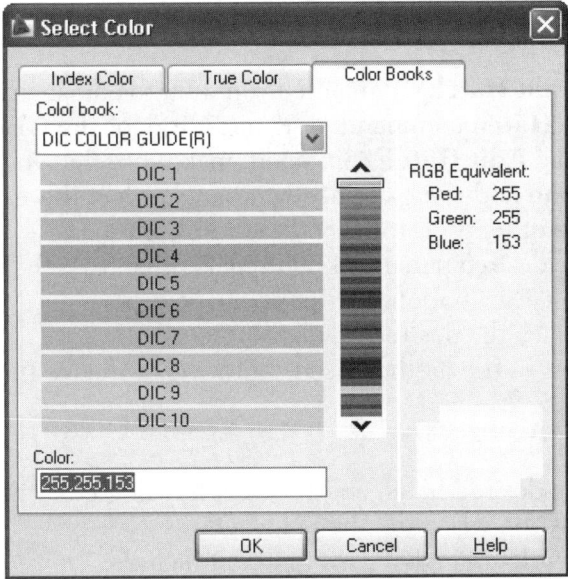

- Now, select one of the nine gradient patterns:

- Select whether your pattern is symmetrical (center) and the angle of the pattern:

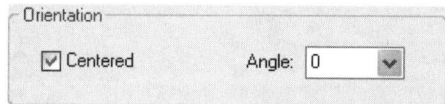

- The rest of the steps are identical to the **Hatch** command.

HOW TO EDIT AN EXISTING HATCH OR GRADIENT

- Use the **Edit Hatch** command if you want to edit an existing hatch (whether using the **Hatch** command, drag-and-drop, or the **Gradient** command).
- To start the **Edit Hatch** command, make sure that you are at **Home** tab on the **Ribbon** and using the **Modify** panel, select the **Edit Hatch** button.
- There are other ways to reach the same command:
- Select the desired hatch and right-click; then, from the shortcut menu select the **Hatch Edit** option.
- Double-click the desired hatch.
- Regardless of the method used, AutoCAD will give the following prompt:

```
Select hatch object:
```

- Select the desired hatch and the Hatch dialog box will appear. Change the settings as you wish, and then click **OK**.
- Other ways to edit a hatch or gradient include:
  - Quick Properties
  - Properties
  - Double-clicking

Quick Properties

- Whenever you select a hatch, the Quick Properties window will appear where you can make the edits you need (not all of the properties are listed here but the most important ones are):

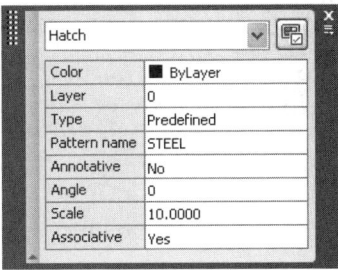

Properties

- Select the hatch, right-click, and select **Properties** from the shortcut menu. The following **Properties** palette will appear:

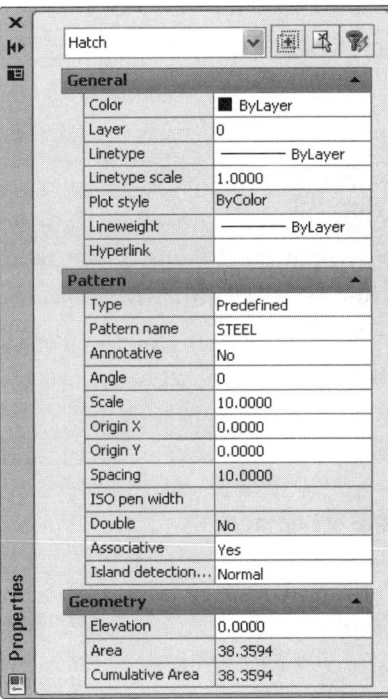

- In the **Properties** palette you can edit all the data related to the hatch selected (some of the settings will be applicable to User hatch patterns such as spacing and double).

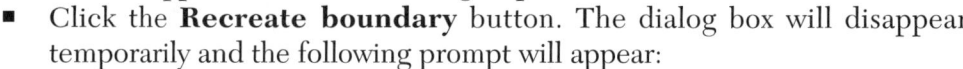

Recreate boundary

- If you hatched an area and the boundary was lost for some reason, but the hatch was kept, you can use this option to recreate the boundary of an existing hatch.
- Use any method to edit the hatch without boundary and the hatch dialog box will appear. Take the following steps:

- Click the **Recreate boundary** button. The dialog box will disappear temporarily and the following prompt will appear:

```
Enter type of boundary object [Region/Polyline] <Polyline>:
```

- Type **P** for polyline, or **R** for Region, and the following prompt will appear:

```
Associate hatch with new boundary? [Yes/No] <Y>:
```

- Type **Y** for yes, and **N** for no.
- The dialog box will appear again, click **OK** to finish the command.

EDIT HATCHING (METRIC)

Workshop 11-A
1. Start AutoCAD 2009.
2. Open the **Workshop_11.dwg** file.
3. Select the AR-CONC hatch, right-click, then select **Hatch Edit**. The dialog box of Hatch Edit will appear. Change the **Scale** of the hatch to **75**.
4. Click **Preview**, then press [Enter] to accept the changes you made.
5. Double-click the ANGLE hatch, and change the Angle to 45.
6. Click **Preview**, then press [Enter] to accept the changes you made.
7. Save the file and close it.

EDIT HATCHING (IMPERIAL)

Workshop 11-B
1. Start AutoCAD 2009.
2. Open the **Workshop_11.dwg** file.
3. Select the AR-CONC hatch, right-click, then select **Hatch Edit**. The dialog box of Hatch Edit will appear. Change the **Scale** of the hatch to **2.5**.
4. Click **Preview**, then press [Enter] to accept the changes you made.
5. Double-click the ANGLE hatch, and change the Angle to 45.

- See the following illustration to differentiate between the two types:

True Type fonts   Shape files fonts

Font Style

- If you select a True Type font, you will be able to select the Font Style. You have the following choices to choose from:
  - Regular
  - Bold
  - Bold Italic
  - Italic
- See the following illustration:

Regular   Bold   Bold/Italic   Italic

Annotative

- This is an advanced feature, which we will discuss later.

Height

- Next, specify the height of the text. See the following illustration:

- As you can see from the illustration, the Height mentioned in the dialog box is for the capital letters. Automatically two-thirds of the height will be for the small letters, and one-third will be for letters with a descendent below the baseline.
- There are two methods for specifying the height of text:
  - Leave the value to be equal to 0 (zero), which means you will have to specify the height each and every time you use this style.
  - Specify a height value, which will be used always once you have created this style.

Effects

- There are five effects you can add to your text:
- **Upside down** effect, as in the following:

Bag   Bɐ9

Normal   Upside down

- **Backwards** effect, as in the following:

Bag   gaB

Normal   Backwards

- **Width Factor** effect, as in the following:

Bag   Bag   Bag

Width Factor=1   Width Factor=1.5   Width Factor=0.75

- **Oblique Angle** effect, as in the following:

Bag   *Bag*   Bag

Oblique Angle=0   Oblique Angle=+15   Oblique Angle=-15

- The **Vertical** effect is only applicable for shx fonts, and it will write the text from top to bottom (good for any shx Chinese fonts).
- When you are done, click the **Apply** button, then the **Close** button.
 - At the left part of dialog box, there is a pop-up list showing **All styles**. Using this list you can show all defined text styles whether used or not, or only the text styles that are used in this drawing.

CREATING A TEXT STYLE (METRIC)

 Workshop 12-A
1. Start AutoCAD 2009.
2. Open the **Workshop_12.dwg** file.
3. Create a text style named **Title** with the following settings:
   a. Font = **Arial**
   b. Font Style = **Bold**
   c. Height = **900**
   d. Width Factor = **2**
4. Create a text style named **Inside_Annot** with the following settings:
   a. Font = **Times New Roman**
   b. Font Style = **Regular**
   c. Height = **300**
   d. Width Factor = **1**
5. Create a text style named **Dimension** with the following settings:
   a. Font = **Arial**
   b. Font Style = **Regular**
   c. Height = **400**
   d. Width Factor = **1**
6. Save the file and close it.

CREATING A TEXT STYLE (IMPERIAL)

 Workshop 12-B
1. Start AutoCAD 2009.
2. Open the **Workshop_12.dwg** file.
3. Create a text style named **Title** with the following settings:
   a. Font = **Arial**
   b. Font Style = **Bold**

    c. Height = **3'-0"**

    d. Width Factor = **2**

4. Create a text style named **Inside_Annot** with the following settings:

    a. Font = **Times New Roman**

    b. Font Style = **Regular**

    c. Height = **1'-0"**

    d. Width Factor = **1**

5. Create a text style named **Dimension** with the following settings:

    a. Font = **Arial**

    b. Font Style = **Regular**

    c. Height = **1'-4"**

    d. Width Factor = **1**

6. Save the file and close it.

SINGLE LINE TEXT

- Single Line Text is the first of two commands you can use in order to write text in AutoCAD.
- Although you write several lines of text in each command, each would be considered a separate object.
- To start Single **Line Text** command, make sure that you are at the **Annotate** tab on the **Ribbon** and using the **Text** panel, select the **Single Line Text** button.
- Either way the following prompt will appear:

```
Current text style:  "arial_09"  Text height:  0.9000
Annotative No
Specify start point of text or [Justify/Style]: (Specify the
start point of the baseline)
Specify rotation angle of text <0>: (Specify the rotation
angle of the baseline)
```

- As noted above AutoCAD will use the current text style to write the desired text. In order to change it, use the **Text** panel, as explained below:

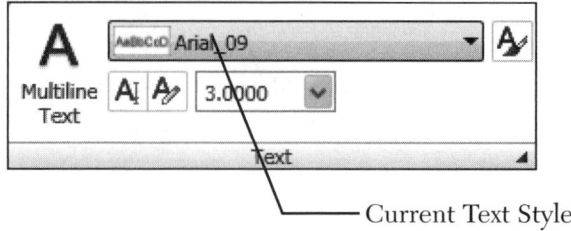

Current Text Style

- After you input these values, start writing. If you want a new line, press [Enter] and the cursor will go to the beginning of a new line. When you are done typing, press [Enter] twice.

MULTILINE TEXT COMMAND

- The **Multiline Text** command simulates Microsoft Word's simplicity in creating text; hence, it is easier for people who have experience using Word.
- All the text you write in a single command will be considered a single object.
- To start the **Multiline Text** command, make sure that you are at the **Annotate** tab on the **Ribbon** and using the **Text** panel, select the **Multiline Text** button.
- Either way AutoCAD will show the following prompt:

```
Current text style:  "arial_09"  Text height:  0.9000
Annotative  No
Specify first corner: (Specify first corner)
Specify opposite corner or [Height/Justify/Line spacing/
Rotation/Style/Width]: (Specify opposite corner)
```

- AutoCAD wants you to select two opposite corners to specify the area that you will write in. Take a look at the following:

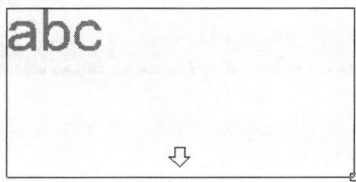

- After you specify the two corners, text editor with a ruler will appear:

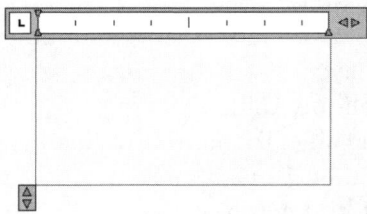

- Automatically AutoCAD will show a new tab called Multiline Text (which will disappear automatically when you are done with this command), which looks like the following:

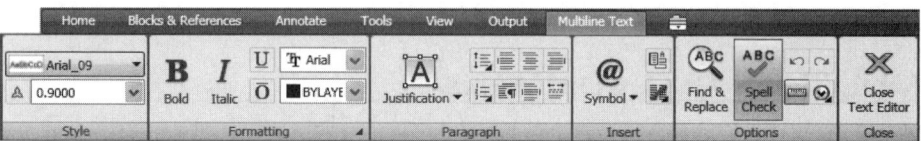

- A blinking cursor will appear in the **text editor** so you can type your desired text. Using the **Multiline Text** tab, you can format the text as you wish.
- If you created a text style (highly recommended) then you will see at the left part of the tab the name of the current text style along with the height.
- In order to format text you should select it first just like you do in MS Word.

Formatting panel

- The **Formatting** panel is as follows:

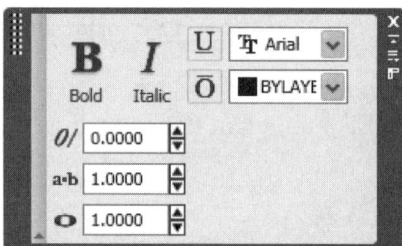

- Use the **Formatting** panel to do all or any of the following:
  - Change the text to Bold
  - Change the text to Italic
  - Change the text to Underlined
  - Change the text to Overlined
  - Change the font (it is recommended to stick with the font specified by the current text style)
  - Change the color of the text (it is recommended to stick with the color of the current layer)
  - Specify the Oblique Angle
  - Specify the Tracking (To increase or decrease the spaces between letters. Values greater than 1 mean more spaces, and vice versa)
  - Specify the Width Factor

Paragraph panel

- The **Paragraph** panel is as follows:

- Use the Paragraph panel to change any or all of the following:
- Change the Justification to one of the following nine options:

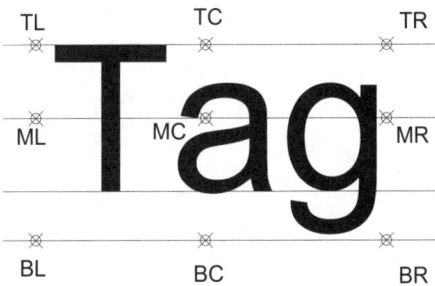

- You can set the Line Spacing of the paragraph. You have the choice of 1.0x, 1.5x, 2.0x, 2.5x, or you can set your own.

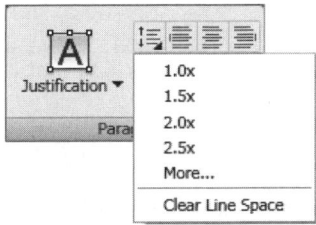

- You can use Numbering; you have three choices, using letters (lowercase or uppercase), numbers, and bullets.

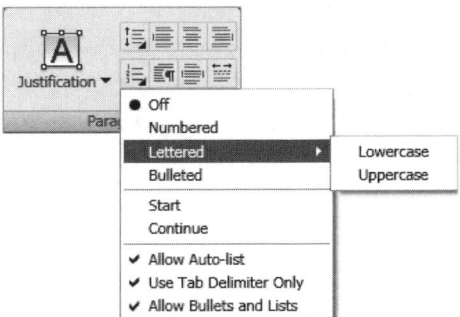

- You can change the justification of the paragraph by using the three buttons Left, Right, Center.
- You can set the Tabs, Left and Right Indent, Paragraph Alignment, Paragraph Spacing, and Paragraph Line Spacing using the Paragraph button. The following dialog box will appear:

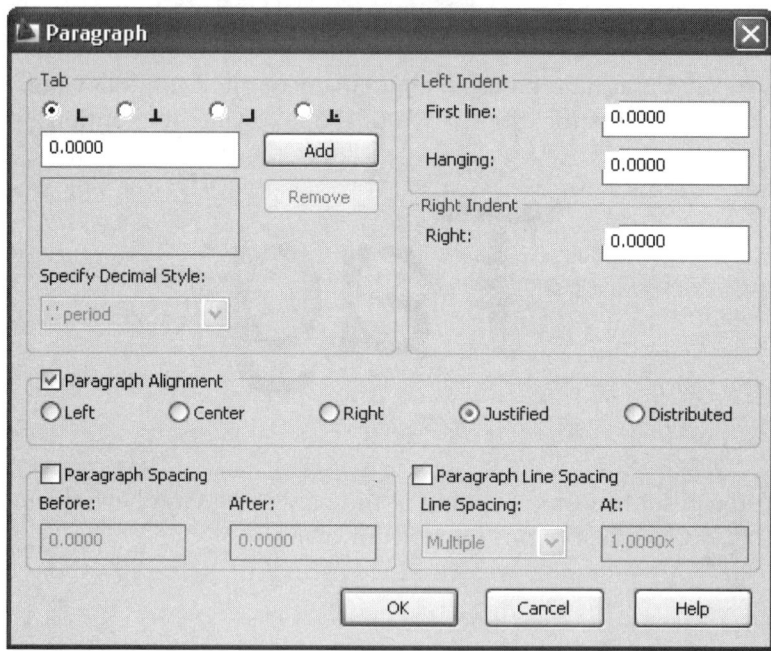

- You can set the paragraph to be justified from left or right using the Justify button.
- Or you can set to distribute the text over the line width using the Distribute button.

Insert panel

- The **Insert** panel is as follows:

- You can add Symbols to your text. If you click the **Symbol** button the following menu will appear, where you can select to add one of 20 available symbols:

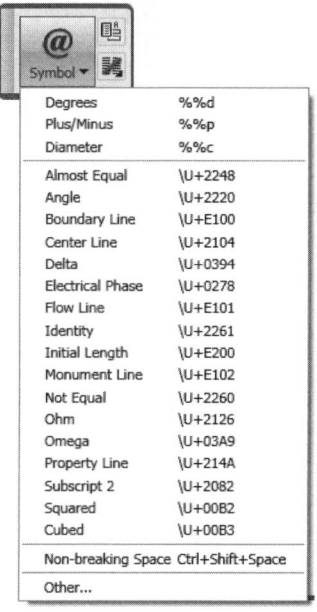

Options panel

- The **Options** panel is as follows:

- Using the Options panel you can do all or any of the following:
- Find and Replace text, where the following dialog box will appear:

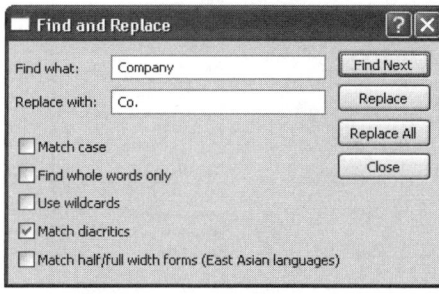

- You can Spell Check the text you wrote using this button. When you click this button a dotted red line will appear underneath the misspelled word, just like the following example:

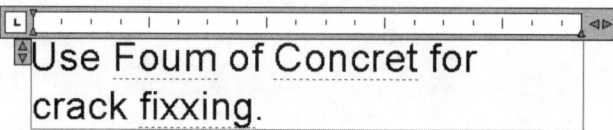

- Go to the misspelled word and right-click. A suggestion of the right spelling will appear at the top of the shortcut menu, like the following:

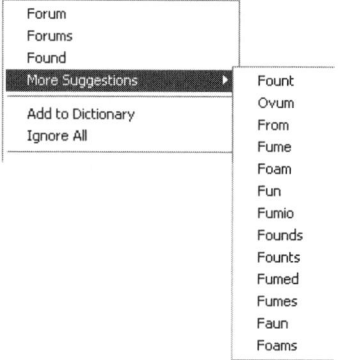

- Select one of the suggested words, or select Add to Dictionary, or Ignore all incidences of the misspelled word.
- You can Undo and Redo any Text command you performed.
- You can select to show the ruler or hide it.
- You can click to show all the available options using the small arrow. The following menu will appear:

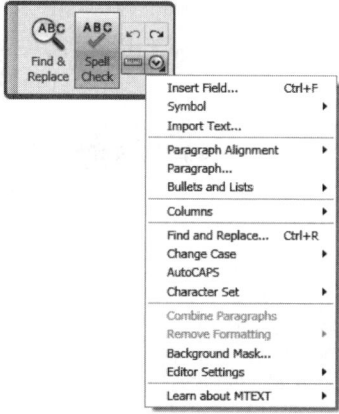

- In the Options shortcut menu there is a very handy command that you can utilize in a very good way, which is **Import Text**.
- If you created a non-formatted text (*.txt) using any editor such as Notepad, you can bring the text to the In-Place editor, and then format it. Select **Import Text** and the following dialog box will appear:

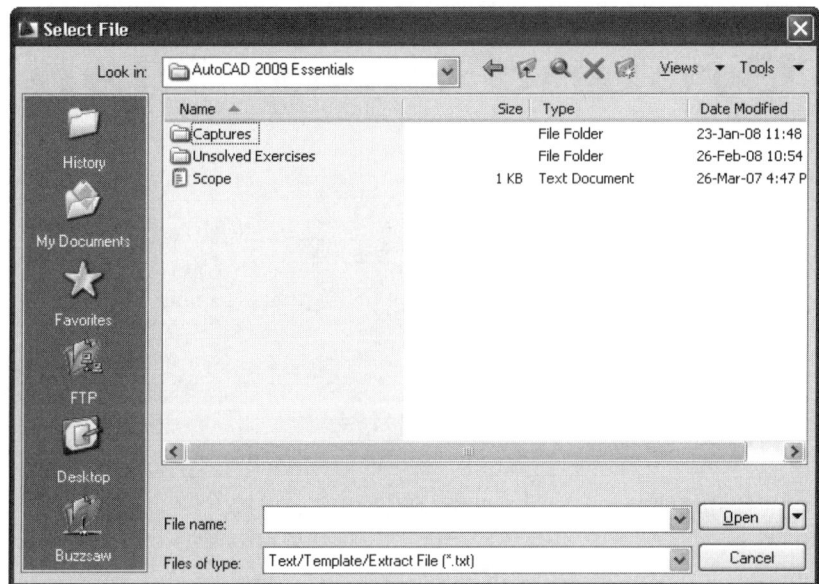

- Select the desired drive and folder, then select the desired txt file. Once you click **Open**, you will see the text in the editor for formatting.

Set indents

- Setting indents in the In-Place editor is identical to the process in MS Word. See the following illustration:

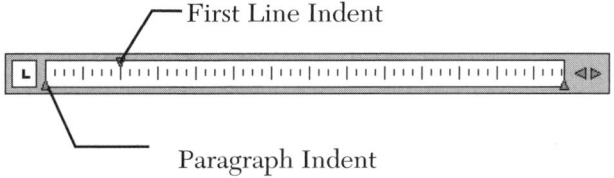

- Move the **First Line Indent** to specify where the first line will start.
- Move the **Paragraph Indent** to specify where the next line will start.
- Also you can set **Tabs** for your text by clicking anywhere in the ruler.

WRITING TEXT (METRIC & IMPERIAL)

Workshop 13-A & 13-B
1. Start AutoCAD 2009.
2. Open the **Workshop_13.dwg** file.
3. Looking at the picture below:

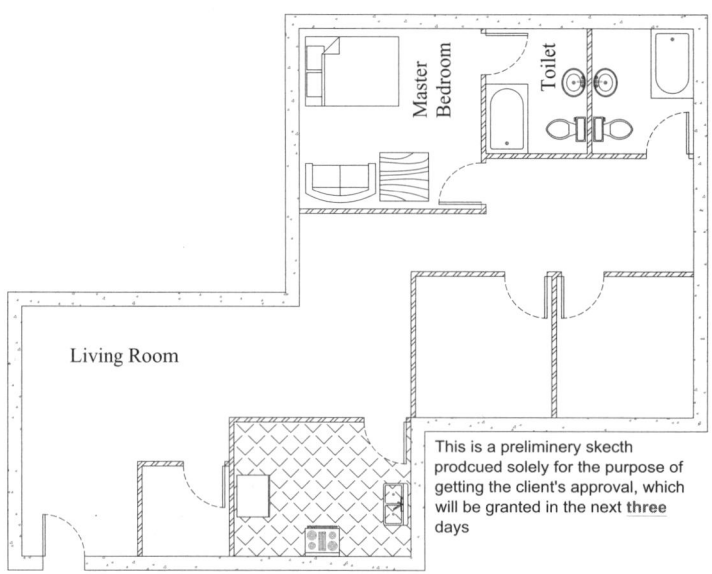

4. Make layer **Text** the current layer.
5. Using Single Line Text (**DTEXT** command) and Text Style **Inside_Annot** type the following words: **Master Bedroom**, **Toilet**, **Living Room**.
6. Using Single Line Text (**DTEXT** command) and Text Style **Title** type the following words: **Ground Floor Plan**.
7. Switch off the **OSNAP** button.
8. Using the **Multiline Text** command, specify the area in the lower right part of the plan as shown above, and using the Text style **Inside_Annot**, import the file named Notes.txt but don't close the editor.
9. Select the word three, and make it red, bold, and underlined. Close the editor.
10. Save the file and close it.

EDITING TEXT

- In order to edit the *contents* of the text, simply double-click the text.
- If you double-click multiline text, the editor will reappear with the **Multiline Text** tab for further adding/deleting or simply reformatting.
- If you double-click single line text, the text will be available for adding and deleting.

- To start the **Edit Text** command, make sure that you are at the **Annotate** tab on the **Ribbon** and using the **Text** panel, select the **Edit** button.
- This command can go with both types of texts.
- Also, you can select multiline text, right-click, and select **Mtext Edit**, which is equivalent to the **mtedit** command.

EDITING TEXT USING QUICK PROPERTIES & PROPERTIES

Single Line Text

- In order to edit the properties of single line text, simply click it. The **Quick Properties** window will appear, where you can make some changes such as the following:

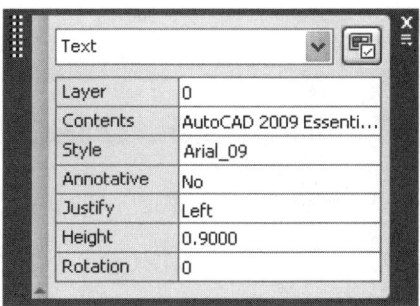

- You can change the Layer, Contents, the Style, Annotative status, Justification, Height, and finally the Rotation angle.

- If you want to do more editing, select Properties, and you will see the following:

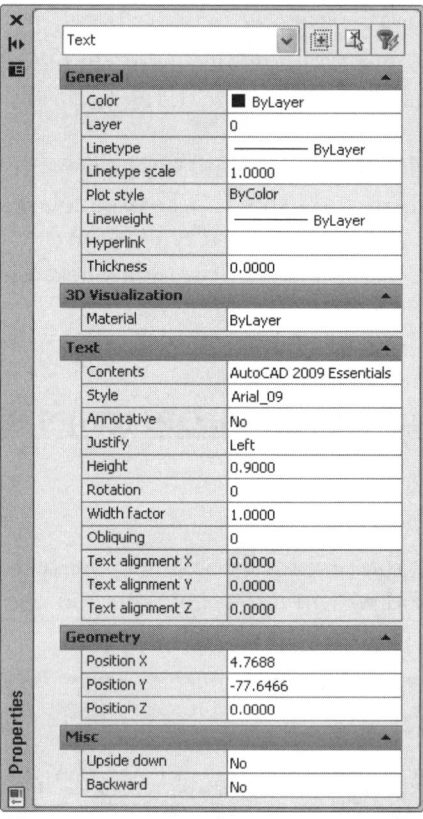

- You can change the **General** properties of the single line text (Color, Layer, Linetype, etc.).
- You can change the Contents of the text, and other properties such as Style, Justification, Height, Rotation, etc.).
- You can change the Geometry of the text (position of X, Y, and Z).
- Finally, you can change the **Miscellaneous** properties of the single line text such as Upside down and Backward.

Multiline Text

- In order to edit the properties of multiline text, simply click it. The **Quick Properties** window will appear, where you can make changes such as the following:

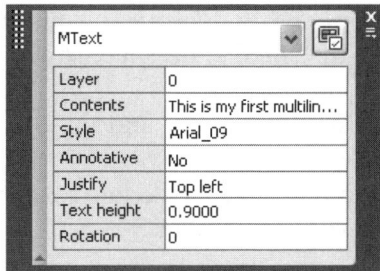

- You can edit the same things you can change in Single Line text.
- In order to have full editing power, you need to use the **Properties** command, where you will see the following:

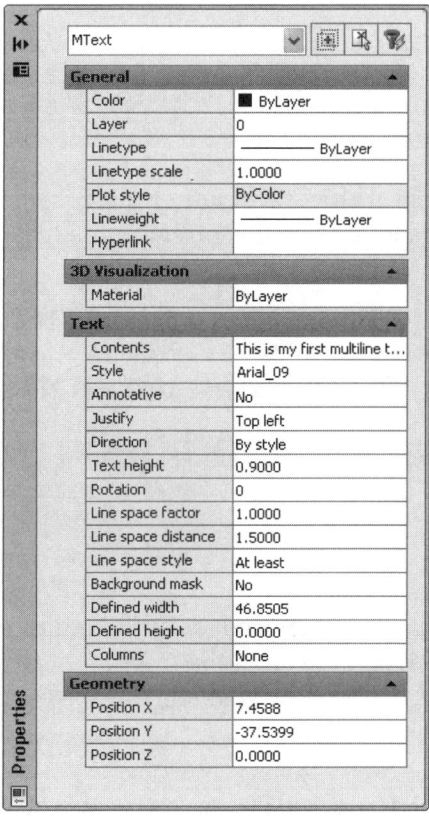

- You can change the General properties of the multiline text (Color, Layer, Linetype, etc.).
- You can change the contents of the multiline text and other properties such as Style, Justification, Direction, Height, Rotation, etc.).

- You can change the specific features of multiline text such as Line space factor, Line space distance, Line space style, Background mask, Defined width, and Defined height.
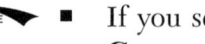 - If you select both single line text and multiline text, you change only the **General** properties.
- You can select either multiple single line text or multiple multiline text, and change their properties in one step.

TEXT & GRIPS

- If you click (single click) over a single line text, you will see the following:

Elevation

- The grip appears at the start point of the Baseline.
- On the other hand, if you click on multiline text you will get the following:

The Elevation and
the Cross-Sections
will be modified
together

- The grips appear in the four edges of the multiline text. This is very helpful if you want to change the area the multiline text is occupying.
- You can make it wider by making one of the right-hand grips hot and dragging it like the following:

The Elevation and the
Cross-Sections will be
modified together

- Or, you can make it narrower by making one of the right-hand grips hot and dragging it like the following:

The Elevation and
the
Cross-Sections
will be modified
together

SPELL CHECK & FIND AND REPLACE

Spell Check

- We've already learned how to Spell Check and Find & Replace inside the multiline text editor, but what if we want to check an existing single line or multiline text? We can use the following two tools.
- AutoCAD will spell check the Entire drawing, Current space/layout, or the Selected text.
- To start the **Check Spelling** command, make sure that you are at the **Annotate** tab on the **Ribbon** and using the **Text** panel, click the **Check Spelling** button.
- The following dialog box will appear:

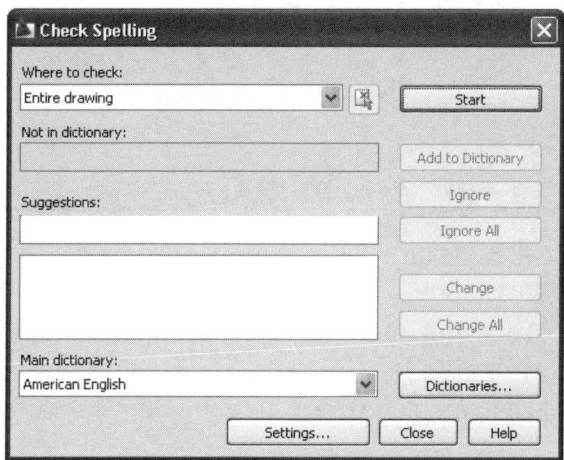

- This is identical to the MS Word spell checker. If AutoCAD finds any misspelled word, it will give you suggestions and you will choose one of them, or you can change the spelling yourself or ignore it.

Find and Replace

- AutoCAD can find any word or part of a word and replace it with another in the entire drawing file.
- To start the **Find and Replace** command, make sure that you are at the **Annotate** tab on the **Ribbon** and using the **Text** panel, take a look at the following illustration:

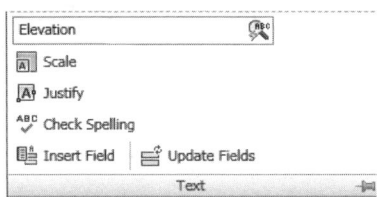

- In the edit box type in the word you want to find, and click the key at the right. AutoCAD will locate the word and show the following dialog box:

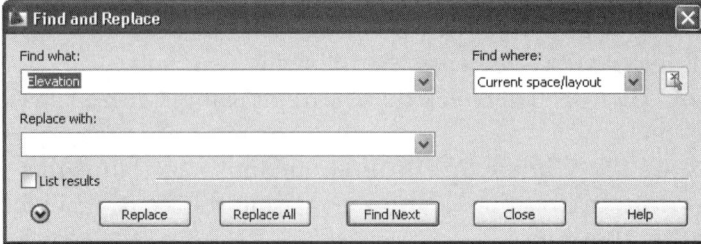

- Under **Replace with**, type the new word(s) you want to use.
- You can search in the **Entire drawing** or search in a selection of the text.
- You have three choices to select from **Find**, **Replace**, and **Replace All**.
- When you are done, click **Close**.

EDITING TEXT (METRIC & IMPERIAL)

Workshop 14-A & 14-B

1. Start AutoCAD 2009.
2. Open the **Workshop_14.dwg** file.
3. Select the Mulitline text and the four grips will appear. Select one of the right grips to make it hot, and stretch it to the right so you will make the text one line less.

4. Double-click the Multiline text, and make the following changes:

   a. Select the word "solely" and make it italic.

   b. Add a comma before the word "which."

   c. Press [Enter] after the last word, to add a new line, and type your initials.

5. While you are in the editor, you can see three words with a dashed, red line beneath them. Spell check these three words and select the correct spelling.

6. Save the file and close it.

TABLE STYLE

- To create a table in AutoCAD, take the following two steps:
- Create a Table style
- Insert and Fill the table
- In **Table Style** you will define the main features of your table.

- To start the **Table Style** command, make sure that you are at the **Annotate** tab on the **Ribbon** and using the **Tables** panel, click the **Table Style** button.
- You will see the following dialog box:

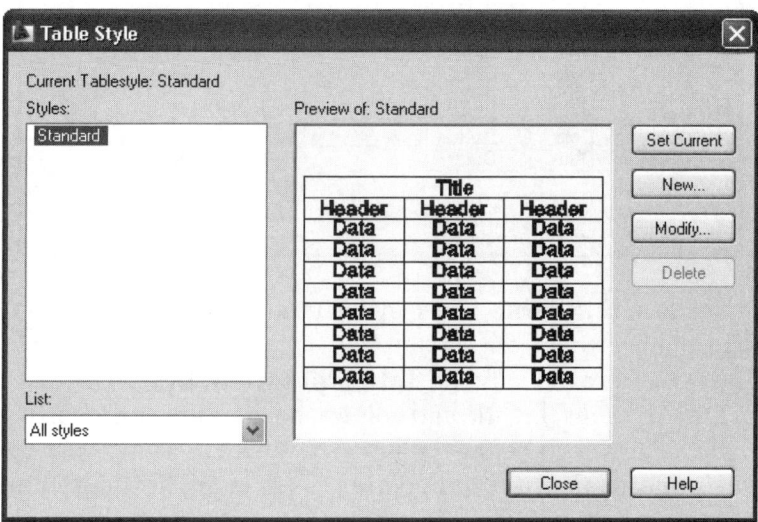

- As you can see, there is a pre-defined style called **Standard**.
- There will be a preview (always), which will show you the changes you are making; hence, it will be easy for you to decide if you've made the right choices.

- To create a new table style, click the **New** button. You will see the following dialog box:

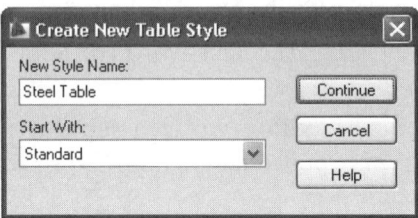

- Type in the name of your new style.
- Select the **Start With** style (you will start with a copy from this style).
- Click the **Continue** button. The following dialog box will appear:

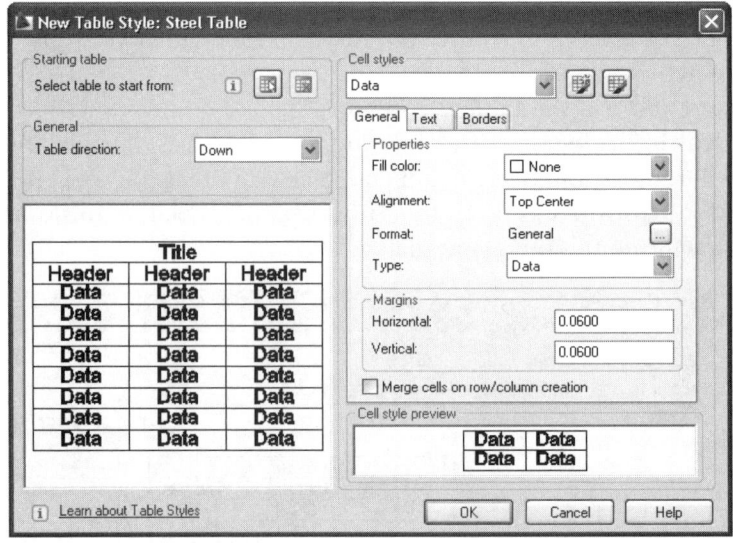

- Under **Starting table** you can select an existing table and copy its style, instead of starting from scratch.
- Under **General** specify the **Table direction**, Up or Down:
    - **Down** means the title and column headers are at the top of the table and the cells will go below them.
    - **Up** means the title and column headers are at the bottom of the table and the cells will go above them.
- Under **Cell styles**, you have three choices to choose from: **Data**, **Header**, and **Title**. This section is used to adjust settings for the table's three parts. You can control the **General** properties, **Text** properties, and **Border** properties of these three parts.

General tab

- The General properties part looks like the following:

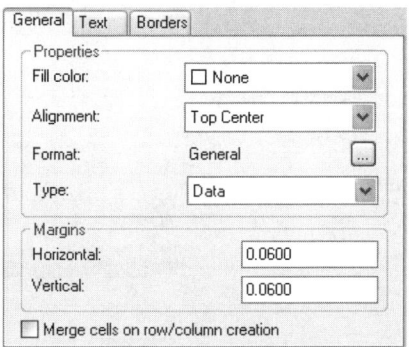

- Here, you can adjust the following settings:
  - **Fill Color**: select whether the cells will have a colored background or not.
  - **Alignment**: select the justification of the text compared to the cell (you have nine choices to select from). The following illustration shows these settings:

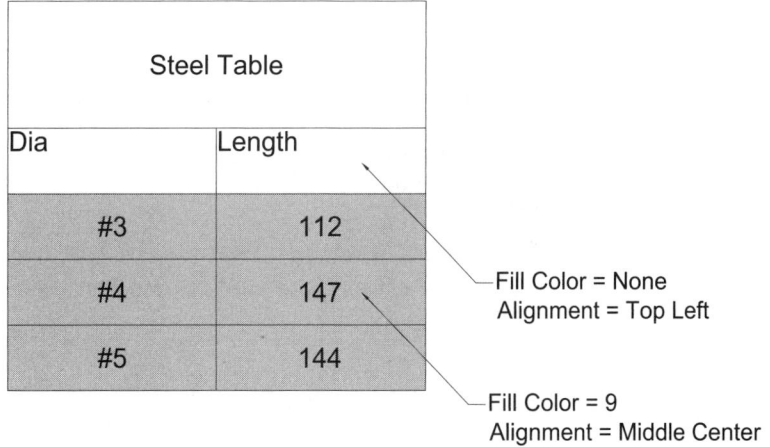

- **Format**: select the format of the numbers.Click on the small button with the three dots and you will see the following dialog box:

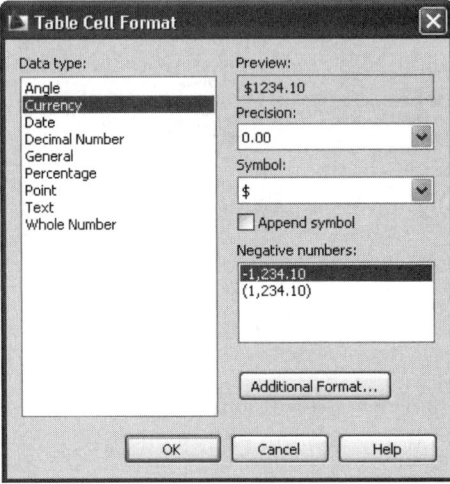

- Set the Type as Data or Label.
- Under Margins control the Horizontal and Verical distances to be taken around the Data relative to the borders.

Text tab

- The Text properties box looks like the following:

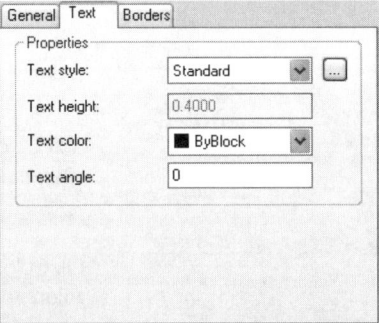

- Here, you can adjust the following settings:
  - The Text style you will use in the cells.
  - Text h eight to be used (this is only applicable if the Text style selected has a Height = 0).
  - Text color to be used (most likely you will use Bylayer or Byblock).
  - Text angle, sets the oblique angle of the text.

Borders tab

- The Border properties box looks like the following:

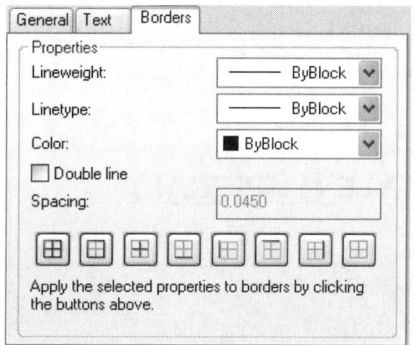

- Here, you can adjust the following settings:
  - Specify the Lineweight, Linetype, and Color of the borders (Byblock, or specify the desired value from the list).
  - Specify whether you want the border to be a single line (default) or a double line. If you specify double line, specify the spacing.
  - Set the type of border (inside, outside, etc.).
- Once you set all the variables, click OK to go back to the first dialog box, where you can do all or any of the following:
- You can select the current style from many available styles. The next time you use the **Table** command, this style becomes the default.
- You can also select one of the existing styles and make any type of modification, and you will get the same dialog box you got when you created this style.

CREATING TABLE STYLE (METRIC)

 Workshop 15-A
1. Start AutoCAD 2009.
2. Open the **Workshop_15.dwg** file.
3. Create a new Table style based on the Standard style and call it **Door Schedule**.
   a. For Title, Text Style = **Inside_Annot**, and Alignment = **Middle Center**
   b. For Data, Text Style = **Inside_Annot**, and Alignment = **Middle Center**

    c. For Column Heads, Text Style = **Inside_Annot**, and Alignment = **Middle Center**

    d. Cell margins, Horizontal = **100**, Vertical = **100**

4. Make it the current style.

5. Save the file and close it.

CREATING TABLE STYLE (IMPERIAL)

Workshop 15-B

1. Start AutoCAD 2009.

2. Open the **Workshop_15.dwg** file.

3. Create a new Table style based on the Standard style and call it **Door Schedule**.

    a. For Title, Text Style = **Inside_Annot**, and Alignment = **Middle Center**

    b. For Data, Text Style = **Inside_Annot**, and Alignment = **Middle Center**

    c. For Column Heads, Text Style = **Inside_Annot**, and Alignment = **Middle Center**

    d. Cell margins, Horizontal = **4,"** Vertical = **4"**

4. Make it the current style.

5. Save the file and close it.

TABLE COMMAND

- To insert a table into an AutoCAD drawing using a predefined style you will use the **Table** command.
- You will specify the number of columns and rows and will fill the cells with the desired data.
- To start the **Table** command, make sure that you are at the **Annotate** tab on the **Ribbon** and using the **Tables** panel, click the **Table** button.

- The following dialog box will appear:

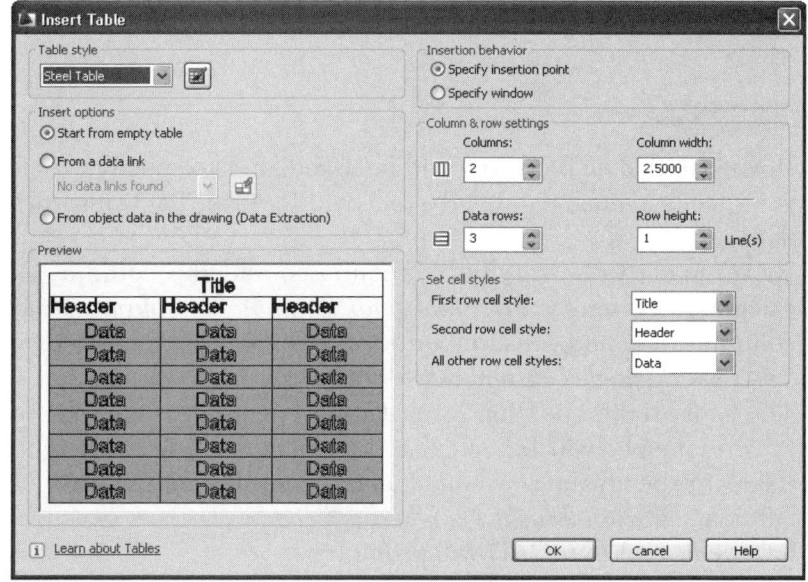

- Select the predefined **Table style name**.

- If you didn't create a Table style before this step, simply click the small button beside the list and start creating the desired Table style.
- Specify the **Insert options**. You have three choices:
- Start from empty table – normally this option should be used.
- From a data link – to bring in data from spreadsheets from MS Excel, etc.
- From object data in the drawing (data extraction) – only if you have block attributes.
- There are two insertion methods:
  - Specify insertion point
  - Specify window

Specify insertion point

- If you use this method, you will specify the upper left corner of the table, and accordingly set up the following data:
  - Number of columns
  - Column width
  - Number of rows (without title and column heads)
  - Row height (in lines)
- Click **OK**, and AutoCAD will prompt:

```
Specify insertion point:
```

- Specify the upper left corner of the table and the table will appear ready to fill in the data. You will first insert the title, the column headers, and then the data. You can move between rows using the [Tab] key on the keyboard to go to the next cell, and [Shift]+[Tab] to go back to the previous cell.

Specify window

- If you use this method, you will be asked later to specify a window, hence, you specify a total height and a total width. Accordingly insert the following data:
- Either specify the number of columns, and the column width will be calculated automatically (*total width/number of columns*) or specify the column width, and the number of columns will be calculated automatically (*total width/single column width*).
- The same thing goes for rows. Either specify the number of rows, and the row height will be calculated automatically (*total height/number of rows*), or specify the row height, and the number of rows will be calculated automatically (*total height/single row height*).
- Click **OK**, and AutoCAD will prompt:

```
Specify first corner:
Specify second corner:
```

- Specify two opposite corners, then the table will be available for your input just like we did in the previous method.
- To edit a cell's content, simply double-click the cell, and it will be available for editing.

INSERTING TABLES (METRIC)

 Workshop 16-A

1. Start AutoCAD 2009.
2. Open the **Workshop_16.dwg** file.
3. Make layer **Text** the current layer.
4. Looking at the picture below, and using Table style **Door Schedule,** add a table just like the one below, using the following specifications:
   a. Specify insertion point
   b. Columns = **5**
   c. Column Width = **2000**
   d. Data Rows = **4**

e.　Row Height = **1** Line(s)

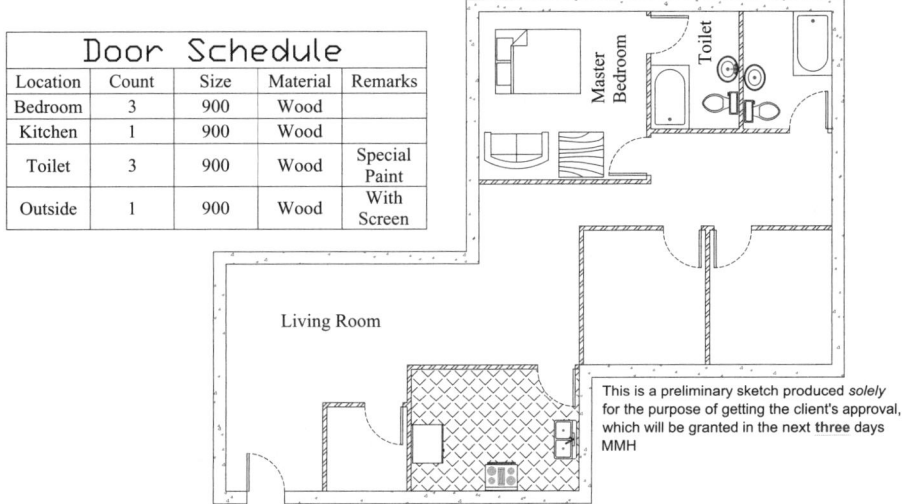

Ground Floor Plan

Door Schedule				
Location	Count	Size	Material	Remarks
Bedroom	3	900	Wood	
Kitchen	1	900	Wood	
Toilet	3	900	Wood	Special Paint
Outside	1	900	Wood	With Screen

Master Bedroom

Toilet

Living Room

This is a preliminary sketch produced *solely* for the purpose of getting the client's approval, which will be granted in the next three days MMH

5.　Save the file and close it.

INSERTING TABLES (IMPERIAL)

Workshop 16-B

1.　Start AutoCAD 2009.

2.　Open the **Workshop_16.dwg** file.

3.　Make layer **Text** the current layer.

4.　Looking at the picture below, and using Table style **Door Schedule**, add a table just like the one below, using the following specifications:

a.　Specify insertion point.

b.　Columns = **5**

c.　Column Width = **6'-8"**

    d.   Data Rows = **4**

    e.   Row Height = **1** Line(s)

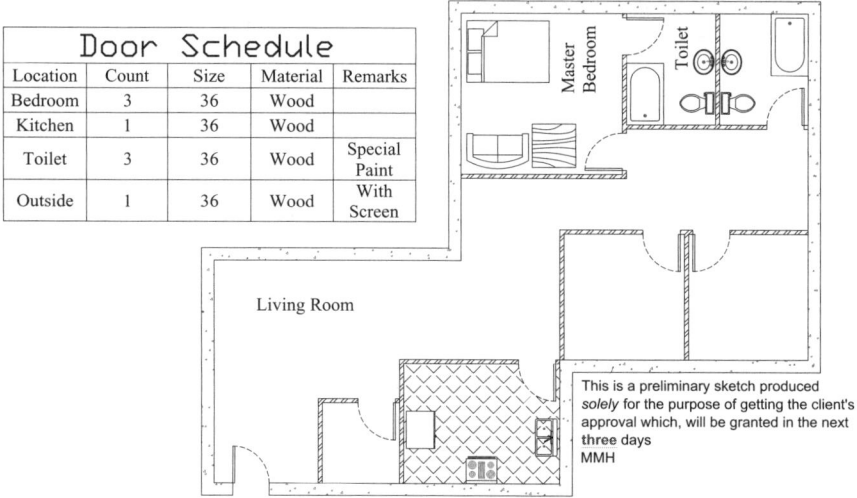

Ground Floor Plan

Door Schedule				
Location	Count	Size	Material	Remarks
Bedroom	3	36	Wood	
Kitchen	1	36	Wood	
Toilet	3	36	Wood	Special Paint
Outside	1	36	Wood	With Screen

Master Bedroom

Toilet

Living Room

This is a preliminary sketch produced *solely* for the purpose of getting the client's approval which, will be granted in the next three days
MMH

5.   Save the file and close it.

CHAPTER REVIEW

1.   The height used in Text Styles is for lowercase letters:
   a.   True.
   b.   False.
2.   There are two types of fonts in AutoCAD: _____ and _____.
3.   There are no similiarities between Text style and Table style:
   a.   True.
   b.   False.
4.   While you are in multiline text editor you can't:
   a.   Import any txt file.
   b.   Format text.
   c.   Change the indents.
   d.   Bring in an MS Word document as OLE.

5. Which of the following statements is NOT true about tables:
   a. There are two methods to insert a table.
   b. You can control the cell style for Title, Header, and Data.
   c. You can convert Multiline text to a table.
   d. You can define the table direction whether down or top.
6. In Table Style, Top Left and Middle are considered _____ options.

CHAPTER REVIEW ANSWERS

1. b
2. shx , ttf
3. b
4. d
5. c
6. Justification

Chapter 9

DIMENSIONING YOUR DRAWING

In This Chapter

◇ Dimension types
◇ Creating Parent and Child dimension styles
◇ Controlling dimension styles
◇ The different types of dimensioning commands
◇ Editing dimensions and editing dimensions with Grips
◇ Creating a Multileader style
◇ Multileader commands

INTRODUCTION

- Dimensioning in AutoCAD is a semi-automatic process; the user will contribute part of the job and AutoCAD will do the rest.
- The user (in linear dimensioning, for instance) will specify three points. The first and the second is the length to be dimensioned, and the third is the position of the dimension line.
- Accordingly, AutoCAD will automatically generate the Dimension block, just like in the following illustration:

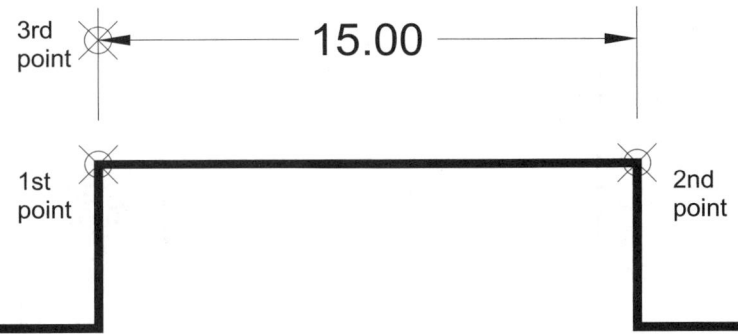

- A Dimension block consists of four parts. They are:
  - Dimension line
  - Extension lines
  - Arrowheads
  - Dimension text
- See the following illustration:

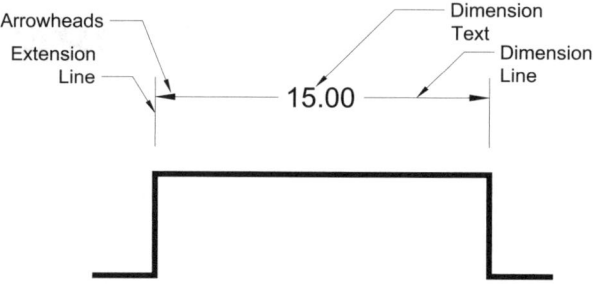

- The Dimensioning process has two phases:
  - Creating Dimension style(s)
  - Putting dimensions over your drawing
- The Dimension style will control the appearance of the Dimension block, so each establishment will set up the style according to their standards.
- Creating a dimension style is a lengthy and tedious job, but it will only be done once, allowing the user to focus on the other job, putting the dimensions over the drawing.

DIMENSION TYPES

- AutoCAD can support linear and aligned dimension types.

Linear and Aligned

- Take a look at the following illustration:

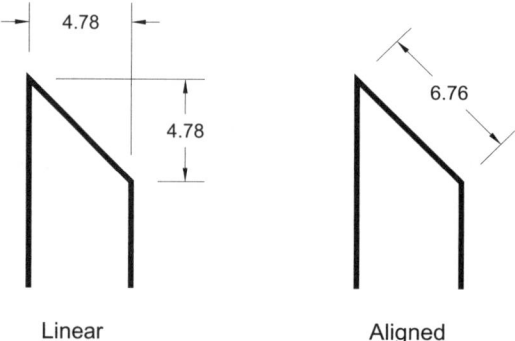

Arc Length, Radius, and Diameter

- Take a look at the following illustration:

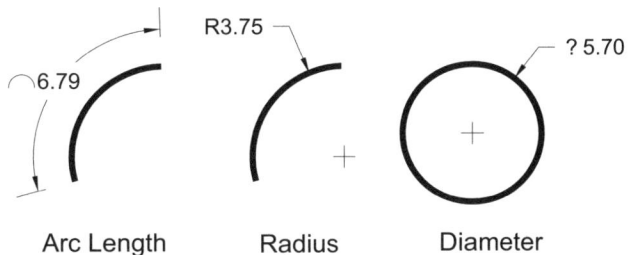

Arc Length   Radius   Diameter

Angular

- Take a look at the following illustration:

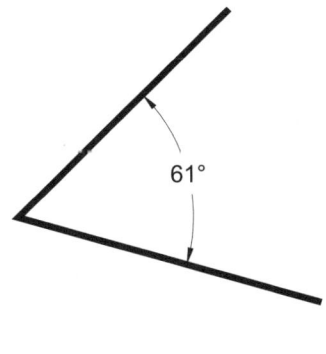

Angular

Continuous

- Take a look at the following illustration:

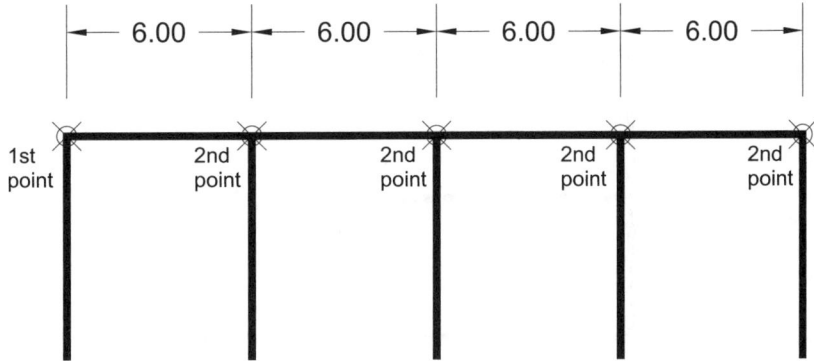

Baseline

- Take a look at the following illustration:

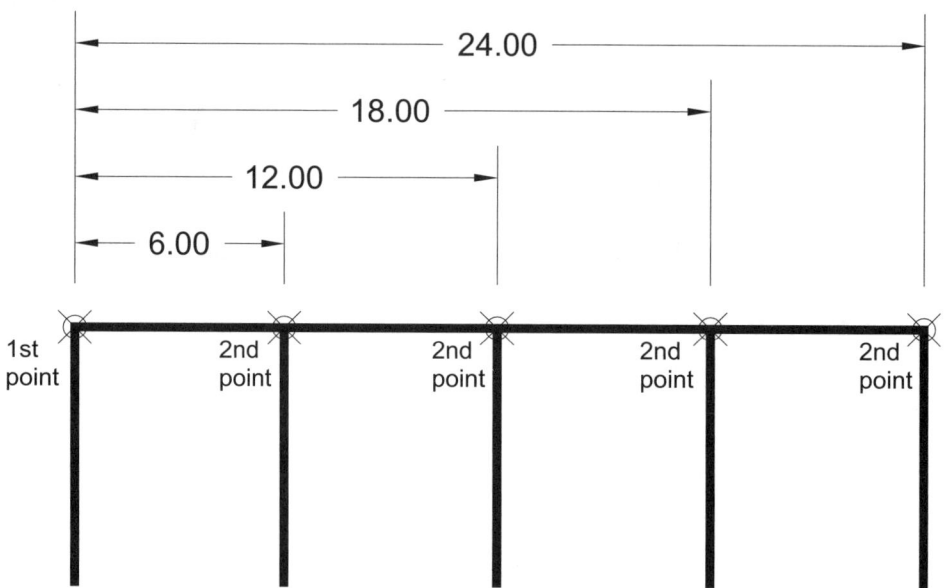

Ordinate

- Take a look at the following illustration:

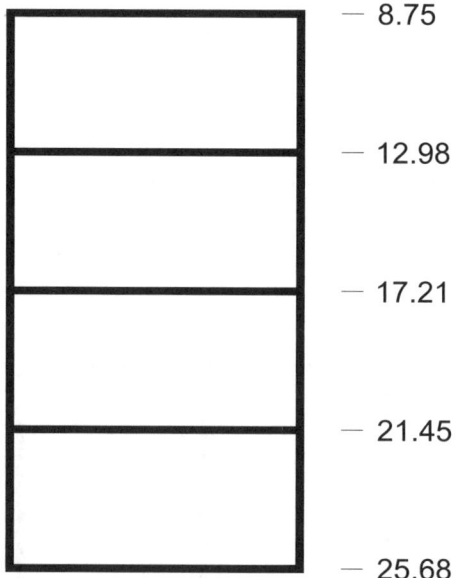

DIMENSION STYLES: THE FIRST STEP

- To start the **Dimension Style** command, make sure that you are at the **Annotate** tab on the **Ribbon** and using the **Dimensions** panel, click the **Dimension Style** button.
- The following dialog box will appear:

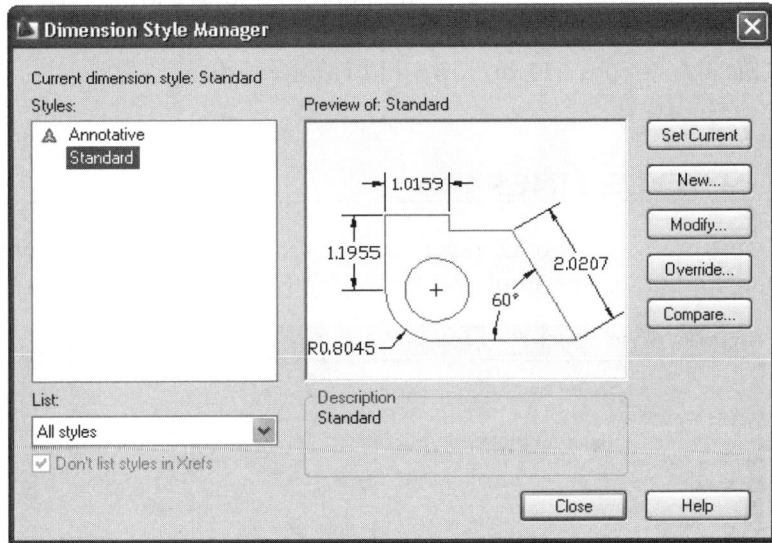

- By default there is a template for the dimension style called **Standard**.
- You can modify this style or create your own (preferable).
- To create a new style, click the **New** button, and the following dialog box will appear:

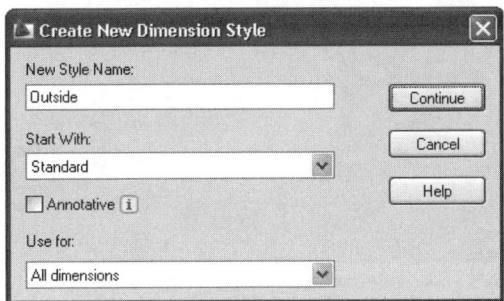

- Type in the new style name using the same naming convention as layers.
- Select the **Start With** style (you will start with a copy of this style).
- Keep **Annotative** off for now.

- By default the changes you make will be implemented for all types of dimensions, but you can create a new dimension style that will affect a certain type of dimension.
- Click the **Continue** button, then you can start modifying the settings. In the following sections we will cover each tab of the Dimension style dialog box.

 ■ In this dialog box whenever you find the **Color** setting, leave it as is as we should control our colors through layers and not through individual objects. This also applies to **Linetype** and **Lineweight**.

DIMENSION STYLE: LINES TAB

- The first tab in the Dimension style dialog box is **Lines**, where we will control Dimension lines and Extension lines. It looks like the following:

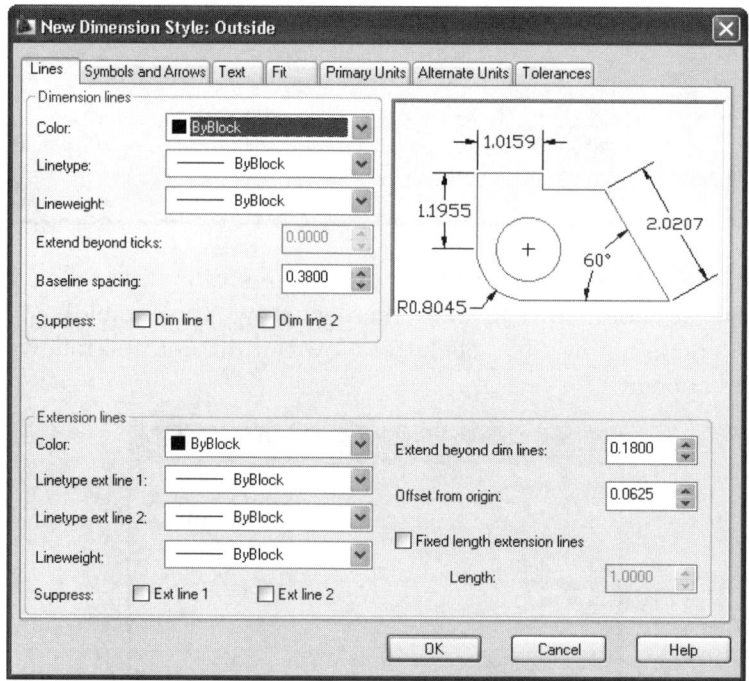

- Under **Dimension lines** control the following settings:
  - The **Color**, **Linetype**, and **Lineweight** of the Dimension line.
  - **Extended beyond ticks** (in order to edit this value, go to the **Symbols and Arrows** tab, and set the **Arrowhead** to be **Architectural tick** or **Oblique**). See the following illustration:

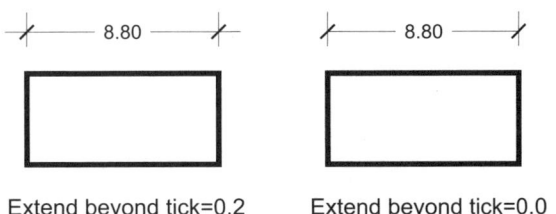

Extend beyond tick=0.2   Extend beyond tick=0.0

- **Baseline spacing**, see the following illustration:

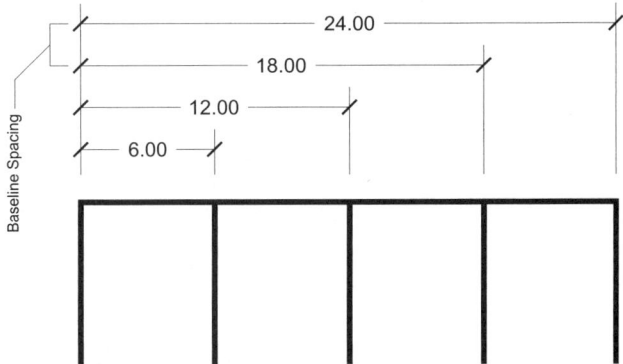

- Select to **Suppress Dim line 1, Dim line 2,** for one of them, or for both. See the following illustration:

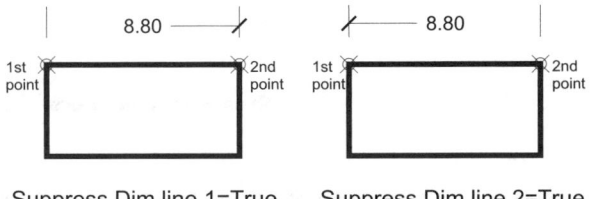

Suppress Dim line 1=True   Suppress Dim line 2=True

- Under **Extension lines** control the following settings:
  - The **Color**, **Linetype**, and **Lineweight** of the Extension lines.
  - Select to **Suppress Ext line 1, Ext line 2,** for one of them, or for both. See the following illustration:

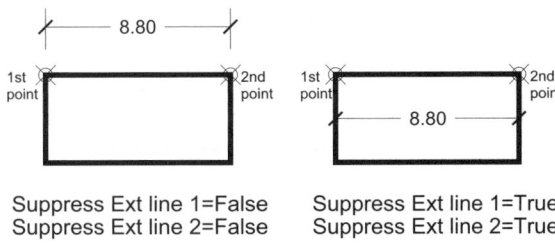

Suppress Ext line 1=False   Suppress Ext line 1=True
Suppress Ext line 2=False   Suppress Ext line 2=True

- Specify **Extend beyond dim lines** and **Offset from origin**. Take a look at the following illustration:

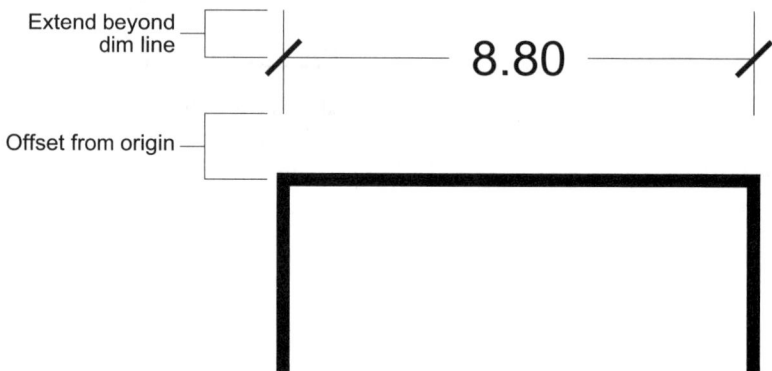

- To set **Fixed length extension lines**, you have to specify the **Length**. In order to understand this setting, see the following example:

Example

- This example will clarify **Fixed length extension lines**:
- Assume we have the following case, and we want to create a linear dimension:

- Before AutoCAD 2006, the only choice was as follows:

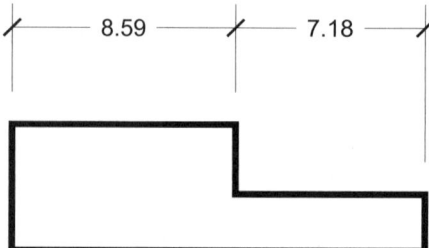

- But in AutoCAD 2009, a new choice, Fixed length extension lines, is available to get the following:

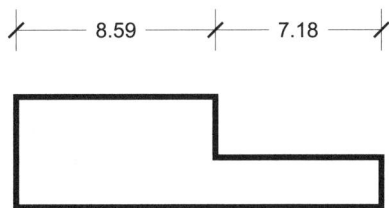

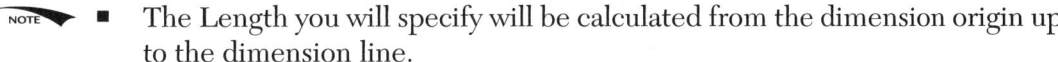

NOTE ➤ ■ The Length you will specify will be calculated from the dimension origin up to the dimension line.

DIMENSION STYLE: SYMBOLS AND ARROWS TAB

- Click the **Symbols and Arrows** tab and you will see the following:

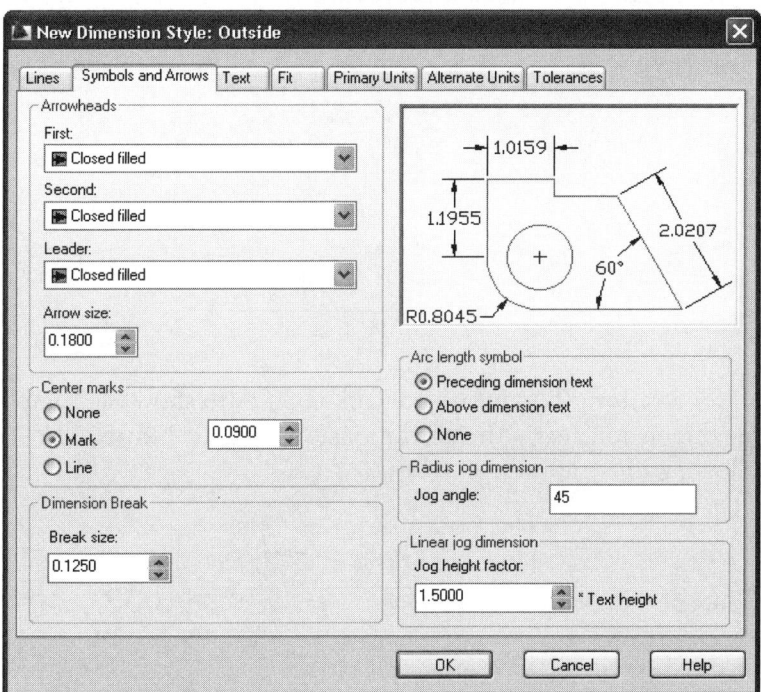

- Under **Arrowheads**, adjust the following settings:
  - The shape of the **First** arrowhead.
  - The shape of the **Second** arrowhead.

- The shape of the arrowhead to be used in the **Leader**.
- The **Size** of the arrowhead.

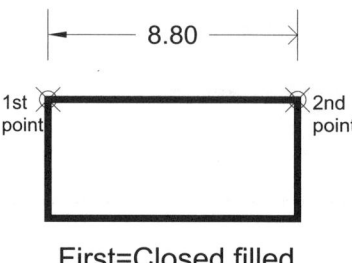

First=Closed filled
Second=Right angle

■ If you change the first, the second will change automatically, but if you change the second the first will not change.

■ Under **Center marks**, adjust the following settings:
  - Select whether to show the Center mark or to show centerlines.
  - Set the **Size** of the Center mark.

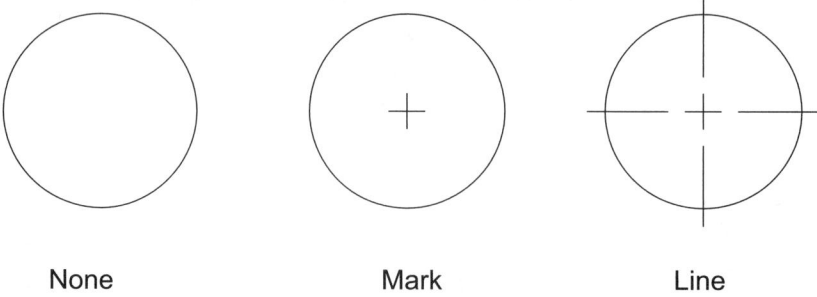

None   Mark   Line

■ Under **Arc length symbol**, control whether to show the symbol **Preceding** the dimension text, **Above** dimension text, or **None**. Take a look at the following illustration:

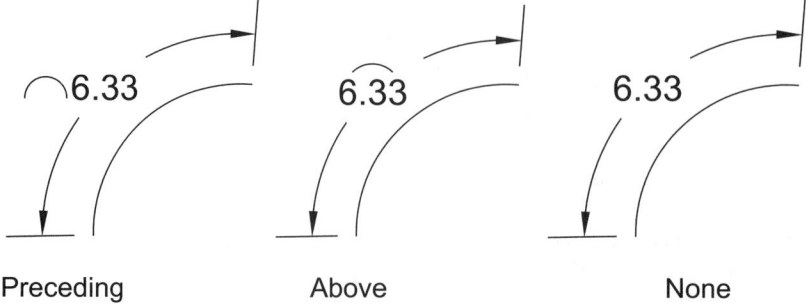

Preceding   Above   None

- Under **Dimension Break**, set the **Break size**, which is the width of the break of the dimension lines in a dimension break.
- Under **Radius dimension jog**, set the value of the **Jog angle**. Take a look at the following illustration:

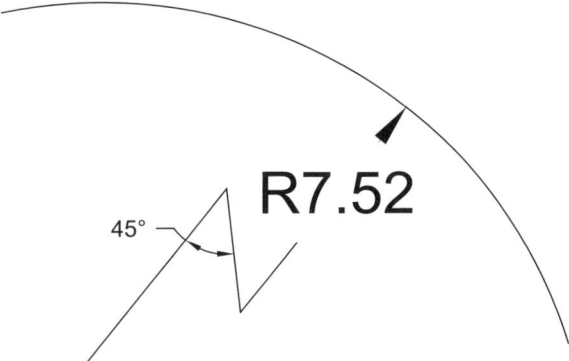

- Under **Linear Jog dimension**, set the **Jog height factor**, as a percentage of the text height. Take a look at the following illustration:

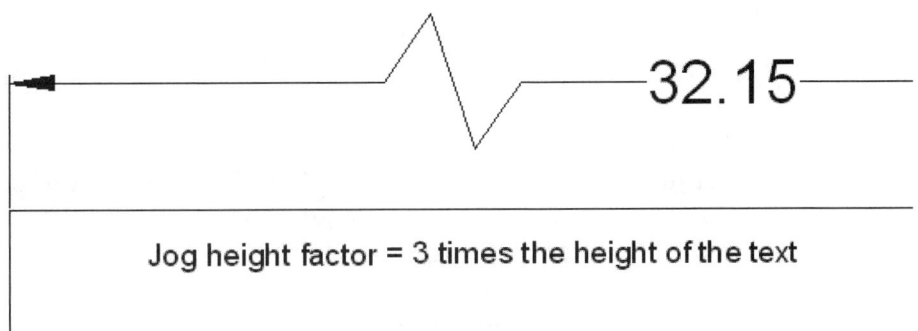

DIMENSION STYLE: TEXT TAB

- Click the **Text** tab and you will see the following:

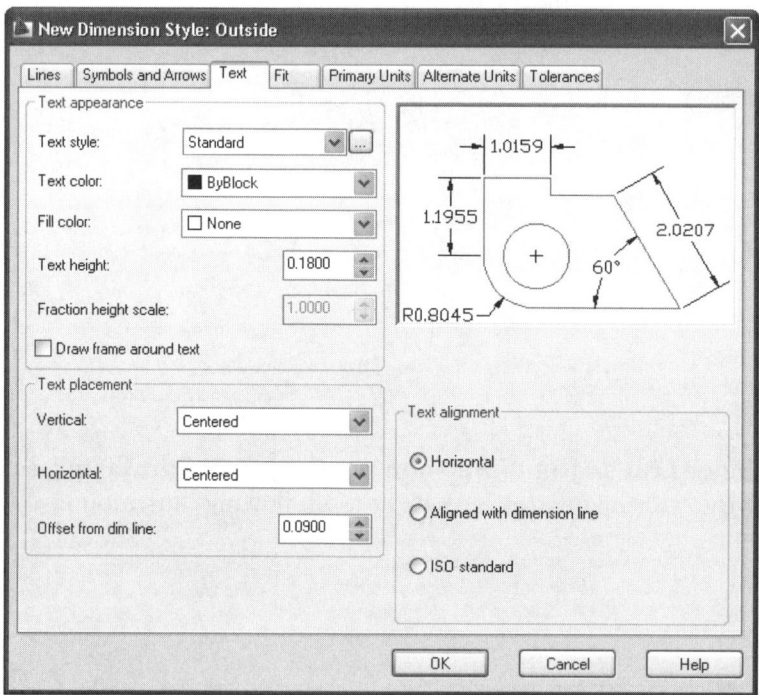

- Under **Text appearance** adjust the following settings:
- Select the desired premade **Text style** to be used to write the dimension text. If you didn't create a Text style prior to this step, you can click the three dots button and create it right now.
  - Specify the **Text color**.
  - Specify the **Fill color**, which is the background color for the dimension text.
- Input the **Text height** (this only applicable if the assigned Text style has a text height = 0.0).
- If you go to the **Primary Units** tab and make the **Unit format Architectural** or **Fractional**, then the dimension text will appear something like 1 1/4. The question here is whether you want the fraction to appear with less height than the ordianry number, accordingly, set **Fraction height scale**.
- Select whether to a **Draw frame around** the dimension text.

- As an introduction to **Text placement**, take a look at the following illustration:

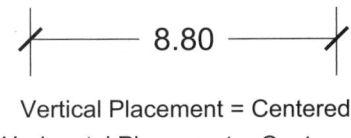

Vertical Placement = Centered
Horizontal Placement = Centered

- Under **Text placement** adjust the following settings:
- Select the **Vertical** placement. You have four choices: Centered, Above, Outside, and JIS (Japan Industrial Standard). Take a look at the following illustration:

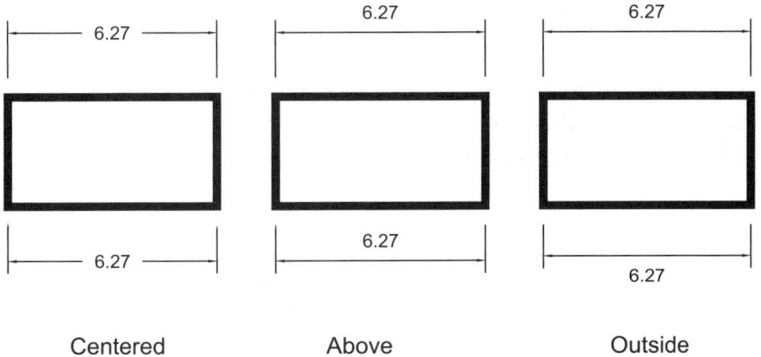

Centered   Above   Outside

- As for **Above**, set the **Offset from dim line**, which is the distance between dimension lines, and the baseline of the dimension text. Take a look at the following illustration:

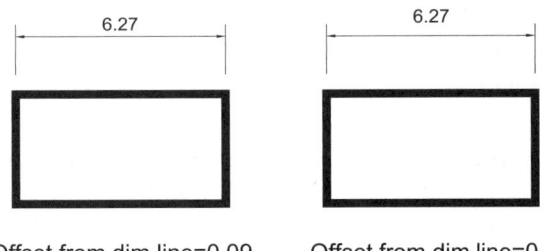

Offset from dim line=0.09   Offset from dim line=0.2

■ Select the **Horizontal** placement. You have five choices: Centered, At Ext Line 1, At Ext Line 2, Over Ext Line 1, and Over Ext Line 2. Take a look at the following illustration:

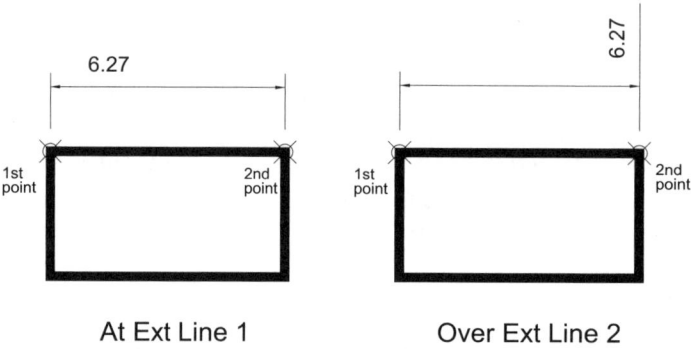

■ Under **Text alignment**, control whether the text will be **Horizontal** always, **Aligned with dimension line**, or according to the **ISO standard**. Take a look at the following illustration:

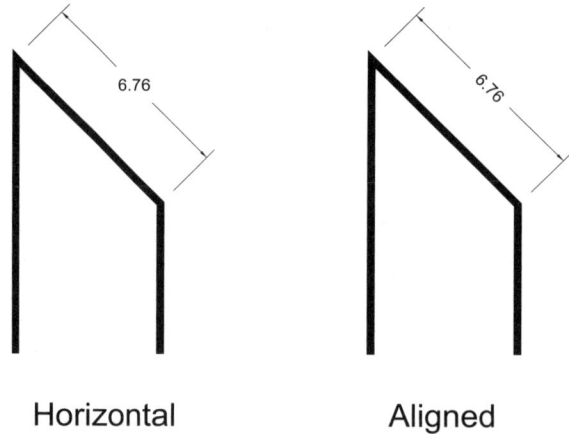

NOTE ■ The only difference between **Aligned with dimension line** and **ISO standard** is with the Radius and Diameter types, where the first is considered like the other types aligned with the dimension line, and ISO standard considers it a special case to be horizontal.

DIMENSION STYLE: FIT TAB

- Click the **Fit** tab and you will see the following:

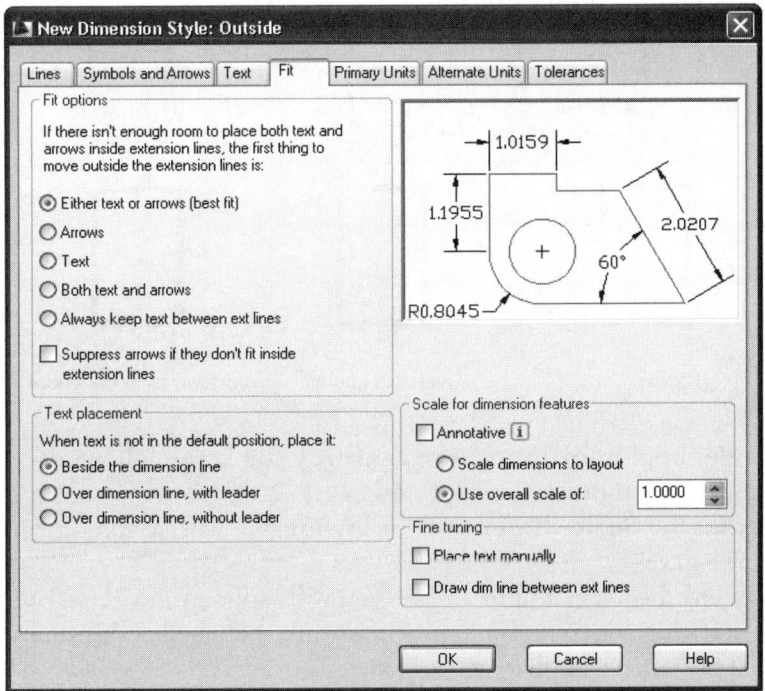

- As an introduction to the **Fit** tab, notice that there are three things within the two Extension lines: Dimension line, Arrowheads, and Dimension text. AutoCAD will put them all inside the two Extension lines when the distance is comfortable enough for all of them. But what if there is not enough room? We will discuss that answer here.
- Under **Fit options** adjust the following settings:
  - Select one of the five options to decide how AutoCAD will treat Arrowheads and Dimension text.
  - Select whether to Suppress arrows if they don't fit inside extension lines.

- Under **Text placement**, control the placement of the text. If it doesn't fit inside the extension lines, you have three options to choose from: **Beside the dimension line**, **Over the dimension line with leader**, and **Over the dimension line without leader**. Take a look at the following illustration:

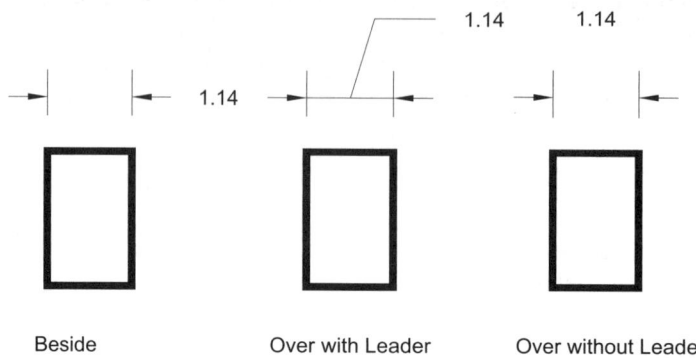

Beside   Over with Leader   Over without Leader

- Under **Scale for dimension features** adjust the following settings:
  - Keep **Annotative** off for now.
  - Set the **Scale dimension to layout** (we will discuss layouts in the next chapter).
- For any distance, length, or size you will input a value. **Use overall scale of** is a setting which will magnify or shrink the whole values in one step. This will not affect the distance measured.
- Under **Fine tuning** adjust the following settings:
  - If you don't trust AutoCAD to place your text in the right place, you can choose to let AutoCAD allow you to Place the dimension text manually.
  - Also, you can choose to force AutoCAD to Draw the dimension line between extension lines, whether the distance is appropriate or not.

DIMENSION STYLE: PRIMARY UNITS TAB

- Click the **Primary Units** tab and you will see the following:

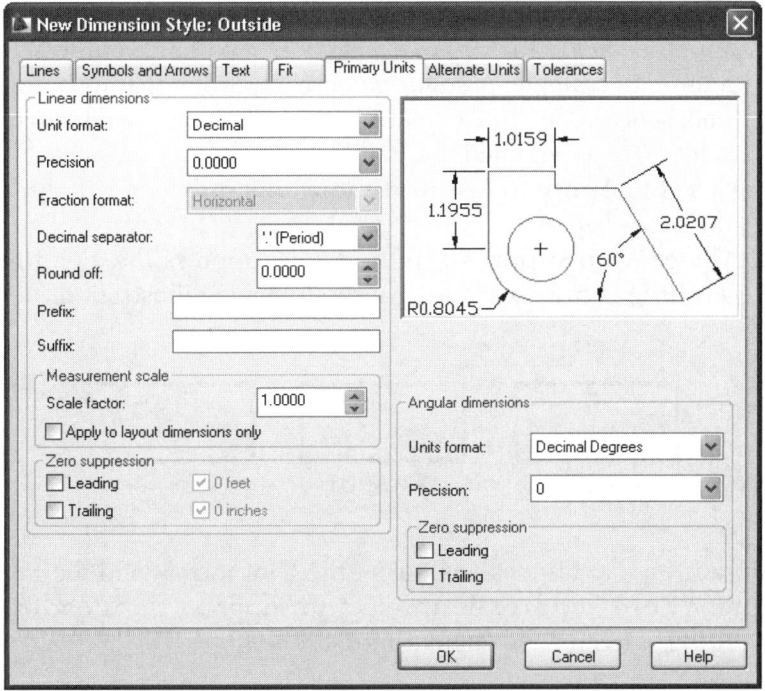

- As an introduction to the **Primary units**, let us assume that your client wants the dimension in decimal format, and one other sub-contractor wants it in Architectural format. The solution for that would be to show two numbers for each dimension; the first will be the **Primary Units** and the second will be the **Alternate Units**. In this tab we will cover the **Primary Units**.
- Under **Linear dimensions** adjust the following settings:
  - Choose the **Unit format**, selecting one of six formats.
  - Select the **Precision** of the unit format selected.
  - If you select the Architectural or Fractional format, then specify the **Fraction format**: **Horizontal**, **Diagonal**, and **Not Stacked**.
  - If you select **Decimal**, then specify the **Decimal Separator**: **Period**, **Comma**, and **Space**.
  - Specify the **Round off** number. If you select, for instance 0.5, then AutoCAD will round off any dimension to the nearest 0.5.
- Input the **Prefix** and/or the **Suffix** to illustrate this part. Take a look at the following illustration:

- Under **Measurement scale** adjust the following:
    - Input the **Scale factor**. To explain the importance of this setting, let's take look at an example: Assume we have a drawing that uses the millimeter as unit; hence, a length of 10 m will be 10,000. But in the dimension we want the value 10 to appear, and not 10,000; hence, we set the Scale factor to 0.001.
    - Select to **Apply to layout dimensions only** (we will discuss layouts in the next chapter).
    - Under **Zero suppression**, select to suppress the **Leading** and/or the **Trailing** zeros. Take a look at the following illustration:

- Under Angular dimensions, select the Unit format and the Precision.
- Under **Zero suppression**, select to suppress the **Leading** and/or the **Trailing** zeros for the angular measurements.

DIMENSION STYLE: ALTERNATE UNITS TAB

- Click the **Alternate Units** tab and you will see the following:

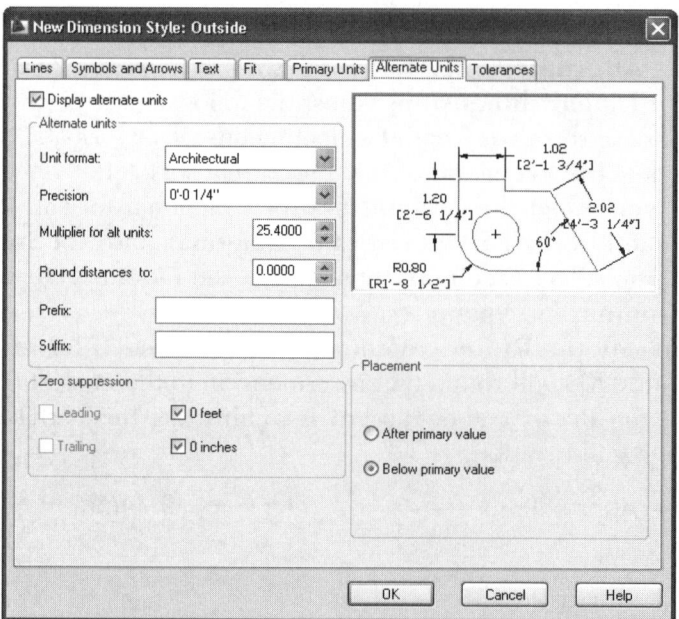

- If you want two numbers to appear for each dimension, click on **Display alternate units**.
- Specify the Alternate Unit format, its Precision, the Multiplier for all units' value, the Round distance, the Prefix, the Suffix, and the Zero suppression criteria.
- Specify whether to show the alternate units **After primary value** or **Below primary value**.

DIMENSION STYLE: TOLERANCES TAB

- Click the **Tolerances** tab and you will see the following:

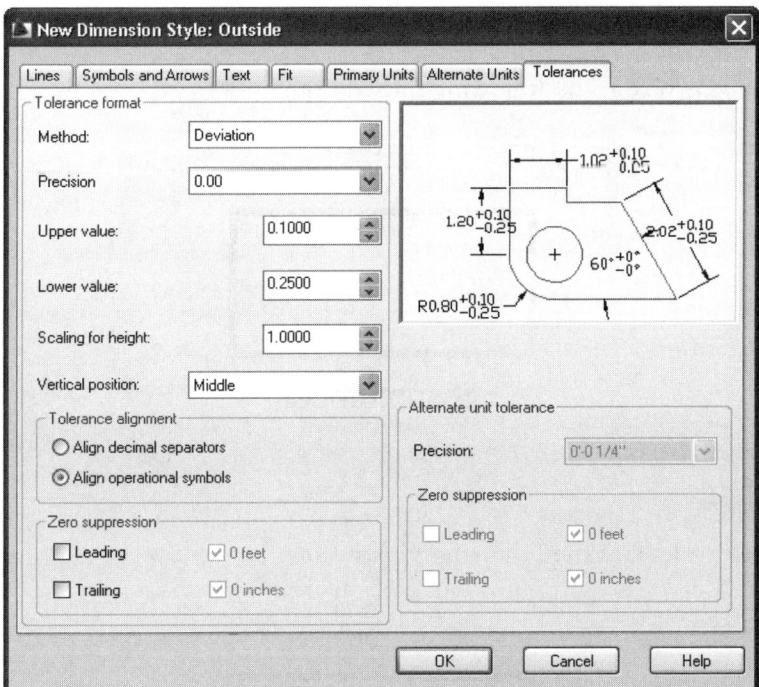

- There are several ways to show the tolerances:
  - None
  - Symmetrical
  - Deviation
  - Limits
  - Basic

None

- Take a look at the following illustration:

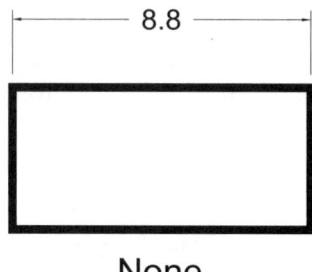

None

Symmetrical

- Take a look at the following illustration:

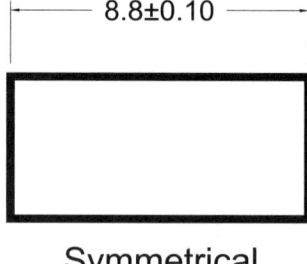

Symmetrical

Deviation

- Take a look at the following illustration:

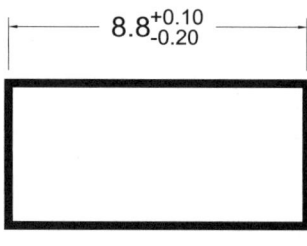

Deviation

Limits

- Take a look at the following illustration:

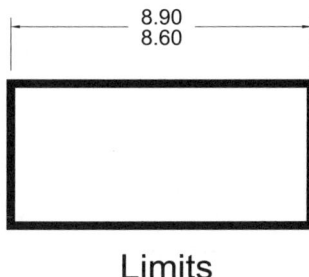

Limits

Basic

- Take a look at the following illustration:

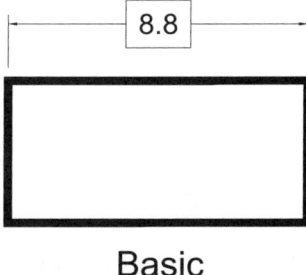

Basic

- Under **Tolerance format** adjust the following:
  - Specify the desired **Method**, one of the above mentioned methods.
  - Specify the **Precision** of the numbers to be shown.
- If you select **Symmetrical** specify the **Upper value**.
- For Deviation and Limits specify the Upper and Lower value.
- If you want the tolerance values to appear smaller than the dimension text, specify **Scaling for height**.
- Specify the **Vertical position** of the dimension text with regard to the tolerance values whether **Bottom**, **Middle**, or Top.
- If you are showing **Alternate units**, specify the **Precision** of the numbers under the **Alternate units' tolerance**.
- Accordingly, specify the **Zero suppression** for both the **Primary Units** tolerance and the Alternate units' tolerance.

DIMENSION STYLE: CREATING A CHILD STYLE

- Sometimes you need a dimension style identical to almost all types of dimensions except for Diameter.
- In this case, we create a dimension style for all types (we call Parent), and then we create a child dimension style from it.
- Take the following steps:
  - Create your parent dimension style.
  - Select it from the list in the dimension style dialog box.
  - Click the **New** button to create a new style.
- The following dialog box will appear:

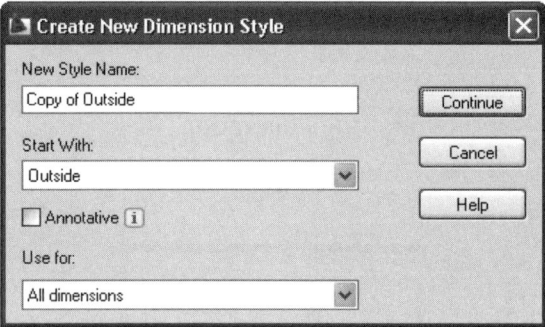

- For **Use for** select **Radius** (for example) and the dialog box will change to:

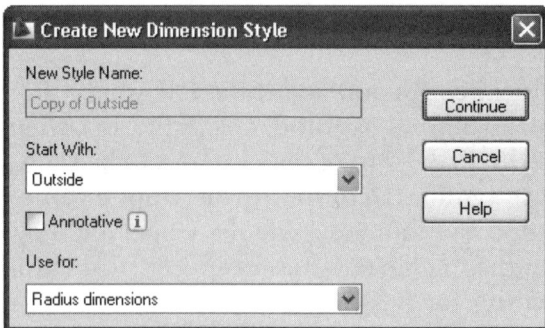

- Now click **Continue** and make the changes you want. These changes will affect only the Radius dimensions.
- In the **Dimension Style** dialog box you will see something like:

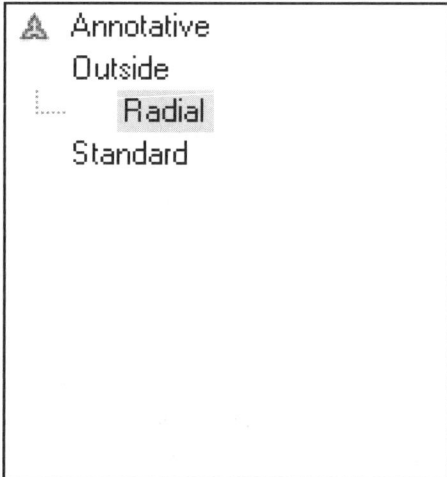

CONTROLLING DIMENSION STYLES

- Once you have created more than one dimension style you can control these dimension styles using the following buttons:

Set Dimension style current

- While you are in the Dimension Style dialog box, select the desired dimension style and click the **Current** button.
- While you are at the **Annotate** tab and using the **Dimensions** panel, use the pop-up list to set the current dimension style:

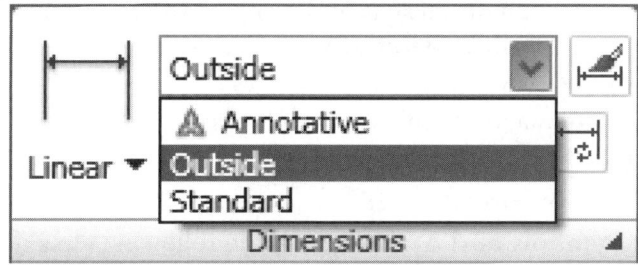

Modify Dimension style

- While you are in the Dimension Style dialog box, select the desired dimension style and click the **Modify** button. The same dialog box will appear for more editing.

Delete Dimension style

- There are two conditions that must be met in order to delete a dimension style:
- It should not be used in the current drawing.
- It should not be the current dimension style.
- It should not have any child style (if it does, delete the child first, then delete the parent).
- If these two conditions are fulfilled, then select the desired dimension style to be deleted, and press [Del] on the keyboard (you can select it and right-click, then select **Delete**). The following dialog box will appear:

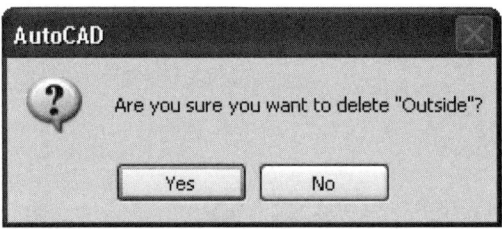

- If you click **Yes**, it will be deleted, and if you click **No**, the whole process will be canceled.

CREATING DIMENSION STYLES (METRIC)

Workshop 17-A

1. Start AutoCAD 2009.
2. Open the **Workshop_17.dwg** file.
3. Create a new dimension style and name it **Outside**, starting from **Standard**, and Use for **All dimensions**. (Anything not mentioned below leave it to the default value or setting.)
4. Under **Line** make the following changes:
   a. Extend beyond dime line = 0.25
   b. Offset from origin = 0.15
5. Under **Symbols and Arrows** make the following changes:
   a. Arrowhead, First = Oblique
   b. Arrow size = 0.25
6. Under **Text** make the following changes:
   a. Text style = Dimension
   b. Text placement, Vertical = Above
   c. Text alignment = Aligned with dimension line

7. Under **Fit** make the following changes:
   a. Use overall scale = 1000
8. Under **Primary Units** make the following changes:
   a. Linear dimension, Precision = 0.00
   b. Suffix = m
   c. Scale Factor = 0.001
9. Create a new style and name it **Inside**, starting from **Outside**, and use for **All dimensions**.
10. Under **Lines** make the following changes:
    a. Extension lines, Suppress Ext line 1 = on, Ext line 2 = on
11. Under **Symbols and Arrows** make the Arrow size = 0.20.
12. Under Text make the following changes:
    a. Text style = Standard
    b. Text height = 0.25
13. Under **Fit** make the following changes:
    a. Fine tuning, Placc text manually = on
14. Make a child dimension style from **Outside** for **Radius dimensions.**
15. Under **Symbols and Arrows** make the following changes:
    a. Arrowheads, Second = Closed filled
16. Under **Text** make the following changes:
    a. Text alignment = ISO Standard
17. Save the file and close it.

CREATING DIMENSION STYLES (IMPERIAL)

Workshop 17-B
1. Start AutoCAD 2009.
2. Open the **Workshop_17.dwg** file.
3. Create a new dimension style and name it **Outside**, starting from **Standard**, and Use for **All dimensions**. (Anything not mentioned below leave it to the default value or set ting.)
4. Under **Line** make the following changes:
   a. Extend beyond dime line = 3/4"
   b. Offset from origin = 1/2"
5. Under **Symbols and Arrows** make the following changes:
   a. Arrowhead, First = Oblique

    b. Arrow size = 3/4"

6. Under **Text** make the following changes:

    a. Text style = Dimension

    b. Text placement, Vertical = Above

    c. Text alignment = Aligned with dimension line

7. Under **Fit** make the following changes:

    a. Use overall scale = 12

8. Under **Primary Units** make the following changes:

    b. a. Unit Format = Architectural, Precision = 0'-0"Suffix = ft

9. Create a new style and name it **Inside**, starting from **Outside**, and use for **All dimensions**.

10. Under **Lines** make the following changes:

    a. Extension lines, Suppress Ext line 1 = on, Ext line 2 = on

11. Under **Text** make the following changes:

    a. Text style = Standard (change the font to be Arial)

    b. Text height = 3/4"

12. Under **Fit** make the following changes:

    a. Fine tuning, Place text manually = on

13. Make a child dimension style from **Outside** for **Radius dimensions**

14. Under **Symbols and Arrows** make the following changes:

    a. Arrowheads, Second = Closed filled

15. Under **Text** make the following changes:

    a. Text alignment = ISO Standard.

16. Save the file and close it.

DIMENSIONING COMMANDS: INTRODUCTION

- Dimensioning commands insert dimensions using the points specified by the user.

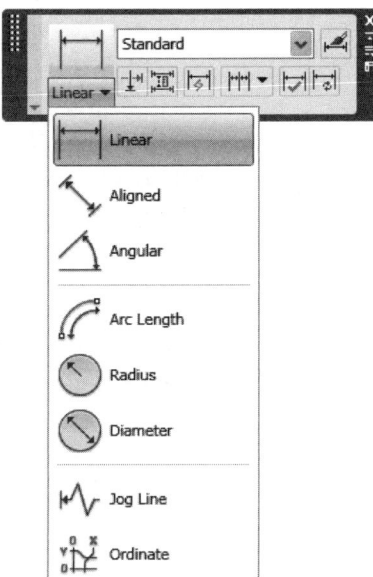

- You will find all commands in the **Annotate** tab under the **Dimensions** panel.
- See the following illustration:
- More commands can be found in the hidden part of the **Dimensions** panel. Take a look at the following illustration:

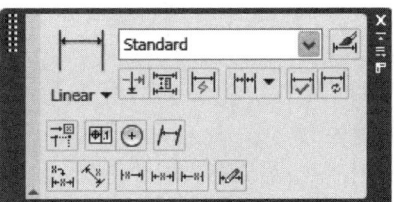

- So, for the purpose of this book, all dimensioning commands you need will be found in the **Dimensions** panel.

DIMENSIONING COMMANDS: LINEAR

- The **Linear dimensioning** command is used to create a horizontal or vertical dimension.
- To start the **Linear** command, make sure that you are at **Annotate** tab on the **Ribbon** and using the **Dimensions** panel, click the **Linear** button.
- The following prompt will appear:

```
Specify first extension line origin or <select object>:
(Specify the first point)
Specify second extension line origin: (Specify the second
point)
Specify dimension line location or
[Mtext/Text/Angle/Horizontal/Vertical/Rotated]: (Specify the
location of the dimension line)
```

- • There are three steps to follow:
- ■ Specify the first point of the dimension distance to be measured.
- ■ Specify the second point of the dimension distance to be measured.
- ■ Specify the location of the dimension block by specifying the location of the dimension line.

The following is the result:

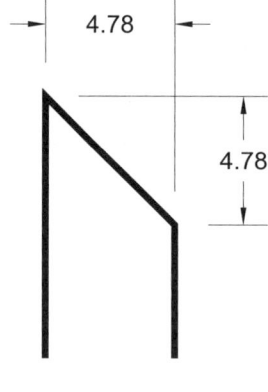

Linear

- ■ You can use the other options available, including:
    - • Mtext
    - • Text
    - • Angle
    - • Horizontal
    - • Vertical
    - • Rotated

Mtext

- ■ To edit the measured distance in the **MTEXT** command.

Text

- ■ To edit the measured distance in the **DTEXT** command.

Angle

- To set up the angle of text.

Horizontal

- To create a horizontal dimension.

Vertical

- To create a vertical dimension.

Rotated

- To create a dimension line parallel to another angle given by the user. As in the case of projecting a distance over another angle.

DIMENSIONING COMMANDS: ALIGNED

- The Aligned dimensioning command is used to create a dimension parallel to the measured distance.
- To start the **Aligned** command, make sure that you are at the **Annotate** tab on the **Ribbon** and using the **Dimensions** panel, click the **Aligned** button.
- The following prompt will appear:

```
Specify first extension line origin or <select object>:
(Specify the first point)
Specify second extension line origin: (Specify the second
point)
Specify dimension line location or
[Mtext/Text/Angle]: (Specify the location of the dimension
line)
```

- There are three steps to follow:
  - Specify the first point of the dimension distance to be measured.
  - Specify the second point of the dimension distance to be measured.
  - Specify the location of the dimension block by specifying the location of the dimension line.

- The following is the result:

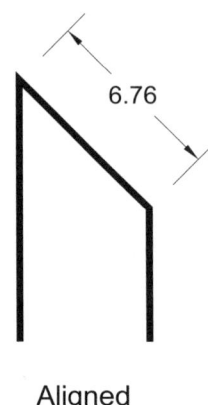

Aligned

- The rest of the options are just like the **Linear** command.

LINEAR AND ALIGNED DIMENSIONS

Exercise 32

1. Start AutoCAD 2009.
2. Open the **Exercise_32.dwg** file.
3. Create a new layer and call it **Dimension**. Make the Color = **White** and make it current.
4. Make the following modification to the current dimension style (i.e., Standard):
   a. Under **Symbols and Arrows** make the Arrow size = **0.10.**
   b. Under **Text** make the Text height = **0.15.**
   c. Under **Primary Units** make the Linear Precision = **0.00.**
5. Make the linear and aligned dimensions as shown:

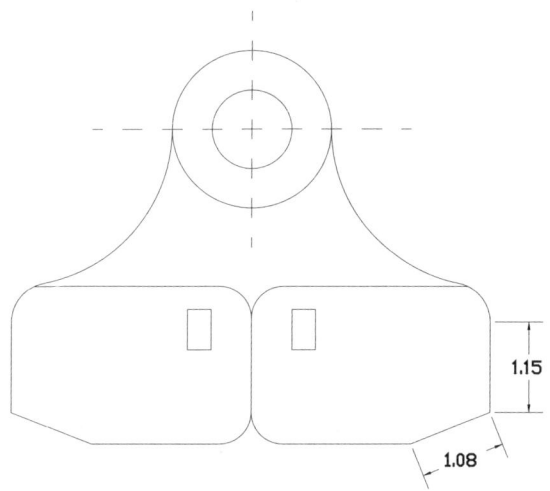

6. Save the file and close it.

DIMENSIONING COMMANDS: ANGULAR

- The Angular dimensioning command is used to create an Angular dimension.
- To start the **Angular** command, make sure that you are at the **Annotate** tab on the **Ribbon** and using the **Dimensions** panel, click the **Angular** button.
- There are four ways to place an angular dimension in AutoCAD. They are:
  - Select an arc and AutoCAD will measure the included angle.
  - Select a circle. The position which you select the circle from will be the first point and the center of the circle will be the second point. AutoCAD will ask you to specify any point on the diameter of the circle, and will place the angle accordingly.
  - Select two lines. AutoCAD will measure the inside angle or the outside angle.
  - Select a vertex, which will be considered a center point, then AutoCAD will ask you to specify two points and will measure the inside angle or the outside angle.
- The following prompts will appear:

Select arc, circle, line, or <specify vertex>: *(Select the desired method as discussed above—assume we select arc)*
Specify dimension arc line location or [Mtext/Text/Angle]: *(Specify the dimension block location)*

- This is the result you will get:

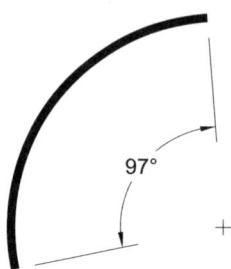

DIMENSIONING COMMANDS: ARC LENGTH

- The Arc Length dimensioning command is used to create a dimension showing the length of a selected arc.
- To start the **Arc Length** command, make sure that you are at the **Annotate** tab on the **Ribbon** and using the **Dimensions** panel, click the **Arc Length** button.
- The following prompt will appear:

```
Select arc or polyline arc segment: (Select the desired arc)
Specify arc length dimension location, or [Mtext/Text/Angle/
Partial/Leader]: (Specify the location of the dimension
block)
```

- There are two steps to follow:
  - Select the desired arc.
  - Specify the location of the dimension block.
- The following is the result:

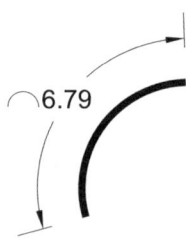

Arc Length

- The options Mtext, Text, and Angle were already discussed in the **Linear** command section.

Partial

- If you want Arc Length to measure part of the arc, and not the entire arc, accordingly specify two points on the arc. The result will look something like this:

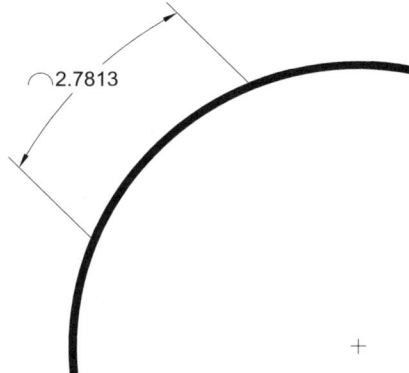

Leader

- For the arc with an angle more than 180 you may add a leader, just like the example below:

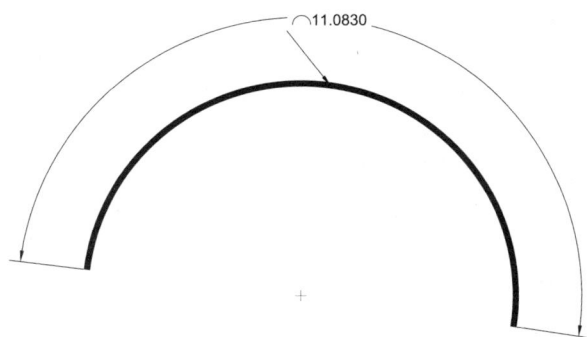

DIMENSIONING COMMANDS: RADIUS

- The Radius dimensioning command is used to put a Radius dimension on an arc and/or circle.
- To start the **Radius** command, make sure that you are at the **Annotate** tab on the **Ribbon** and using the **Dimensions** panel, click the **Radius** button.
- The following prompts will appear:

```
Select arc or circle: (Select the desired arc or circle)
Specify dimension line location or [Mtext/Text/Angle]:
(Specify the location of the dimension block)
```

- There are two steps to follow:
  - Select the desired arc or circle.
  - Specify the location of the dimension block.
- This is the result you will get:

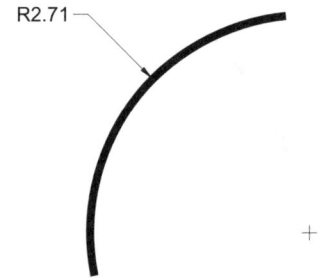

DIMENSIONING COMMANDS: DIAMETER

- The Diameter dimensioning command is used to put a diameter dimension on an arc and/or circle.
- To start the **Diameter** command, make sure that you are at the **Annotate** tab on the **Ribbon** and using the **Dimensions** panel, click the **Diameter** button.
- The following prompts will appear:

```
Select arc or circle: (Select the desired arc or circle)
Specify dimension line location or [Mtext/Text/Angle]:
(Specify the dimension block location)
```

- This is the result you will get:

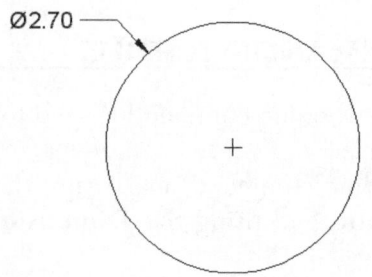

DIMENSIONING COMMANDS: JOG LINE

- The Jog Line dimensioning command is used to add (or remove) a jog line on Linear or Aligned dimension lines.
- To start the **Jog Line** command, make sure that you are at the **Annotate** tab on the **Ribbon** and using the **Dimensions** panel, click the **Jog Line** button.
- The following prompts will appear:

```
Select dimension to add jog or [Remove]: (Select the desired
linear or aligned)
Specify jog location (or press ENTER): (Click on the desired
place)
```

- If there is a previous jog, you can remove it by selecting the Remove option. The following prompt will appear:

```
Select jog to remove: (Click on the desired existing jog)
```

 ■ It is preferable to choose **Nearest** as your running **OSNAP** in order to specify the place of the jog.

DIMENSIONING COMMANDS: ORDINATE

- The Ordinate dimensioning command is used to add several measurements to objects relative to a certain point.
- To start the **Ordinate** command, make sure that you are at the **Annotate** tab on the **Ribbon** and using the **Dimensions** panel, click the **Ordinate** button.
- The **Ordinate** command allows you to set dimensions relative to a datum, either in X or in Y. Take a look at the following illustration:

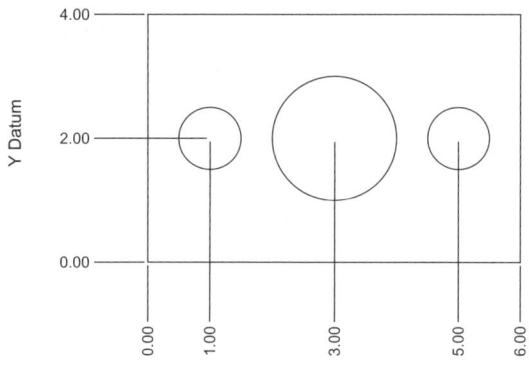

■ You have to change the UCS origin location to the desired location so the readings will be right, otherwise, the values will be relative to the current 0,0.

■ AutoCAD will give the following prompts:

```
Specify feature location: (Click on the desired point)
Specify leader endpoint or [Xdatum/Ydatum/Mtext/Text/Angle]:
(Specify the dimension location)
```

■ By default, when you select a point, you may go in the direction of X or in Y. If you want the **Ordinate** command to go specifically in the direction of X, then select the **Xdatum** option, and select **Ydatum** if you want to go specifically in the direction of Y.

■ The rest of the options were discussed in the Linear command section.

ANGULAR, ARC LENGTH, RADIUS, DIAMETER AND DIMENSIONS

 Exercise 33

1. Start AutoCAD 2009.

2. Open the **Exercise_33.dwg** file.

3. Make the following modification to the current dimension style (i.e., Standard):

   a. Under **Text,** change the current text style to use the **Arial** font.

4. Create the four types of dimensions as shown:

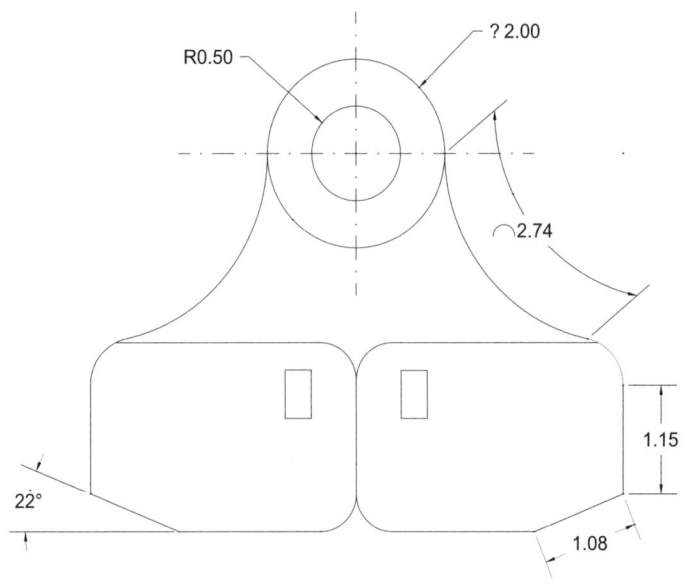

5. Save the file and close it.

JOG LINE & ORDINATE

Exercise 34

1. Start AutoCAD 2009.
2. Open the **Exercise_34.dwg** file.
3. Create the ordinate and jog line as shown below:

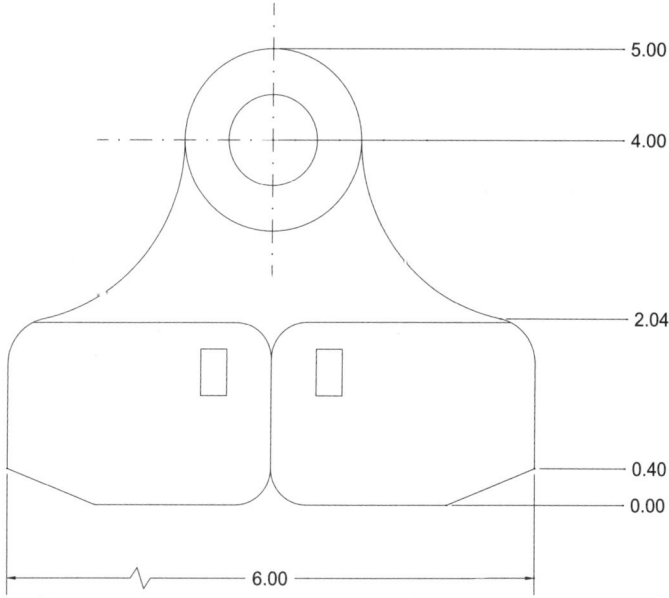

4. Save the file and close it.

DIMENSIONING COMMANDS: CONTINUE

*   After you put a dimension in your drawing (i.e., Linear, Aligned, Angular, or Ordinate), you can ask AutoCAD to continue using the same type, and to allocate it along the first one.
*   Using the Continue dimensioning command will allow you to use many dimensions quickly.
*   To start the **Continue** command, make sure that you are at the **Annotate** tab on the **Ribbon** and using the **Dimensions** panel, click the **Continue** button.

If no dimension was created in this session

- The following prompts will appear:

```
Select continued dimension: (Select either Linear, Aligned,
Ordinate, or Angular)
```

- AutoCAD will consider the selected dimension as the base dimension, and will continue accordingly.

If the dimension was created in this session

- The following prompt will appear:

```
Specify a second extension line origin or [Undo/Select]
<Select>: (Specify the second point of the last Linear,
Aligned, Ordinate, or Angular, or select an existing
dimension)
```

- AutoCAD will give you the ability to do one of three things:
- If you already created a linear dimension (for example), then you can continue by specifying the second point. Considering the second point of the first dimension is the first point of the continuing dimension.
- Also, you can select an existing dimension, and continue from there.
- Or, you can undo the last continue dimension.
- Take a look at the following illustration:

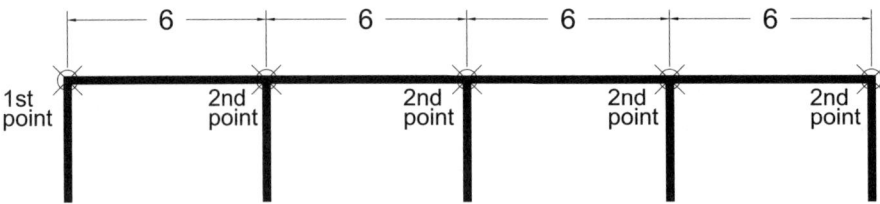

DIMENSIONING COMMANDS: BASELINE

- The **Baseline** command is just like the **Continue** dimensioning command except the dimensions will be always related to the first point you selected.
- To start the **Baseline** command, make sure that you are at the **Annotate** tab on the **Ribbon** and using the **Dimensions** panel, click the **Baseline** button.
- All the prompts and the procedures are identical to the **Continue** command.

▪ Take a look at the following illustration:

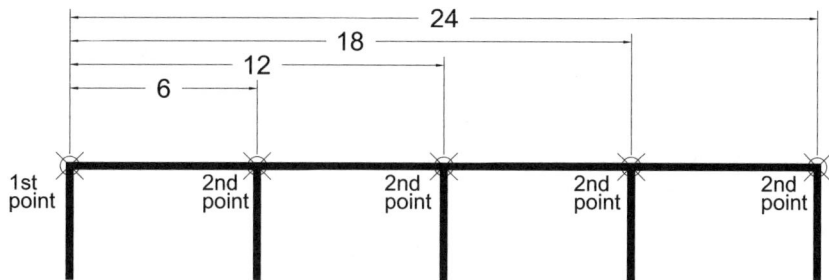

CONTINUOUS AND BASELINE DIMENSIONS

Exercise 35
1. Start AutoCAD 2009.
2. Open the **Exercise_35.dwg** file.
3. Create the Continuous and Baseline dimensions as shown:

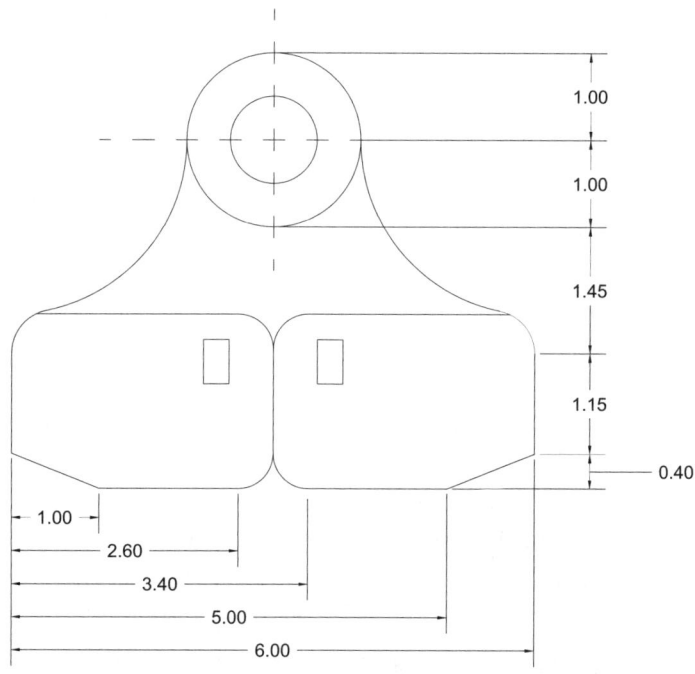

4. Save the file and close it.

DIMENSIONING COMMANDS: QUICK DIMENSION

- The Quick Dimension command is used to place a group of dimensions in a single step.
- To start the **Quick Dimension** command, make sure that you are at the **Annotate** tab on the **Ribbon** and using the **Dimensions** panel, click the **Quick Dimension** button.
- The following prompt will appear:

```
Select geometry to dimension: (Either by clicking, Window,
or Crossing)
Specify dimension line position, or [Continuous/Staggered/
Baseline/Ordinate/Radius/ Diameter/datumPoint/Edit/seTtings]
<Continuous>:
```

- At this prompt you can right-click, and the following shortcut menu will appear:

- From this shortcut menu, you can select the proper dimension type: Continuous, Staggered, Baseline, Ordinate, Radius, or Diameter.
- Select the type and then specify the dimension line location; a group of dimensions will be placed in a single step.
- Take a look at the **Staggered** example below:

DIMENSION BLOCKS AND GRIPS

- You can edit dimension blocks using Grips.
- If you click a dimension block, five grips will appear, just like the following:

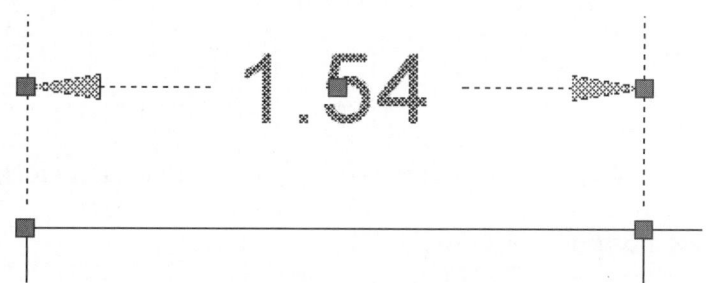

- From the above illustration, we can see that grips appear in the following places:
  - The two ends of the dimension line.
  - The two origins of the dimension line.
  - The dimension text.
- You can change the position of the text by clicking its grip and moving it parallel to the dimension line.
- You can change the position of the dimension line by clicking one of the two grips and moving it closer to or farther from the origin.
- You can change the measured distance by moving one of the two grips of the origin so the distance will change accordingly.
- See the following example:

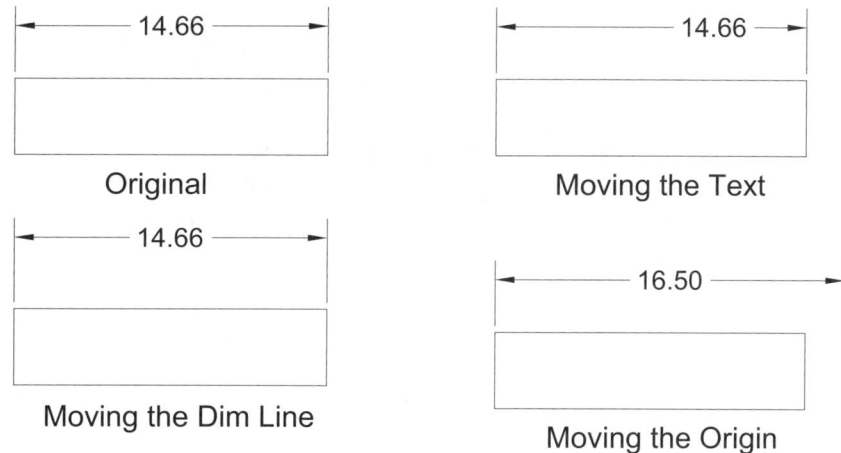

■ Also, if you select a dimension block and right-click, the following shortcut menu will appear (the part only concerning the dimension is shown below):

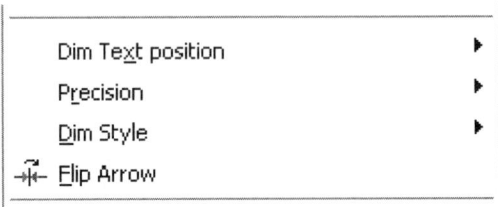

■ You can change four things in the selected dimension block.

Dim Text position

■ You can change the position of the dimension text, with the following options:
  • **Above dim line**: it will change it from any other position to **Above**.
  • **Centered**: it will change it from any other postion to **Centered**.
  • **Home text**: it will restore back to its original position according to its dimension style.
  • **Move text alone**: it will give you the option of positioning the text freely in any place you want.
  • **Move with leader**: to do the same as above, but with a leader.
  • **Move with dim line**: you move both the dimension text and the dimension line in a single step.

Precision

■ This will allow you to set the number of decimal places for the number shown.
■ You can start from no decimal places, up to 8 decimal places.

Dim Style

■ The changes made using this method can be saved in a new dimension style. Use the option **Save as New Style** and type in a new name.
■ You can change the dimension style of any dimension block in the drawing. The existing dimension styles will appear. Select the new desired dimension style.

Flip arrow

■ To flip the arrows from inside to outside, and vice versa.
■ The process will be done only on one of the arrows and not two.

DIMENSION BLOCK PROPERTIES

- Select a dimension block, then right-click and select **Properties**. The following dialog box will appear:

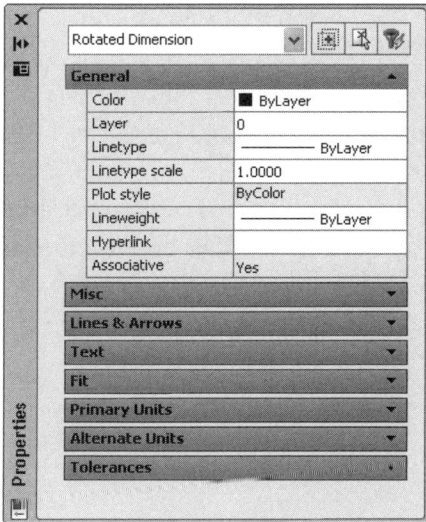

- Under **General**, you will see the general properties of the selected dimension block.
- Then you will see Misc, Lines & Arrows, Text, Fit, Primary Units, Alternate Units, and Tolerances. If you compare these to the **Dimension Style** command, which we discussed, you will find them identical, which means you can change any of the characteristics of the dimension block after we place it in **Properties**.

QUICK DIMENSION AND EDITING

Exercise 36
1. Start AutoCAD 2009.
2. Open the **Exercise_36.dwg** file.
3. Using Quick Dimension and using crossing, select all the lines and the two arcs at the bottom of the shape.
4. Deselect the two arcs along with the middle vertical line and press [Enter], then right-click and select Baseline and put it in a convenient place beneath the shape.
5. Select the dimension with value = 1.00 (at the most left). Five grips will appear.

6. Make sure that Middle in **OSNAP** is turned on, and select the upper right grip to make it hot and move it to the middle point of the right horizontal line.

7. The value of the dimension should read 1.80. Press [Esc] twice.

8. Select the same dimension block again, and move the dimension line closer to the shape. Press [Esc] twice.

9. Select the lower dimension with value = 6.00.

10. Right-click, and change the Precision of the number to 0.0000, and make it above the dim line.

11. Select the dimension with value = 5.00, and show the Properties pallete.

12. Change the Arrow 1 & Arrow 2 to be Oblique, and the arrow size = 0.3.

13. The shape should look like the following:

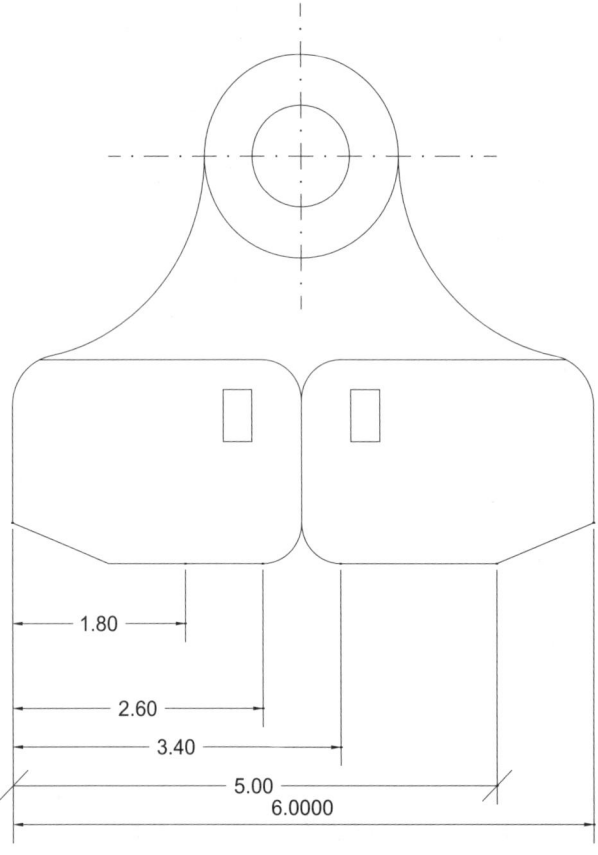

14. Save the file and close it.

MULTILEADER: INTRODUCTION

- Leader in AutoCAD is an arrow pointing to part of the drawing, with two lines and some text that explain certain facts about that part.
- Multileader can be one arrow, with a single set of lines, or multiple arrows with multiple sets of lines. Take a look at the illustration below for single leader:

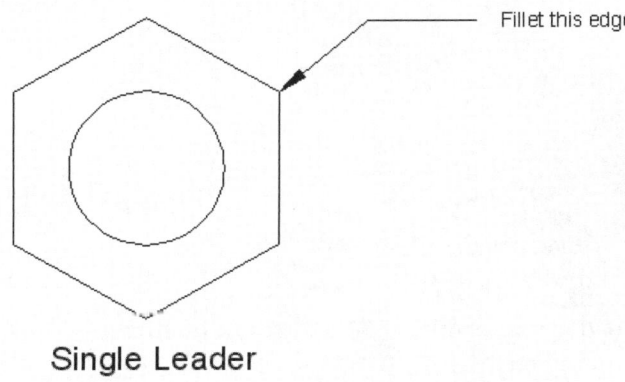

Single Leader

- Take a look at the following illustration for multileader:

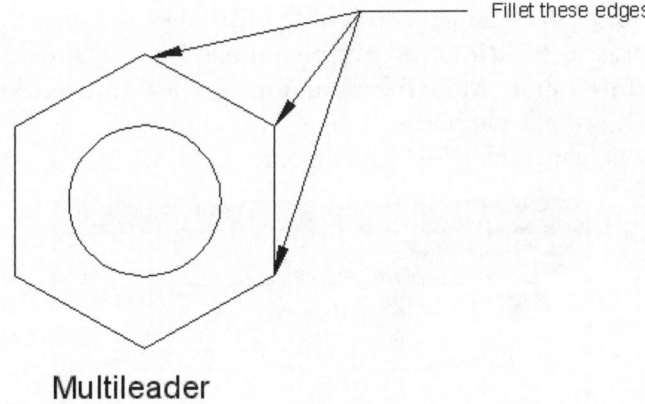

Multileader

 - Normally you will create a single leader, then using other commands you can create a multileader from it.

- You will specify (by default) two points; the first one is where the arrow will be pointing to, and the second will be the body of the leader. The angle of the leader will be specified by the user, but another small horizontal landing will be added automatically. To understand this take a look at the illustration below:

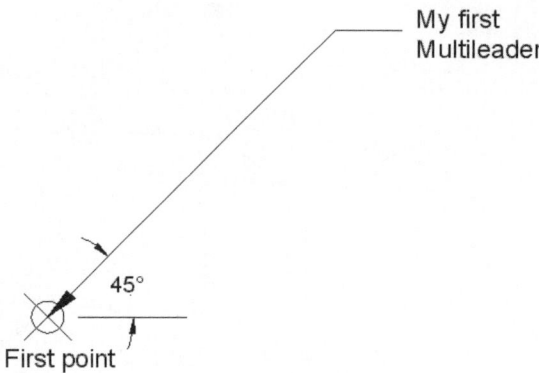

- Multileader has its own style and set of commands, which we will discover in upcoming pages.

MULTILEADER: CREATING THE STYLE

- As we discussed in the Dimension Style section, you will use the Multileader Style to set the characteristics of the Multileader block.

- To start the **Multileader Style** command, make sure that you are at the **Annotate** tab on the **Ribbon** and using the **Multileader** panel, click the **Multileader Style** button.
- The following dialog box will appear:

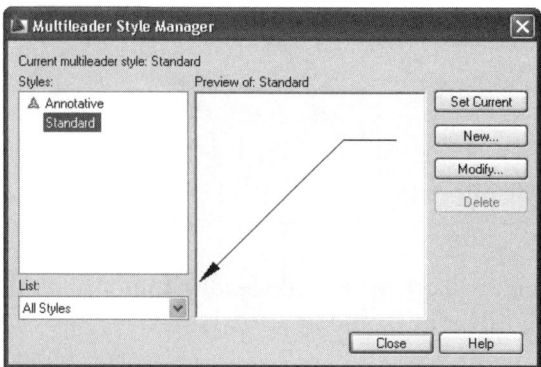

- To create a new style click the **New** button and the following dialog box will appear:

- Type the name of the new style, and select the existing style that you want to start with. Click **Continue** to start modifying the Multileader style.
- You will see three tabs:
  - Leader Format
  - Leader Structure
  - Content
- We will discuss each one of these in the coming pages.

Leader Format

- You will see the following dialog box:

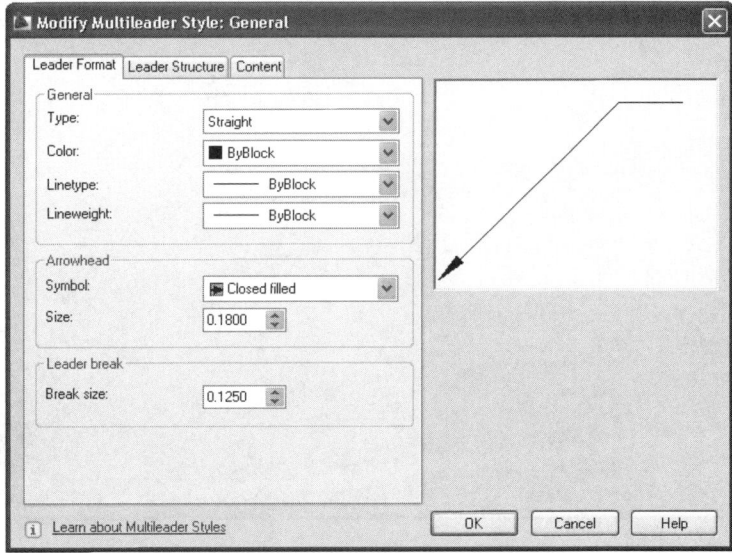

- Control the leader type. You have three choices:
  - Straight
  - Spline
  - None

- Take a look at the following illustration:

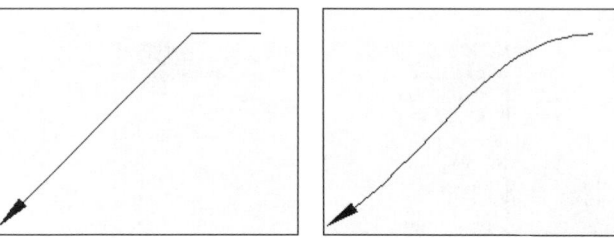

- Control the **Color**, **Linetype**, and **Lineweight** just like we discussed in the **Dimension Style** command section.
- Choose the **Arrowhead Symbol** (out from 20 different existing shapes) and its size.
- If there is any Dimension Break? How much will the break of the Multileader be? Answer this question by setting the **Break size** value.

Leader Structure

- You will see the following dialog box:

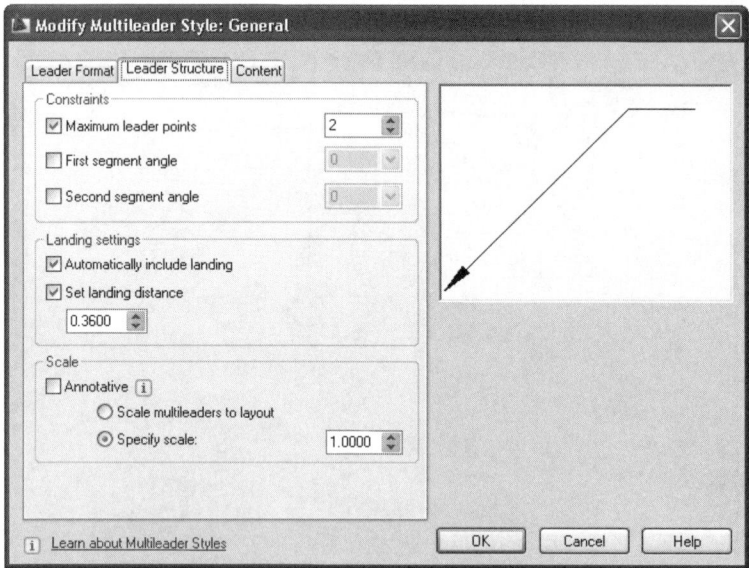

- Specify the **Maximum leader points**. As we discussed earlier, by default this value is 2, but you can specify more points.
- By default you will specify the **First segment angle** on the screen, and a small horizontal landing (**Second segment**) will be added, but you can set the angle values for both in the Multileader style.

- Choose whether to **Automatically include a landing**. If yes, what is the **landing length?**
- Select whether the Multileader will be Annotative (this part will be discussed later).

Content

- You will see the following dialog box:

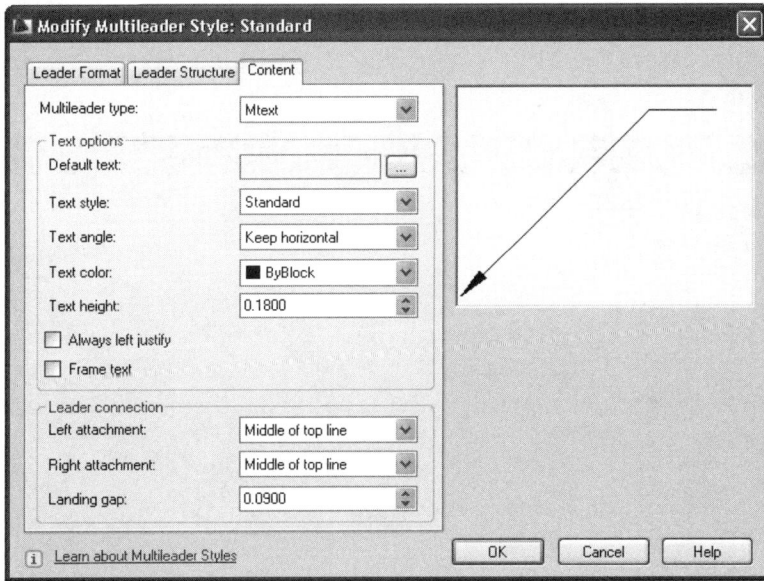

- There are two types of Multileader:
  - With Multiline text
  - With a block (Either pre-defined or user-defined)
- Take a look at the following illustration:

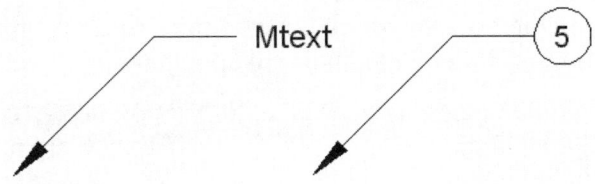

- By default Mtext (Multiline text) is selected. The settings to adjust are:
  - If there is any text that should appear each time, type it in **Default text**.

- Specify the **Text style**.
- Specify the **Text angle** (Keep horizontal, Right-reading, or As inserted).
- Specify **Text Color** and **Text height** (if Text Style height = 0).
- Specify whether to make the text **Always left Justify**, or not, and with a **Frame**, or not.
- Control the position of the text relative to the landing for both left and right leader lines.
- Control the gap distance between the end of the landing and the text.

■ If you select the Multileader type to be **Block**, you will see the following dialog box:

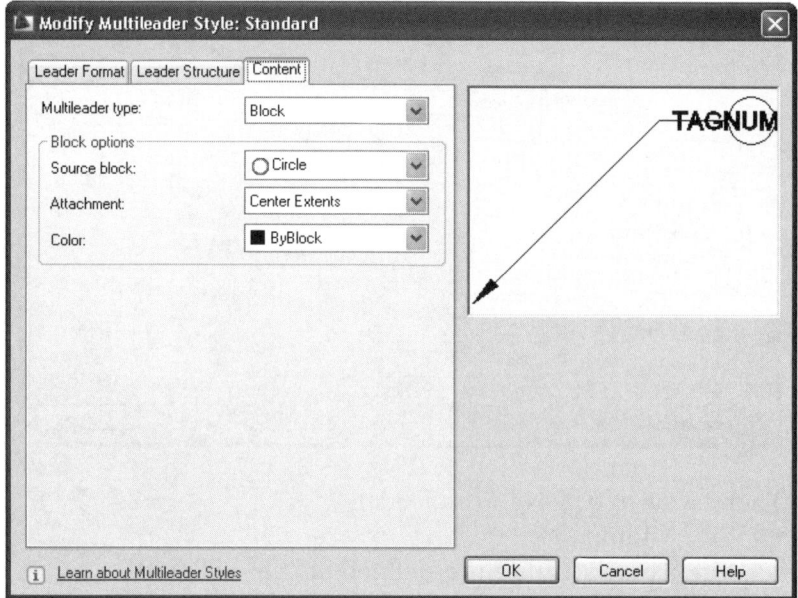

■ Control the following settings:
  - Specify the **Source block** (choose from the list) or select User defined, and the following dialog box will appear:

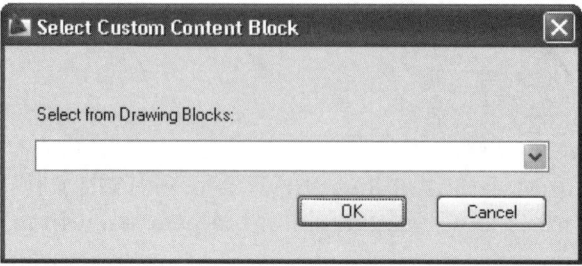

- Type the name of the desired block, and click **OK**.
- Specify the **Attachment** position.
- Specify the **Color** of the Attachment.

MULTILEADER: COMMANDS

- After you finish creating the Multileader Style, you are now ready to insert the multileaders your drawing needs.
- You will always start with the **Multileader** command, which will insert a single leader.
- To start the **Multileader** command, make sure that you are at the **Annotate** tab on the **Ribbon** and using the **Multileaders** panel, click the **Multileader** button.
- The following prompts will appear:

```
Specify leader arrowhead location or [leader Landing first/
Content first/Options] <Options>: (Specify the point which
the arrow should point to)
Specify leader landing location: (Specify the angle and the
length of the leader)
```

- Type the text you want to appear in the leader.

- Click the **Add Leader** button to add more leaders (arrows) to an existing single leader. The following prompts will appear:

```
Select a multileader:
1 found
Specify leader arrowhead location:
Specify leader arrowhead location:
```

- Click the **Remove Leader** button to remove some leaders from an existing multileader. The following prompts will appear:

```
Select a multileader:
1 found
Specify leaders to remove:
Specify leaders to remove:
```

- Click the **Align** button to align several multileaders to be in the same line. The following prompts will appear:

```
Select multileaders: 1 found
Select multileaders: 1 found, 2 total
Select multileaders: (Press [Enter])
Current mode: Use current spacing
Select multileader to align to or [Options]:
Specify direction:
```

- Click the **Collect** button to collect several multileaders to a group in a single leader. This command works only with leaders containing blocks. You will see the following prompts:

```
Select multileaders:
Select multileaders: (Press [Enter] when you are done)
Specify collected multileader location or [Vertical/
Horizontal/Wrap] <Horizontal>:
```

MULTILEADER

Exercise 37
1. Start AutoCAD 2009.
2. Open the **Exercise_37.dwg** file.
3. Make the Multileader style Free current.
4. Create a multileader to the right chamfer and type "Chamfer these edges."
5. Add a leader to the existing leader and make it point to the left chamfer.
6. Make the Multileader style Block current.
7. Create a multileader to the inner circle and type the number 1.
8. Do the same to the outer circle and type the number 2.
9. If the two leaders are not aligned properly use the **Align** command to align them.
10. The shape should look like the following:

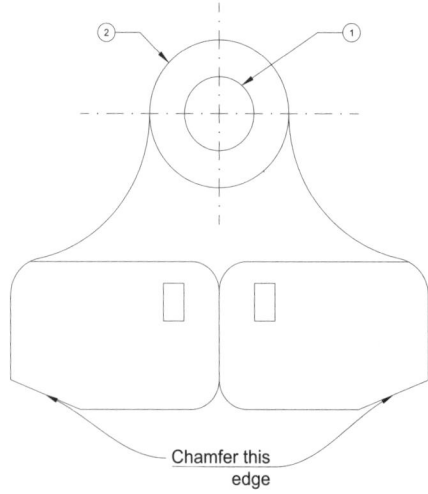

11. Save the file and close it.

CREATING DIMENSIONS IN THE PLAN (METRIC)

Workshop 18-A

1. Start AutoCAD 2009.
2. Open the **Workshop_18.dwg** file.
3. Make layer **Dimension** the current layer.
4. Make the following layers frozen: **Furniture, Hatch,** and **Text**.
5. Using **Outside** and **Inside** dimension styles create the dimensions for the outer and inner dimensions as shown:

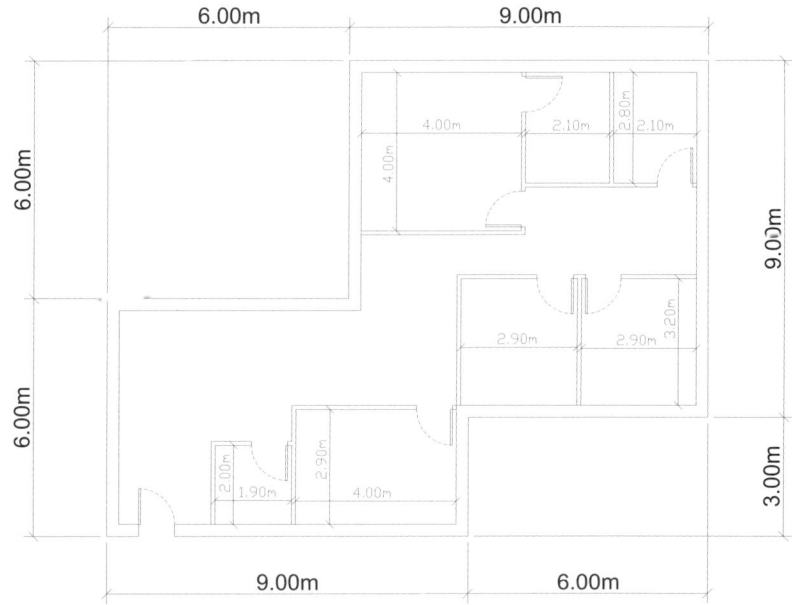

6. Save the file and close it.

CREATING DIMENSIONS IN THE PLAN (IMPERIAL)

Workshop 18-B

1. Start AutoCAD 2009.
2. Open the **Workshop_18.dwg** file.
3. Make layer **Dimension** the current layer.
4. Make the following layers frozen: **Furniture**, **Hatch**, and **Text**.
5. Using **Outside** and **Inside** dimension styles create the dimensions for the outer and inner dimensions as shown:

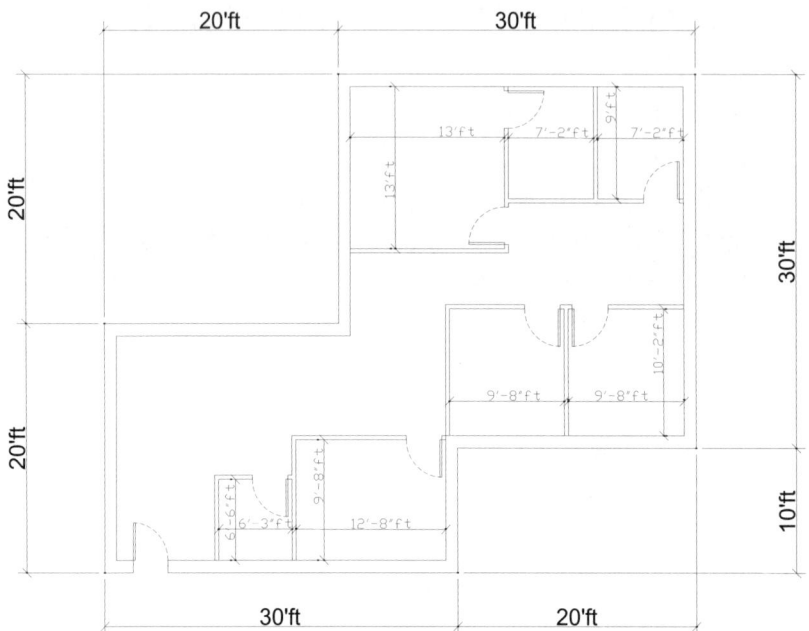

6. Save the file and close it.

NOTES

CHAPTER REVIEW

1. You can ONLY create dimension styles that will affect all dimension types.
   a. True.
   b. False.
2. _____ and _____ are two types of dimensions you can use with arcs.
3. Which of the following is not an AutoCAD dimension command:
   a. dimlinear
   b. dimarc
   c. dimchordlength
   d. dimaligned
4. You have to have two lines to create an Angular dimension.
   a. True.
   b. False.
5. Which of the following is a type of Tolerance in AutoCAD:
   a. Deviation.
   b. Symmetrical.
   c. Limits.
   d. All of the above.
6. In order to make a dimension style _____ double-click the name in the dimension style dialog box.

CHAPTER REVIEW ANSWERS

1. b
2. Arc length, Jogged, Radius, Diameter
3. c
4. b
5. d
6. current

Chapter 10   PLOTTING YOUR DRAWING

In This Chapter

◊ Model Space vs. Paper Space
◊ Creating Layouts
◊ Page Setup
◊ Creating viewports in layout using multiple methods
◊ Editing and scaling viewports
◊ Creating Plot Styles
◊ Plot command
◊ DWF plotting

INTRODUCTION

- Before AutoCAD 2000, almost all AutoCAD users plotted from Model Space, which is the place they created their design in.
- But in AutoCAD 2000, **Layouts** made it easy for everybody to shift their attention to the new method, which encompasses many new features, surpasses plotting in Model Space.
- Also, in AutoCAD 2000, a new feature was introduced called Plot Style, which allows you to use color-independent configuration plotting.
- No doubt, AutoCAD 2000 was a flagship version in more than one aspect, but the new improvements in plotting process made it the most important.

MODEL SPACE VS. PAPER SPACE

- Model Space is the place where you create the drawing, with all of the modification processes.
- When you think about plotting, you should use Paper Space.
- There is only one Model Space in each drawing file.

- Before AutoCAD 2000, there was only one Paper Space per drawing file.
- From AutoCAD 2000 and on, the name of Paper Space changed to Layout.
- You can create as many layouts as you wish in each drawing file.
- Each Layout will be connected to Page Setup where you will specify at least three settings. They are:
  - The Plotter you will send the drawing to.
  - The Paper size you will use.
  - Paper orientation (Portrait or Landscape).
- To show the importance of this feature, let's take a look at the following example: say we have a company who owns A0 plotter, A2 printer, along with A4 laser printer. The staff will use all of these printers to print a single drawing.
- If you use Model Space, you will change the setup of the printer, paper size, and paper orientation, along with the drawing area to be plotted each and every time you want to print.
- But if you create three layouts with the proper Page Setup and Viewports, each time you want to print, simply go to the Layout and give the command **Plot**, which will save time, effort, and money!

INTRODUCTION TO LAYOUTS

- Each layout consists of the following elements:
  - **Page Setup**, where you will specify the printer (or plotter), the paper size, paper orientation, and other things that will be covered later in this chapter.
  - **Objects**, such as blocks (e.g., the title block), text, dimensions, and any other desired object.
  - **Viewports**, which will be covered separately in the following pages.
- Take a look at the following illustration:

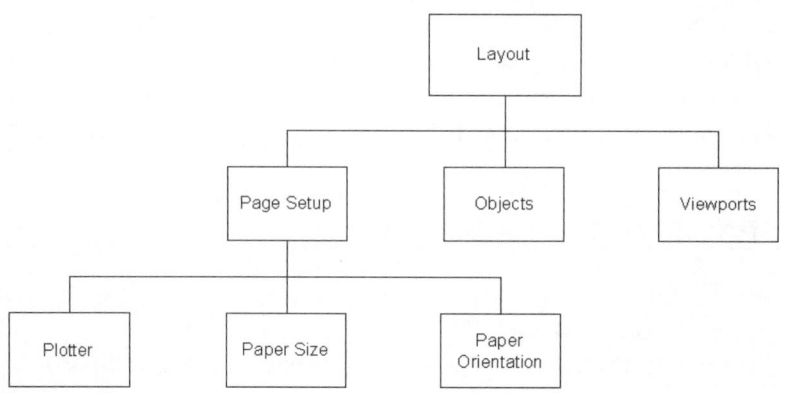

- Each layout should have a name. AutoCAD will give it a temporary name, but you can change it as you wish.
- By default when you create a new drawing using the *acad.dwt* template, two layouts, Layout1, and Layout2 will be created for use.
- You can select the option in the **Page Setup Manager** dialog box to appear when you click on a layout for the first time in order to set the printer, paper size, etc.
- **Layouts** and **Page Setup** will be saved in the drawing file.
- By default page setup has no name, but you can name it, accordingly, and use it in other layouts in the current drawing file, or in other drawings.

HOW DO YOU SWITCH BETWEEN MODEL SPACE AND LAYOUTS?

- By default, when you start a new drawing, AutoCAD will be in Model Space.
- On the Status bar you will find the following:

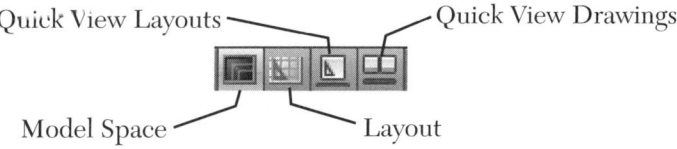

- Before you click on the **Layout** button, click the **Quick View Layouts** button to see the available layouts saved in your drawing.
- Take a look at the illustration below:

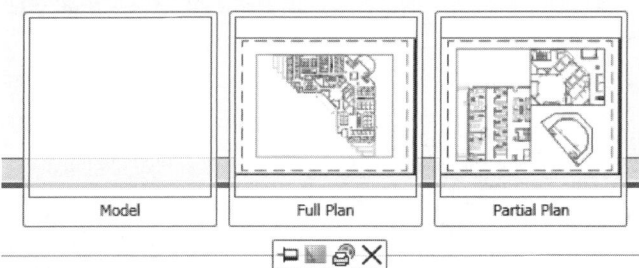

- From the illustration you can see two layouts. You can choose which to view by clicking on the small view. Also, you can **Publish**, create a **New Layout**, and you can choose to **Pin Quick View Layouts**.
- In order to jump from Model Space to Layout and vice versa, click on the Model Space and Layout buttons on the Status Bar.

- Also, you can right-click either, and the following shortcut menu will appear:

- Select the only option, and you will see at the lower left corner of the graphical area the following tabs:

- This is essential to what we will learn in the next few pages.

HOW DO YOU CREATE A NEW LAYOUT?

- There are several ways to create a new layout. These include:

New Layout

- A very simple method: right-click on any existing layout name and a shortcut menu will appear, select the **New Layout** option.
- A new layout will be added with a temporary name. You can rename using the right-click menu and selecting the **Rename** option.

Using a template

- You can bring any layout defined inside a template, and use it in your current drawing file.
- Right-click on any existing layout and a shortcut menu will appear. Select the **From template** option and the following dialog box will appear:

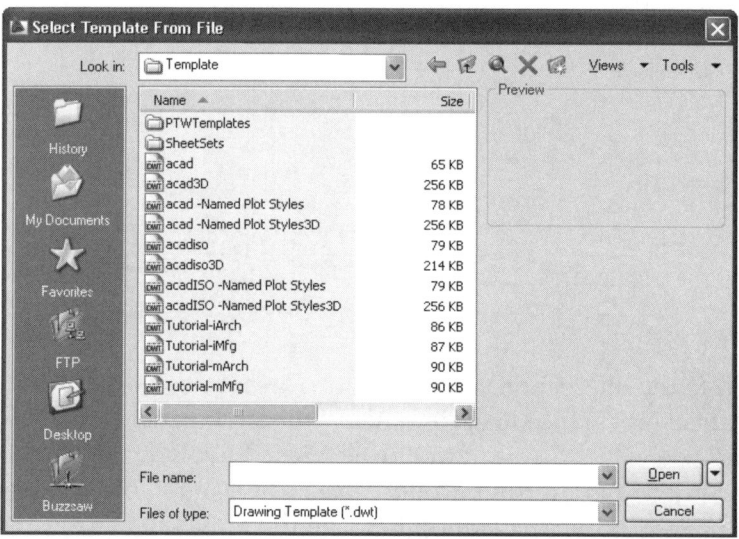

- Select the desired template, and click **Open**. The following dialog box will appear:

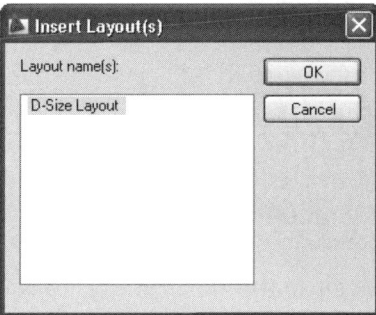

- Click on one of the listed layouts and click **OK**.

Move or Copy

- Using this option you can move a layout from its current position to the left or to the right. Also, you can create a copy of an existing layout.
- Select the desired layout that you want to create a copy from and right-click, a shortcut menu will appear. Select the **Move or Copy** option and the following dialog box will appear:

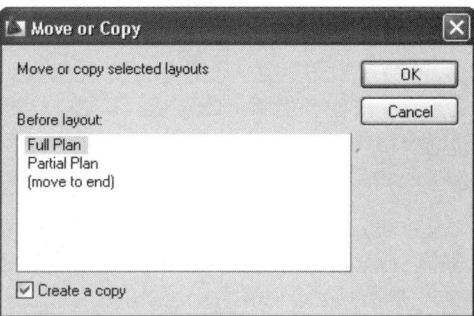

- From the upper dialog box you can see there are two existing layouts. Select one of them and click the checkbox **Create a copy**.
- Rename the new layout.
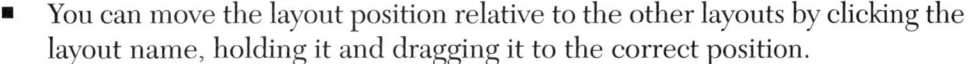 ■ You can move the layout position relative to the other layouts by clicking the layout name, holding it and dragging it to the correct position.

Copying using the mouse

- You can also copy any desired layout by taking the following steps:
  - Click the name of the desired layout to be copied.
  - Hold the [Ctrl] key on the keyboard.

- Hold and drag the mouse to the new position of the newly copied layout.
- Rename the new layout.

WHAT IS PAGE SETUP MANAGER?

- As we discussed previously each layout will have a Page Setup linked to it.
- The **Page Setup Manager** is the dialog box in which you will create, modify, delete, and import Page setups for layouts.
- The easiest way to issue this command is to select the desired layout, right-click, and then select **Page Setup Manager**.
- The following dialog box will appear:

- At the top, you will see the **Current layout** name, and at the bottom you will see **Selected page setup details**.
- A checkbox which allows you to **Display** Page Setup Manager **when creating a new layout** (highly recommended).
- To create a new Page Setup click the **New** button. The following dialog box will appear:

- Type in the name of the new Page Setup and click **OK**. The following dialog box will appear:

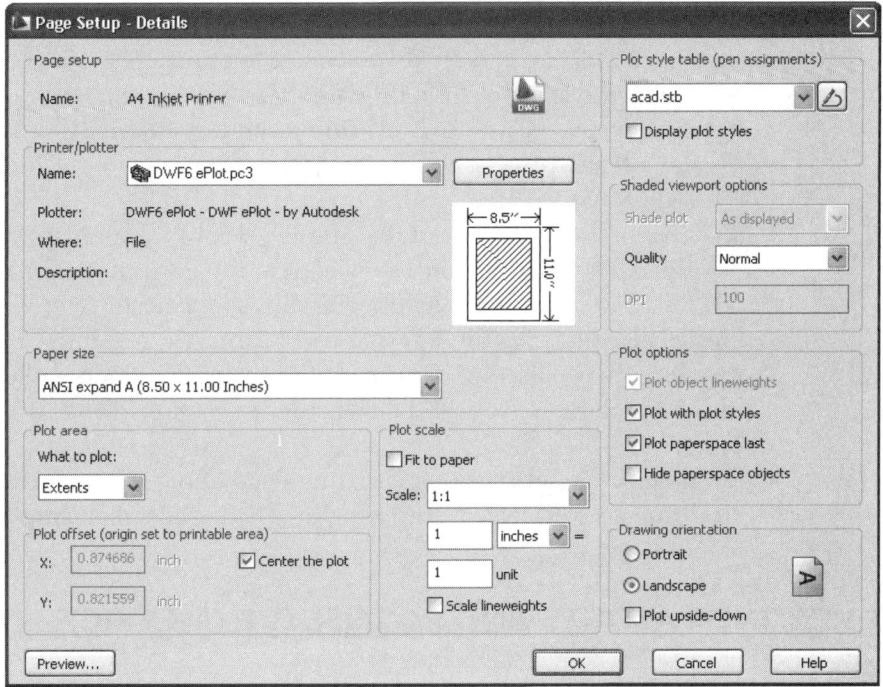

- Specify the **Name** of the printer, or the plotter you want to use (this printer should be installed and configured ahead of time).
- Specify the **Page Size** to be used.
- Specify **What to plot**. You have three choices: **Display**, **Layout**, and **Window**. If you use Layout (as this book recommends) always leave it as **Layout**.

- Specify the **Plot Offset** (by default it is **Center the plot**).
- Specify the **Plot Scale**. If you want to plot from Layout then you will use the viewports (will be discussed shortly), and you will specify plot scale for each viewport. Accordingly, you will set this Plot scale to 1 = 1. Specify if you want to **scale lineweights**.
- Specify the **Plot style table (pen assignment)**, which will be discussed later in this chapter. Specify whether to **Display** the effects of the **plot style** on the layout.
- If you are plotting a 3D drawing and you want to plot it as shaded or rendered, then specify the **Quality** of the shading or rendering.
- Specify the **Plot options**, which are:
  - Specify to plot the objects with their lineweight as specified for each object and layer. This will be available only if you specify **None** for the **Plot style** setting.
  - Specify to let the Plot Style control the objects and layers lineweight.
  - By default Paper Space objects will be printed first, and then the Model Space objects. Specify if you want the opposite to occur.
  - Specify to show or hide the Paper Space objects.
  - Specify the **Paper orientation**, whether **Portrait** or **Landscape**. By default the printer will start printing from top-to-bottom, specify if you want the opposite.
- When you are done, click **OK**. The Page Setup you create will be available for the current layout, and any layout in the current drawing file.
- To link any layout in your drawing file to a certain Page Setup, go to the desired layout, start the **Page Setup Manager**, select the Page Setup from the list, then click **Set Current**. (You can also double-click the name of the Page Setup.) Now, the current layout is linked to the Page Setup you select.
- To modify the settings of an existing Page Setup click **Modify**.
- To bring a saved Page Setup from an existing file click **Import**.

CREATING LAYOUTS AND PAGE SETUP (METRIC)

Workshop 19-A
1. Start AutoCAD 2009.
2. Open the **Workshop_19.dwg** file.
3. Make sure the current layer is **Viewports**.
4. Using Status bar, right-click the Layout1 icon, and select **Display Layout and Model tabs**.
5. Right-click on the name of any existing layout, and select **From template**.

6. Select the template file **Tutorial-mArch.dwt**.

7. Select the layout name **ISO A1 Layout**.

8. Go to **ISO A1 Layout**, and delete the only viewport in the layout (select its frame, and press the [Del] key).

9. Go to Layout1, and right-click the name of the layout, and select **Page Setup Manager**.

10. Create a new Setup and call it **Final**.

11. Input the following settings:

    a. Printer = **DWF6 ePlot.pc3**

    b. Paper Size = **ISO A3 (420 x 297 MM)**

    c. Orientation = **Landscape**

    d. Plot scale = **1:1**

12. Make **Final** the current setup.

13. Erase the existing viewport.

14. Make layer **Frame** current, and insert the file with name **ISO A3 Landscape Title Block.dwg** using 0,0 as the insertion point.

15. Save the file and close it.

CREATING LAYOUTS AND PAGE SETUP (IMPERIAL)

 Workshop 19-B

1. Start AutoCAD 2009.

2. Open the **Workshop_19.dwg** file.

3. Make sure the current layer is **Viewports**.

4. Using the Status bar, right-click the Layout1 icon, and select **Display Layout and Model tabs**.

5. Right-click on the name of any existing layout, and select **From template**.

6. Select the template file **Tutorial-iArch.dwt**.

7. Select the layout name **D-Size Layout**.

8. Go to **D-Size Layout**, and delete the only viewport in the layout (select its frame, and press the [Del] key).

9. Go to Layout1, and right-click the name of the layout, and select **Page Setup Manager**.

10. Create a new Setup and call it **Final**.

11. Input the following settings:

    a. Printer = **DWF6 ePlot.pc3**

    b. Paper Size = **ANSI B (17 x 11 Inches)**

    c. Orientation = **Landscape**

    d. Plot scale = **1:1**

12. Make **Final** the current page setup.

13. Erase the existing viewport.

14. Make layer **Frame** current, and insert the file with name **ANSI B Landscape Title Block.dwg** using 0,0 as the insertion point.

15. Save the file and close it.

LAYOUTS AND VIEWPORTS

- After you complete these three steps:
  - Creating a new layout
  - Creating a Page Setup
  - Linking a Page Setup to the layout
- You will see the following image:

- The outer frame is the real paper size.
- The inner frame (dashed) is the truncated paper size, which is the paper size minus margins of the printer.
- Each printer comes from the manufacturer with built-in margins for all sides.

- AutoCAD can read these margins from the printer driver accordingly.
- This means that each user should read the manual of the printer in order to know the exact margins. This will prove vital when you want to create the frame block of the company or establishment they work in, because users should create it within the truncated paper size and not the full size.
- The above proves that printing from layouts is WYSIWYG (What You See Is What You Get).
- Also, by default you will see that a single viewport of your drawing appears at the center of the paper size.
- As we said in the beginning of this chapter, we have only one Model Space, yet we can have as many Layouts as we wish. *Viewport* is a rectangular shape (or any irregular shape) that contains a view of your Model Space.
- There are two types of Viewports:
  - Model Space Viewports, which are always tiled, cannot be scaled, and the arrangement of viewports shown on the screen cannot be printed.
  - Layout Viewport, which can be tiled or separated, can be scaled, and the arrangement of viewports shown on the screen can be printed.
- Take a look at the following illustration:

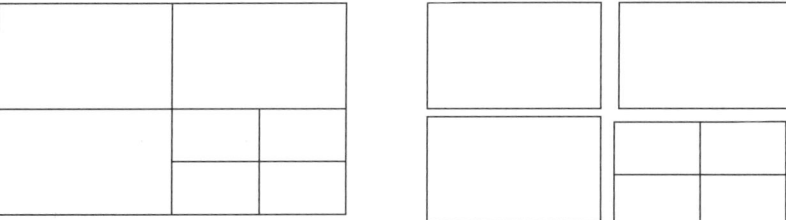

Model Space Viewports   Paper Space Viewports

ADDING VIEWPORTS

- You can add viewports to layouts using several methods:
  - Adding a single rectangular viewport, or multiple rectangular viewports.
  - Adding a single polygonal viewport.
  - Converting an object to be a viewport.
  - Clipping an existing viewport.
- In the following pages we will discuss each method.

Single or multiple rectangular viewport

- You can add single or multiple rectangular viewports in any layout, and as many as you wish. You have to specify two opposite corners in order to specify the area of the viewport(s).

- To start the **New Viewport** command, make sure that you are at the **View** tab on the **Ribbon** and using the **Viewports** panel, click the **New** button.
- The following dialog box will appear:

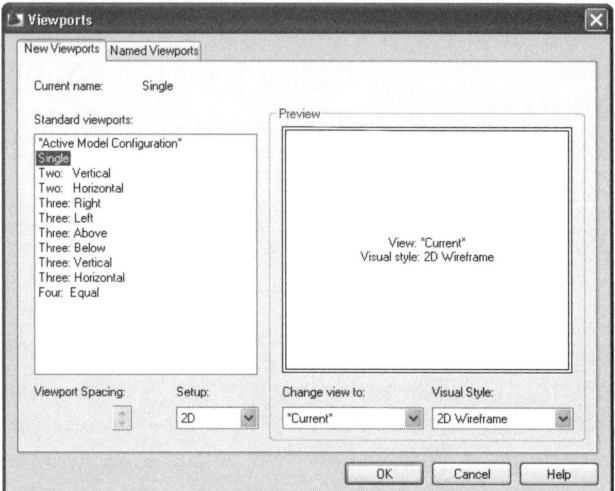

- From **Standard viewports** select **Single**, then click **OK**. The following prompt will appear:

```
Specify first corner or [Fit] <Fit>:
Specify opposite corner:
```

- Just like we specify a window (when we select objects), specify two opposite corners and a single viewport will be created.
- Using the same dialog box:

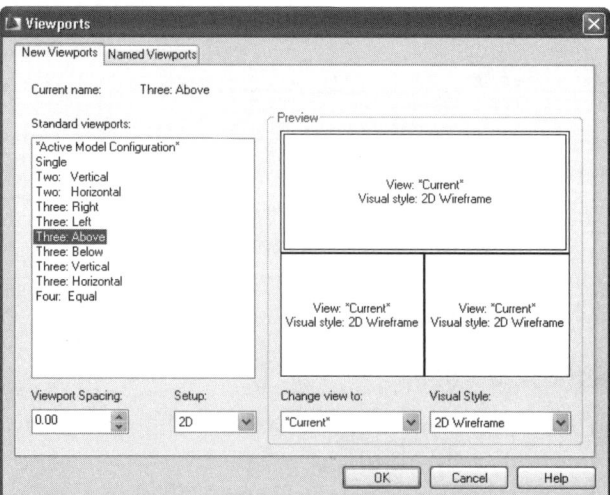

- Specify the arrangement you like. You can have two (Horizontal or Vertical), or six different arrangements for three viewports, and one for four viewports.
- If you want the viewports to be tiled, leave the **Viewport Spacing** = 0, otherwise set a new value.
- Click **OK**. AutoCAD will display the following prompt:

```
Specify first corner or [Fit] <Fit>:
Specify opposite corner:
```

- Take a look at the following illustration:

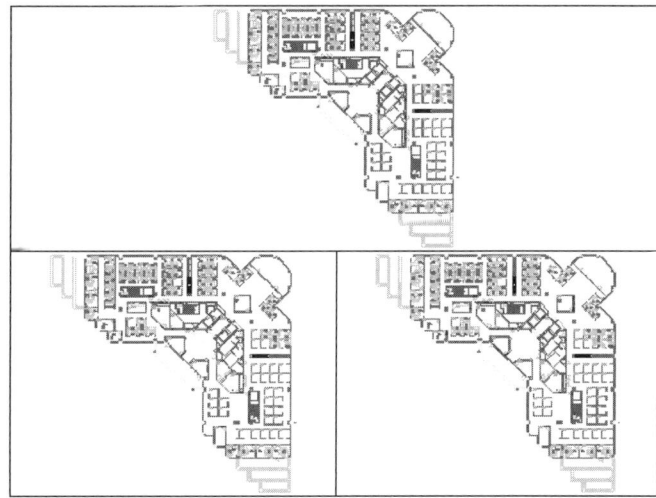

Single polygonal viewport

- This command is used to add a single viewport with any irregular shape consisting of both straight lines and arcs.

- To start the **Polygonal Viewport** command, make sure that you are at the **View** tab on the **Ribbon** and using the **Viewports** panel, click the **Polygonal** button.
- The following prompt will appear:

```
Specify corner of viewport or
[ON/OFF/Fit/Shadeplot/Lock/Object/Polygonal/
Restore/LAyer/2/3/4] <Fit>: _p
Specify start point:
Specify next point or [Arc/Length/Undo]:
Specify next point or [Arc/Close/Length/Undo]:
```

- It is almost identical to the **Pline** command.

- Take a look at the following illustration:

Converting an object to a viewport

- This command is used to convert an existing object to a viewport.
- First, you have to draw the desired object that will be converted to a viewport, such as Circle, Polyline, Ellipse, etc.

- To start the **Converting Object** command, make sure that you are at the **View** tab on the **Ribbon** and using the **Viewports** panel, click the **Object** button.
- The following prompt will appear:

```
Specify corner of viewport or
[ON/OFF/Fit/Shadeplot/Lock/Object/Polygonal/
Restore/LAyer/2/3/4] <Fit>: _o
Select object to clip viewport:
```

- Take a look at the following illustration (circle and pline are converted to viewports):

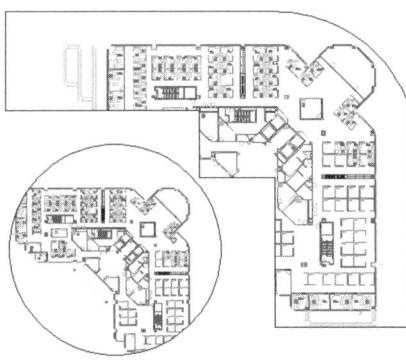

Clipping an existing viewport

- If you have a rectangular viewport, you can change it to an irregular shape by clipping it.
- To start the **Viewport Clip** command, make sure that you are at the **View** tab on the **Ribbon** and using the **Viewports** panel, click the **Viewport Clip** button.
- The following prompt will appear:

```
Select viewport to clip:
Select clipping object or [Polygonal] <Polygonal>:
Specify start point:
Specify next point or [Arc/Length/Undo]:
Specify next point or [Arc/Close/Length/Undo]:
```

- Select first the existing viewport. You can draw a pline beforehand, or you can draw any irregular shape using the **Polygonal** option (which is identical to the Polygonal viewport).
- Take a look at the following illustration:

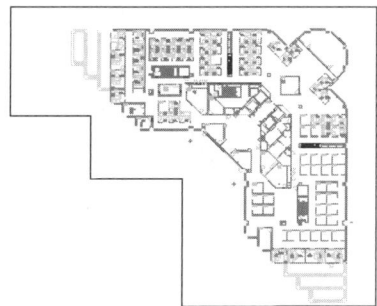

MODEL SPACE AND PAPER SPACE MODES IN LAYOUTS

- In a layout you deal with the viewports in two modes:
  - Paper Space mode
  - Model Space mode

Paper Space Mode

- This is the default mode in any layout.
- On the **Status** bar, you will see the following:

- In this mode you can place the viewports, as we learned in the previous discussion.
- Also, you can deal with the viewports as objects: you can copy, move, stretch, and delete them.

Model Space Mode

- In this mode you will get *inside* the viewport.
- You can zoom in, zoom out, and pan while you are in this mode.
- Also, you can scale each viewport.
- Furthermore, you can change the status of layers for the current viewports.
- There are two ways to enter this mode:
  - Double-click inside the desired viewport.
  - From the Status bar click the **Paper** button, and it will switch to **Model** as shown below:

- In order to switch from Model Space mode to Paper Space mode, simply double-click outside any viewport, or click the Model button on the Status Bar.

MODIFYING, SCALING, AND MAXIMIZING VIEWPORTS

- Each viewport can be modified, scaled, and maximized to fill the whole screen.

Modifying

- Each viewport is considered an object: it can be copied, moved, scaled, and deleted. You have to select each viewport from its border in order to select it.
- You can select viewports first, and then issue the modifying command, or vice versa, you can issue the command, and then select the desired viewports.

Scaling

- Each viewport can be scaled relative to the Model Space units.
- Double-click inside the desired viewport; you will switch to the Model Space mode for this viewport.

- Look at the right side of the Status bar. You will see the following:

- Click the pop-up list which contains the scales. You will see something like the following:

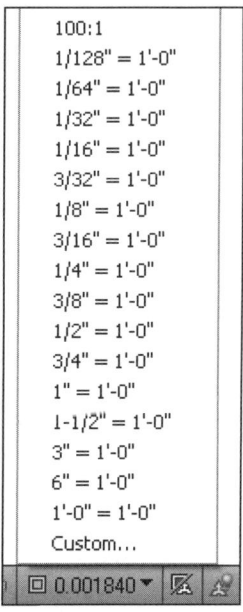

- Select the suitable scale to be used in the viewport.
- If you didn't find the desired scale, select the **Custom** option, and you will see the following dialog box:

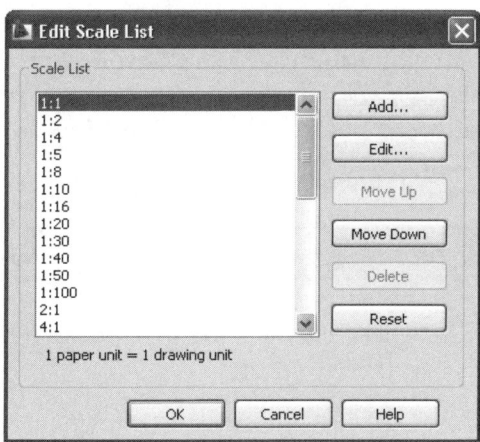

- Click the **Add** button to add a new scale. You will see the following dialog box:

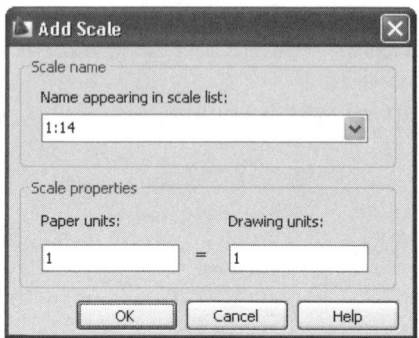

- Type in the desired scale, and then click **OK** twice.
- After you set the scale, you can use the **Pan** command, but if you want to use the **Zoom** command, the scale value will be invalid, hence you would have to repeat the procedure of setting the scale.
- In order to avoid this problem, you can lock the display of the viewport by clicking the golden opened lock on the Status bar (you have to be inside the viewport in order for this to succeed). The golden lock will change to blue and it will be locked.

NOTE ▶
- After you make the scaling of a viewport there are two possible results:
- The scale is perfect to the area of the viewport. Leave it as is.
- The scale is either too small or too big, so either change the scale, or change the area of the viewport.

Maximizing

- After placing and scaling your viewports, there will be small ones and big ones.
- For small ones you can maximize the area of the viewport to be as large as your screen momentarily. You do all of your work, and then put it back to the original size.
- Using the Status bar, click the **Maximize Viewport** button:

- The same button will be changed to the **Minimize button** in order to restore the original size of the viewport.

■ Another way of **Maximizing** the viewport is to double-click the border of the viewport.

FREEZING LAYERS IN VIEWPORT

■ We learned in the previous chapter how to freeze a layer. This tool is effective in both Model Space and Layouts.

■ In Layouts if you freeze a layer it will be frozen in all viewports. So, what if you want to freeze a certain layer(s) in one of the viewports and not the other viewports? To do so, you have to freeze the layer in the current viewport.

■ Do the following:
   • Make the desired viewport current (by double-clicking inside it).
   • Make sure that you are at **Home** tab on the **Ribbon** and using the **Layers** panel, click the icon **Freeze or thaw in current viewport** for the desired layer, just like the illustration below:

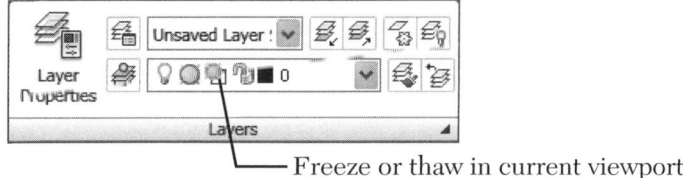

——— Freeze or thaw in current viewport

INSERTING AND SCALING VIEWPORTS (METRIC)

 Workshop 20-A

1. Start AutoCAD 2009.
2. Open the **Workshop_20.dwg** file.
3. Select the **ISO A1 Layout**.
4. Make layer **Viewports** current.
5. Click **OSNAP** off.
6. Using the **Ribbon**, select the **View** tab, and using the **Viewports** panel click the **New** button. Select the arangement **Three: Left**, and set the **Viewport spacing** to 5.

7. Click **OK**, and specify two opposite corners so the three viewports fill the empty space, just like the following:

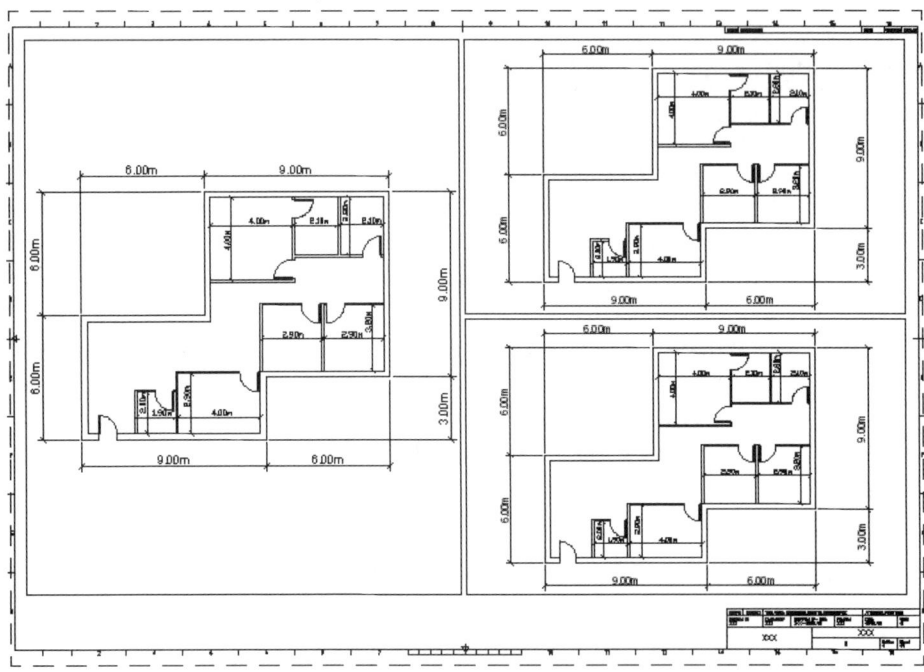

8. Select the big viewport at the left and set the scale to 1:50, the upper viewport scale to 1:20, and finally the lower viewport scale to 1:30.

9. Double-click outside the viewports to move to the **Paper** mode.

10. Freeze layer **Dimension**, and thaw **Furniture**, **Hatch**, and **Text**.

11. Make the big left viewport the current viewport, and freeze only in this viewport layers **Furniture**, **Hatch**, and **Text**.

12. Make the upper viewport current and pan to the Master Bedroom (don't use the zooming facilities). Make the lower viewport current and pan to the Living room.

13. Double-click outside the viewports to move to **Paper** mode.

14. Lock the view in the three viewports.

15. The drawing should look like the following:

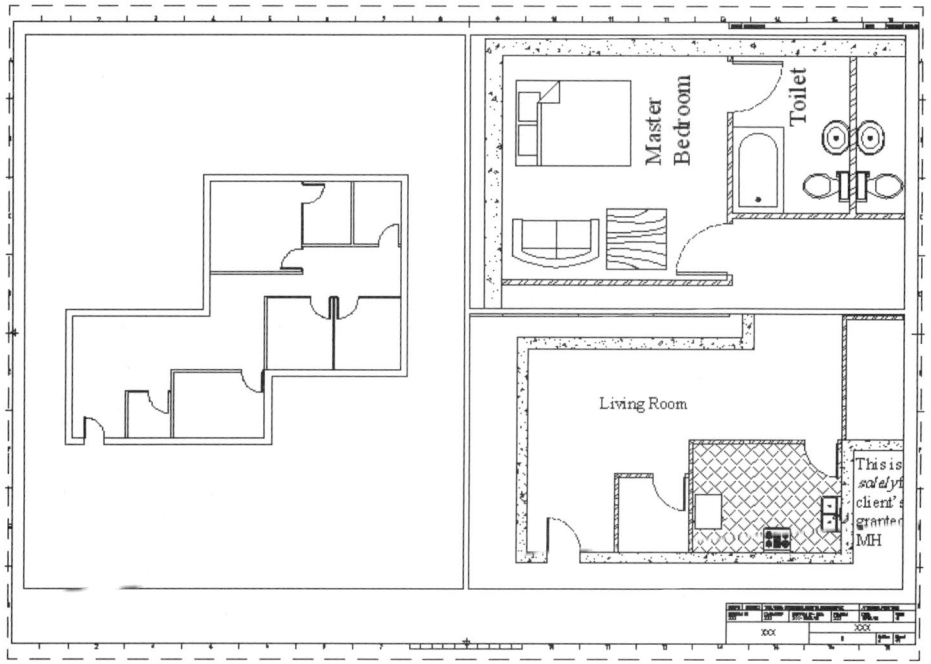

16. Save the file and close it.

INSERTING AND SCALING VIEWPORTS (IMPERIAL)

 Workshop 20-B

1. Start AutoCAD 2009.
2. Open the **Workshop_20.dwg** file.
3. Select the **D-Sized Layout**.
4. Make layer **Viewports** current.
5. Click **OSNAP** off.
6. Using the **Ribbon**, select the **View** tab, and using the **Viewports** panel click the **New** button. Select the arangement **Three: Left**, and set the **Viewport spacing** to 0.35.

7. Click **OK**, and specify two opposite corners so the three viewports fill the empty space, just like the following:

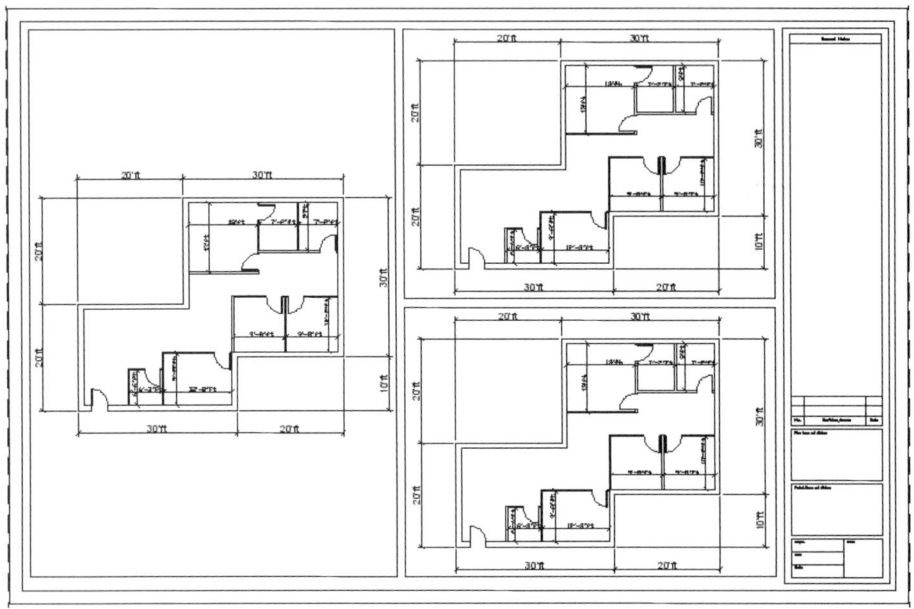

8. Select the big viewport at the left and set the scale to ¼"=1'. The upper and the lower viewports scale to ½"=1'.

9. Double-click outside the viewports to move to **Paper** mode.

10. Freeze layer **Dimension**, and thaw **Furniture**, **Hatch**, and **Text**.

11. Make the big left viewport the current viewport, and freeze only in this viewport layers **Furniture**, **Hatch**, and **Text**.

12. Make the upper viewport current and pan to the Master Bedroom (don't use the zooming facilities). Make the lower viewport current and pan to the Living room.

13. Double-click outside the viewports to move to **Paper** mode.

14. Lock the view in the three viewports.

15. The drawing should look like the following:

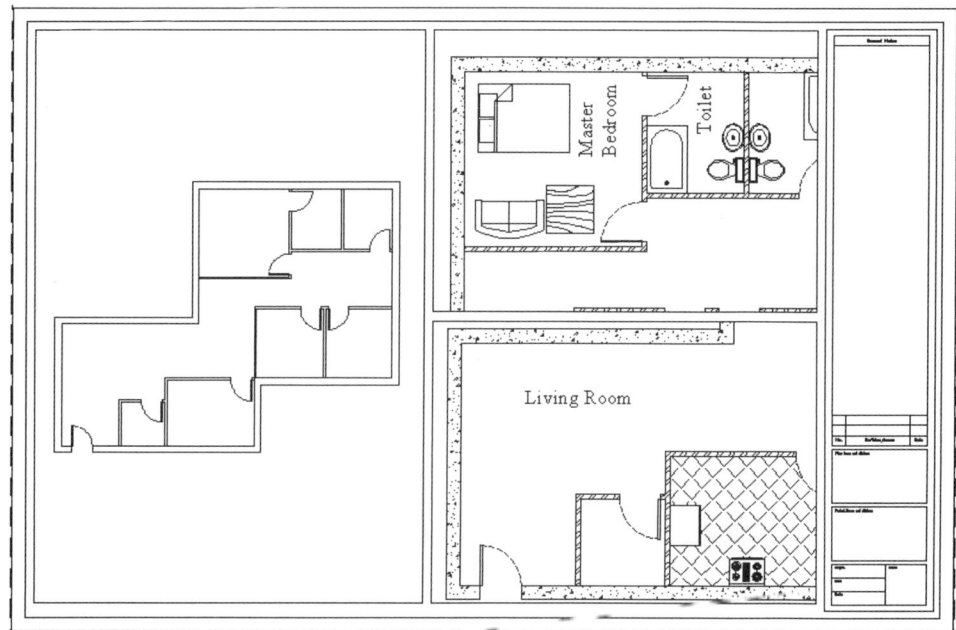

16. Save the file and close it.

PLOT STYLE TABLES: INTRODUCTION

- There are many available colors to use in AutoCAD drawing files but will these colors print? You have to make sure. There are two possibilities:
    - Either you will use the same colors in both the softcopy and the hardcopy of the drawing, or you will assign for each color in the softcopy a different color in the hardcopy.
- To translate the colors between softcopy and hardcopy, we need to create a Plot style.
- There are two types of Plot styles:
    - Color-dependent Plot Style Table
    - Named Plot Style Table

PLOT STYLE TABLES: COLOR-DEPENDENT PLOT STYLE TABLE

- This method is almost the same method that was used prior to AutoCAD 2000; it depends on the colors used in the drawing file.
- Each color used in the drawing file will be printed with a color chosen by the user. Also, you will set the lineweight, linetype, etc., for each color.

- This method is limited because you will have only 255 colors to use.
- Also, if you have two layers with the same color, you be will forced to use the same output color, with the same lineweight, linetype, etc.
- Each time you create a Color-dependent Plot Style Table, AutoCAD will ask you to name a file with the extension *. *ctb*.
- You can create Plot Style tables from outside AutoCAD (using the Control Panel of Windows), or from inside AutoCAD using the Wizards. This will only initiate the command, but the command is the same for both.
- From outside AutoCAD, start the Control Panel of Windows, double-click the **AutoDesk Plot Style Manager** icon, and then double-click the **Add-A-Plot Style Table Wizard**.
- Inside AutoCAD, from the menu browser go to **Tools/Wizards/Add Plot Style Table**.
- Either way the following dialog box will appear:

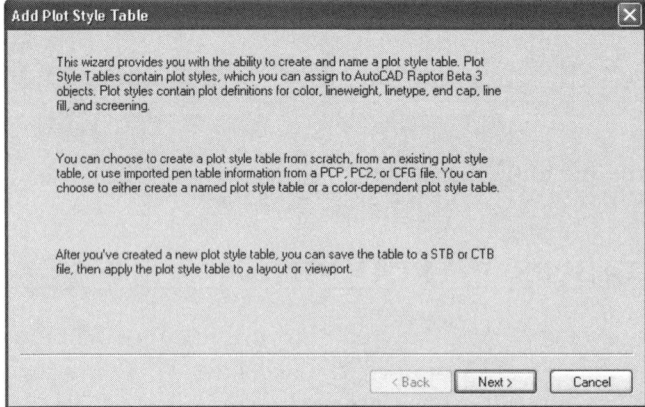

- In the above dialog box, AutoCAD explains the next few steps to be taken. Click **Next**, and the following dialog box will appear:

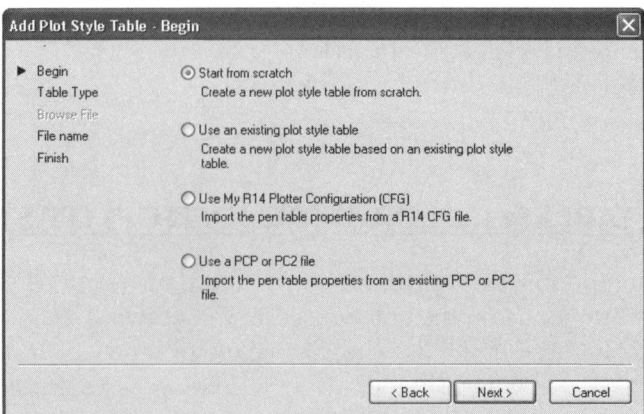

- You have four choices to select from. They are:
  - Create your style from the scratch.
  - Use an existing plot style.
  - Import the **AutoCAD R14 CFG** file, and create a plot style from it.
  - Import the **PCP** or **PC2** file, and create a plot style from it.
- Select **Start from scratch**, and click **Next**. The following dialog box will appear:

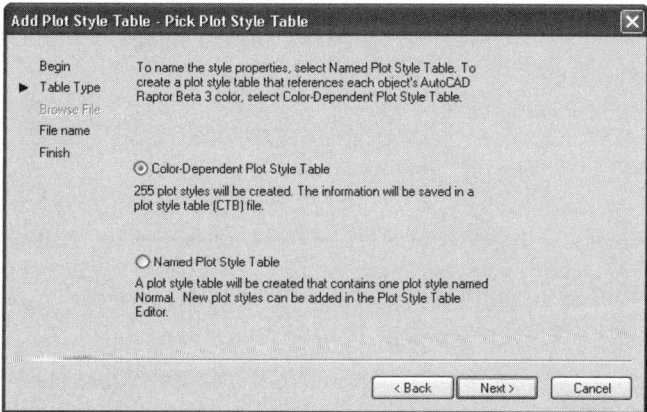

- Select Color-Dependent Plot Style Table, and click Next.
- The following dialog box will appear:

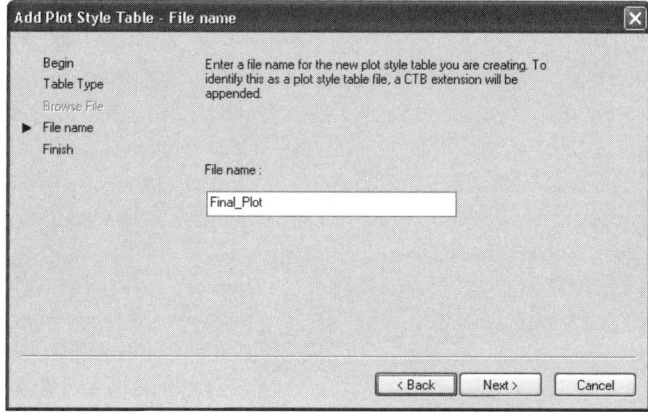

- Type in the name of the plot style, and click **Next**. The following will appear:

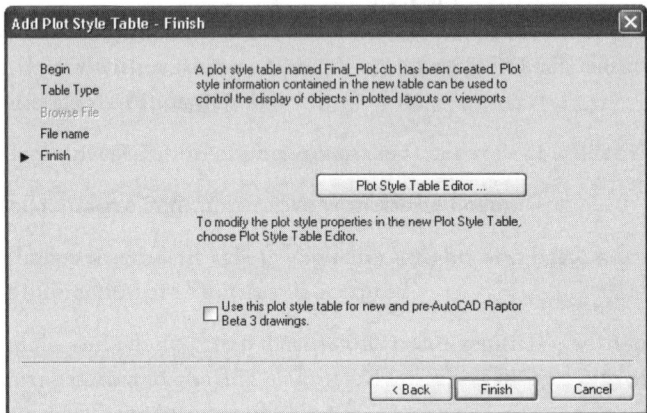

- You can use this plot style table for new and pre-AutoCAD 2009 drawings. Click the **Plot Style Table Editor** button, and you will see the following:

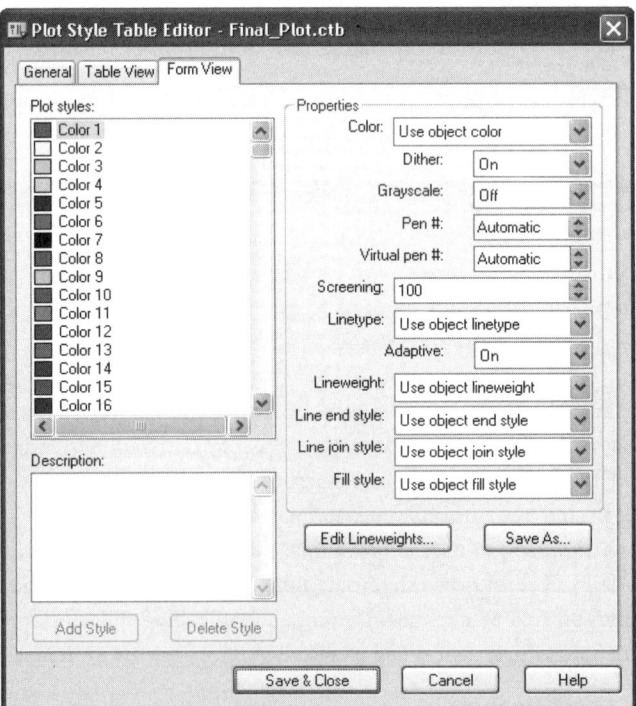

- At the left part, select the color you used in your drawing file, and then at the right part, change all or any of the following settings:

- **Color**: the hardcopy color.
- **Dither**: this option will be dimmed if your printer or plotter doesn't support Dithering. Dither means to allow the printer to give the impression of using more colors than the limited 255 colors of AutoCAD. It is best to leave this option off. It should be on, however, if you want **Screening** to work.
- **Grayscale**: you can translate the 255 colors to grayscale grades (good for laser printer printing).
- **Pen #**: good only for the old types of plotters – pen plotters – which are nowadays obsolete.
- **Virtual pen #**: for non-pen plotters to simulate pen plotters by assigning a virtual pen for each color; it is best to leave it **Automatic**.
- **Scr eening**: this is good for trial printing, which if you input numbers less than 100, will reduce the intensity of the shading and fill hatches. You should turn **Dithering** on so **Screening** will be effective.
- **Linetype**: you can use the object's linetype, or you can set a different linetype for each color.
- **Adaptive**: to change the linetype scale to fit the current line length, so it will start with a segment and end with a segment, and not end with a space. Turn this option off if the linetype scale is important to the drawing.
- **Lineweight**: set the lineweight for the color selected; you have a list of lineweights to select from.
- **Line end style**: to specify the end style for lines; the available end styles are: Butt, Square, Round, and Diamond.
- **Line join style**: to specify the line join (the connection between two lines) style, the available options are: Miter, Bevel, Round, and Diamond.
- **Fill style**: to set the fill style for the area filled in the drawing (good for trial printing).
- Click **Save & Close**. Then click **Finish**.
- To link a Color-Dependent Plot Style to a layout, take the following steps:
  - Go to the desired Layout, then start the **Page Setup Manager**.
  - At the upper right part of the dialog box, change the **Plot style table (pen assignment)** setting to the desired **ctb** file:

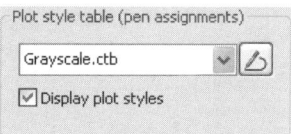

- Click the checkbox **Display plot styles**.
- You can assign for each layout one **ctb** file.
- In order to see the lineweight of the objects you have to switch the **LWT** button on Status bar on.

PLOT STYLE TABLES: NAMED PLOT STYLE TABLE

- This method is the new method introduced in AutoCAD 2000; it does not depend on colors.
- You will create a Plot style and give it a name, and each plot style will include inside it deferent tables, which you will link later on with layers.
- With this method you can have two layers having the same color but that will be printed in different colors, linetypes, and lineweights.
- The **Named Plot Style Table** has a file extension *.stb*.
- The creation procedure of Named Plot Style is identical to Color-Dependent Plot Style, except the last step, which includes the **Plot Style Table Editor** button.
- From outside AutoCAD, start Control Panel, double-click the **AutoDesk Plot Style Manager** icon, then double click the **Add-A-Plot Style Table Wizard**.
- From Inside AutoCAD, select from the menu browser **Tools/Wizards/Add Plot Style Table**.
- Go through the dialog boxes up until you reach the **Plot Style Table Editor** button, click it and you will see the dialog box.
- The Plot Style Table Editor for Named Plot Style, after we clicked the **Add Style** button looks like this:

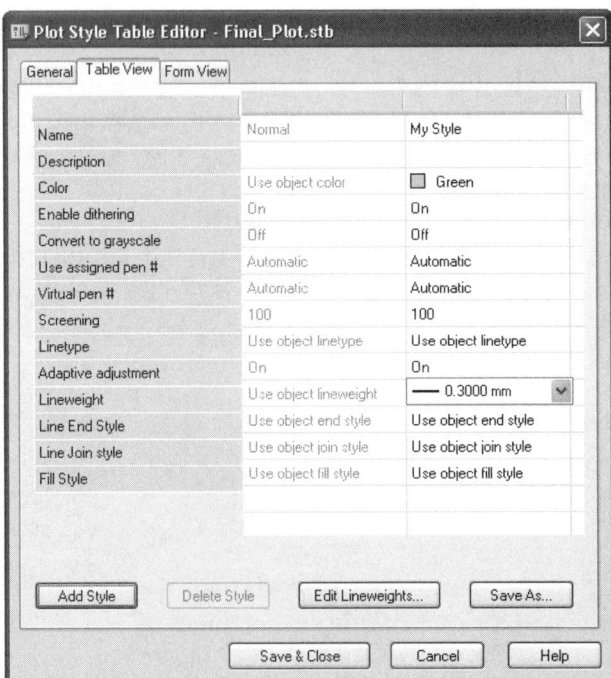

- As you can see you have to change all or any of the following:
  - Type in the Name of the style.
  - Type in any Description for this style.
  - Specify the Color you will use in the hardcopy.
  - The rest is identical to the Color-Dependent Plot Style Table.
  - You can add as many styles as you wish in the Named Plot Style.
  - Click **Save & Close**. Then click **Finish**.
- In order to link a Named Plot Style Table with any drawing, take the following steps:
- You first have to convert one of the **ctb** files to a **stb** file. At the Command Window type **convertctb** and a dialog box with all the ctb files will appear. Select one of them, keeping the same name, or giving it a new name, then click **OK**. The following dialog box will appear:

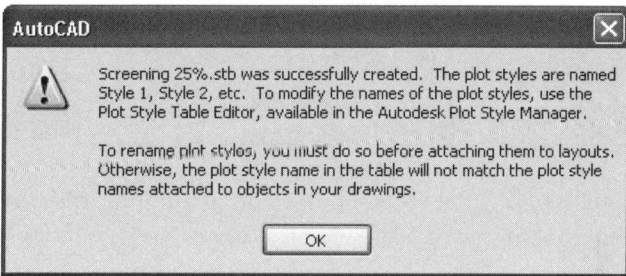

- Convert the drawing from Color-Dependent Plot Style to Named Plot Style. At the Command Window type **convertpstyles**, and the following warning message will appear:

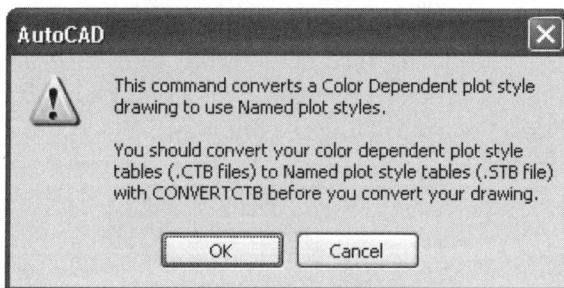

- Click **OK**, and the following dialog box will appear:

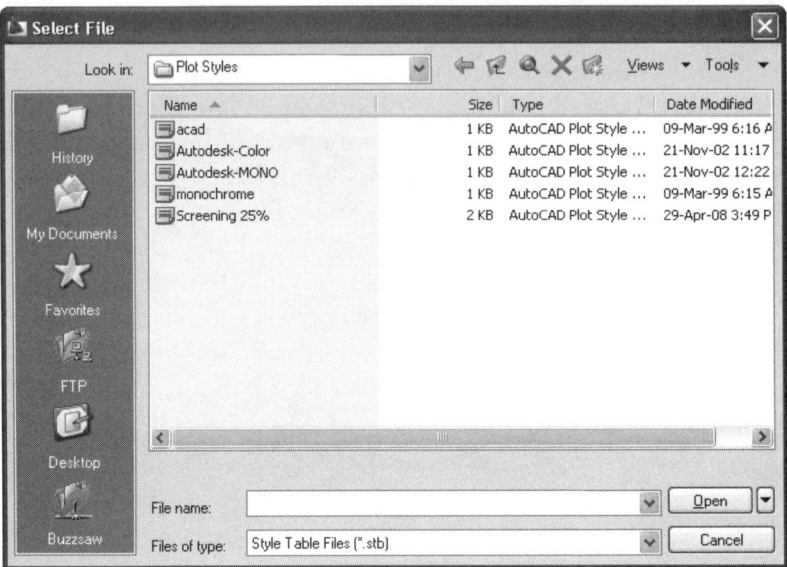

- Select the Named Plot Style Table you just converted, and click **Open**. The following message will appear at the Command Window:

```
Drawing converted from Color Dependent mode to Named plot
style mode.
```

- Because you will use the Named Plot Style Table with layers, the Model Space and all layouts will be assigned the same stb file.
- Go to the desired Layout, then start the **Page Setup Manager**. At the upper right part of the dialog box, change the Plot style table (pen assignment) setting to the desired stb file. Click the checkbox **Display plot styles**, and end the **Page Setup Manager** command.

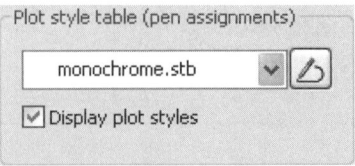

- Go to the **Layer Properties Manager**, and for a certain layer under the **Plot Style** column click **Normal**, and the following dialog box will appear:
- Make sure that the **Active plot style table** is your desired table, then from the list of the **Plot styles**, select the desired plot style to be linked to the selected layer. When done, click OK.

PLOT STYLE TABLES

Exercise 38

1. Start AutoCAD 2009.
2. Open the **Exercise_38.dwg** file.
3. Click Layout1.When the dialog box appears, click **Close** (this means we are accepting the default Page Setup to this layout).
4. Start a new Plot Style Table, and choose Color-dependant. Call this Plot Style **Mechanical_BW**, and make the following changes:

Drawing Color	Plotter Color	Linetype	Lineweight
Color 2	Black	Dashdot	0.30
Color 3	Black	Solid	0.70
Color 4	Black	Solid	0.50
Color 6	Black	Solid	0.50

5. Go to the **Page Setup Manager**, and select **Plot style table** to be **Mechanical_BW**, and turn **Display plot styles** on.
6. Click the **Show/Hide Lineweight** button to see the effect of the lineweight.
7. Save the file as **Exercise_38_1.dwg**.
8. At the Command Window, type **convertctb**, and convert **Mechanical_BW** from a **ctb** to an **stb** file.
9. At the Command Window, type **convertpstyles** to convert the whole drawing to accept Named Plot Styles. Select **Mechanical_BW** when you are asked to select an stb file.
10. Start a new Plot Style Table, and choose Name Plot Style. Call this Plot Style **Design_Process**, and make the following changes:

Style	Description	Color	Linetype	Lineweight
Finished	Design is Final	Black	Solid	0.7
Incomplete	Incomplete Design	Green	Dashed	0.3

11. Go to the **Page Setup Manager**, and select **Plot style table** to be Design_Process, and turn **Display plot styles** on.
12. Start the **Layer Manager** and set the plot style for layer **Base** to be **Finished**, and layers **Shaft**, and **Body** to be **Incomplete**.

13. Click the **Show/Hide Lineweight** button to see the effect of the lineweight.

14. Use the **Regenall** command if things didn't appear correctly.

15. Save the file as **Exercise_38_2.dwg**.

PLOT COMMAND

- The final step in this process is to issue the **Plot** command, which will send your layout to the printer or plotter.
- As a first step go to the desired layout that you want to plot.
- To issue this command, make sure that you are at the **Output** tab on the **Ribbon** and using the **Plot** panel, click the **Plot** icon. The following dialog box will appear:

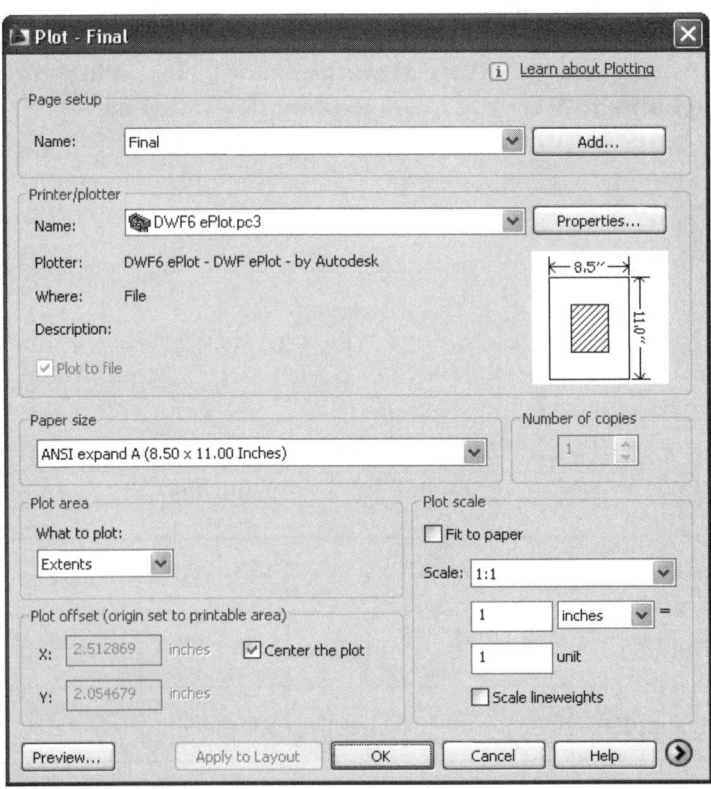

- As you can see all the settings are identical to the Page setup settings.
- If you change any of these settings, AutoCAD will detach the Page setup from the current layout.

- Click the **Apply to Layout** button if you want this Plot dialog box saved with this layout for future use.
- Click the **Preview** button in order to see the final printed drawing on the screen before the real printout so you can decide if your choices of Plot styles and the other settings are correct.

- You can preview your drawing from outside this dialog box using the **Output** tab on the **Ribbon** and using the **Plot** panel. Click the **Preview** button.
- After you are done, click **OK** so the drawing will be sent to the printer.

WHAT ARE DWF FILES?

- Assume one or all of the following cases:
  - You want to share your design with another company, but you are afraid if you send them the **dwg** file they will alter it.
  - Your **dwg** file is very large (more than 1 mb), which may not be accepted by your e-mail server.
  - The recipient doesn't have AutoCAD to view the **dwg** file.
- To solve these problems, AutoCAD offers you the option of plotting to a DWF file (**D**esign **W**eb **F**ormat). This file has the following features:
  - Does not need AutoCAD to open it, instead, free software comes with AutoCAD called **Autodesk Design Review** (which you can download from the Internet free of charge).
  - You can view the file, zoom, pan, measure, markup, and print it.
  - It is small in size so you can send it through e-mail.
  - The recipient can't modify it.

HOW CAN YOU PRODUCE SINGLE PAGE & MULTIPLE PAGE DWFS?

Single Page DWF

- A single page DWF will produce a DWF file that contains a single layout. To create a single page DWF do the following:
- In the **Page Setup Manager** select the printer to be **DWF6 ePlot.pc3**.

- Link this **Page Setup** with the layout you want to print, and click **OK**. Once you plot this layout, the following dialog box will appear:

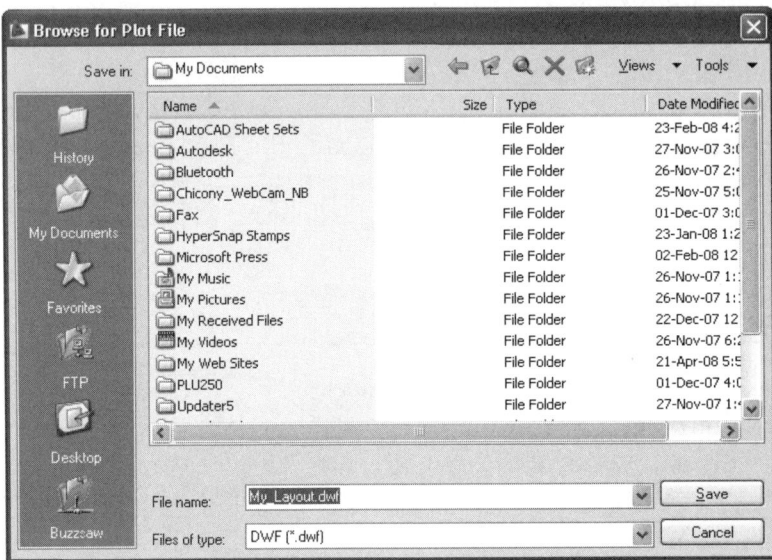

- Select the place in your computer for the file to be saved in, and type the name of the **dwf** file. Click **Save** button.
- In order to see this file, simply double-click it, and Windows will launch the Autodesk Design Review software automatically.
- Here is an example of a single sheet DWF file:

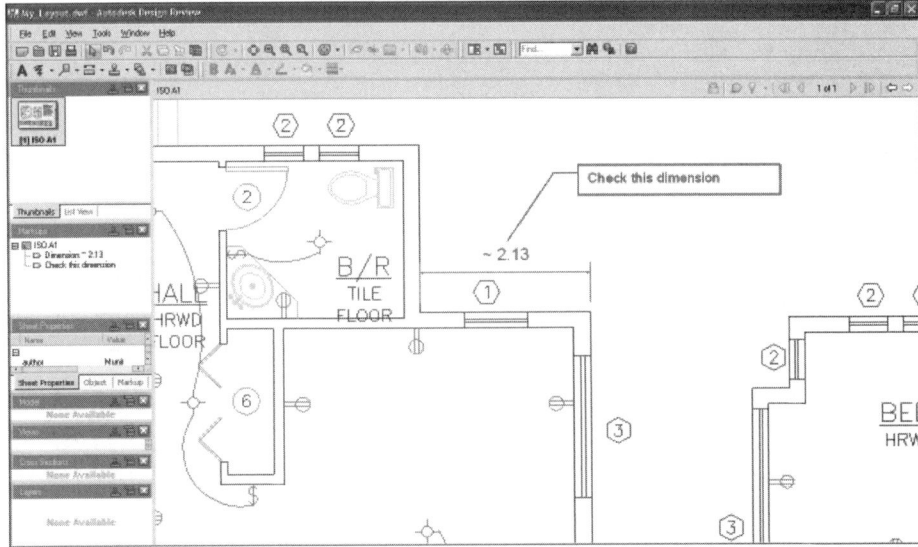

- As you can see, you can create a dimension to measure any distance, and then add a callout which gives instructions for your engineers (this only shows some of the many powerful features of this free software).

Multiple Pages DWF

- This method will produce a DWF file that contains multiple layouts from the current drawing and from other drawings.
- Issue the **Publish** command on the **Ribbon**. Make sure you are at the **Output** tab, and using the **Publish** panel, click the **Publish** button.
- The **Publish** dialog box will appear:

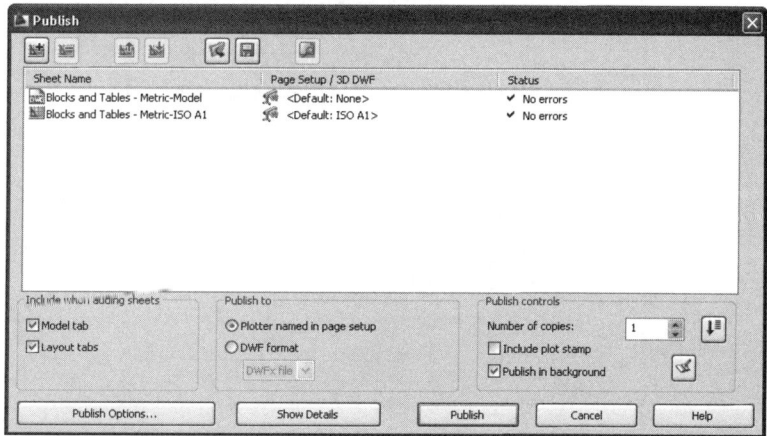

- You will see a list of the current file's Model Space and layouts.
- Select one of the sheets, and use the following buttons:
  - To add more sheets from other drawings, the **Select Drawings** dialog box will be shown to select the desired file.
  - To remove one sheet or more from the list.
  - To move the sheet up in the list.
  - To move the sheet down in the list.
  - To open a sheet list saved previously.
  - To save a sheet list for future printing.
  - To preview the selected sheet (only a single sheet) as we did in **Print Preview**.
  - To include a Plot Stamp in each sheet, click the **Include plot stamp** checkbox.
  - Specify the number of copies.

- Select to publish either to the **Plotter named in Page Setup**, or the **DWF file** (select this option if you want to a DWF file).
- When you add new sheets, would you like to include the Model Space as one of the sheets?
  - Click the **Publish Options** button, and you will see the following dialog box:

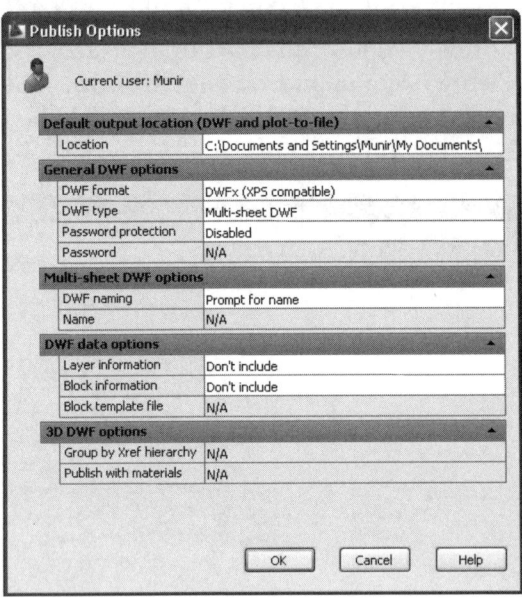

  - Control the following settings:
    - Specify the location of the file.
    - Specify the DWF format (you can save to older versions).
    - Specify if the DWF file will be single sheet or multiple sheet.
    - Select whether to include a Password for the DWF file.
    - If you select multi-sheet, select whether to prompt for the DWF naming.
    - Select whether to include Layer and Block information (such as attributes) in the DWF file.
    - If this is a 3D drawing, specify whether to **Group by Xref hierarchy** and whether to **Publish with materials**.
  - Once you are done, click **OK**.
  - For the selected sheet, you can see more details such as Plot device, Plot size, Plot scale, etc.
  - Once you are done setting all of these things, click the **Publish** button, which will prompt AutoCAD to create the sheets one by one.
  - Below you will see an example of a multi-sheet DWF file.
  - In order to see this file, simply double-click it, and Windows will launch Autodesk Design Review automatically.

- A multi-sheet DWF file:

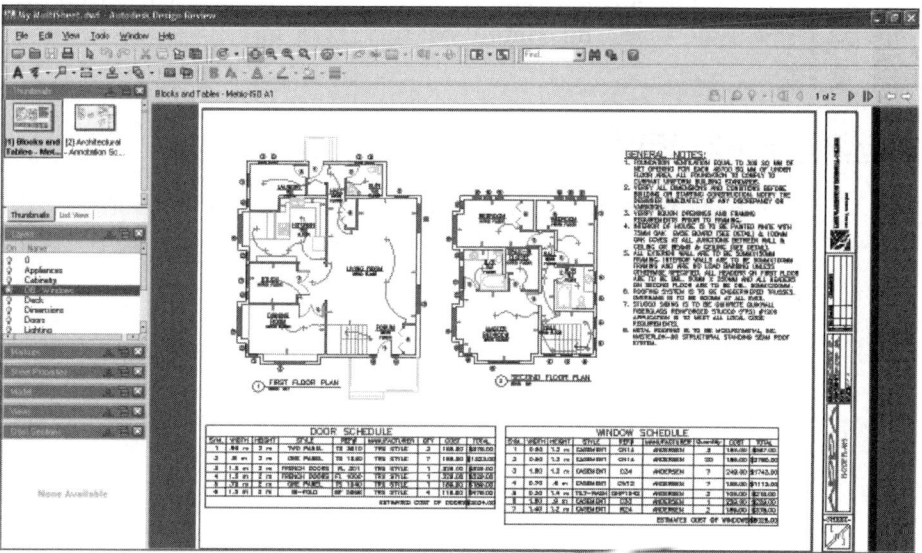

- You can see at the left part of the picture the small box that includes the layers inside the DWF file.
- You can turn off the desired layers in order to visualize the design better.

CREATING MULTIPLE SHEET DWF FILES (METRIC & IMPERIAL)

Workshop 21-A & 21-B

1. Start AutoCAD 2009.
2. Open the **Workshop_21.dwg** file.
3. Start the **Publish** command.
4. Select the Model Space sheet and remove it.
5. Select to **Add new sheets**. Browse for AutoCAD 2009\Sample\Blocks and Tables – Metric.dwg.
6. Remove the Model space sheet.
7. Make the ISO A1 sheet the top sheet.
8. Select to Publish to DWF file.
9. Click **Publish** to create the file. AutoCAD will ask you for the file name and the place to save the file in, specify accordingly.
10. Publish will be performed in the background. You can see this from the tray at the lower right corner of the AutoCAD 2009 window.

11. After the background publishing, browse to the place you saved the file in, and doube-click it. The Autodesk DWF Viewer will start automatically and will show you the contents of the DWF file.

CHAPTER REVIEW

1. Which of the following should you control in Page Setup?
   a. Paper size.
   b. Plotter to send to.
   c. Viewports.
   d. A & B.

2. Layouts contain _____, and you can set a scale for each one.

3. A DWF can be a single sheet ot multiple sheets.
   a. True.
   b. False.

4. You can choose to include Layers in a DWF file.
   a. True.
   b. False.

5. The Named Plot Style table file extension is:
   a. filename.ctb
   b. filename.stb
   c. filename.sbt
   d. filename.bct

6. In the Name Plot Style table, if you assign a plot style to a layer, you need to switch _____ from the Status bar to see this lineweight in the layout.

CHAPTER REVIEW ANSWERS

1. d
2. Viewports
3. a
4. a
5. b
6. Show/Hide Lineweight

Appendix **A** | # CREATING TEMPLATE FILES

In This Chapter
◇ What are template files?
◇ What elements are included in a template file?
◇ How do you create a template file?

INTRODUCTION

- Companies using AutoCAD are always looking for better ways to:
- Unify their work to a certain standard (homemade or international).
- Speed up the process of producing a drawing.
- The answer to these two issues is to create template files.
- Template files will ensure that all the pre-made settings for the drawings are already done in the templates, which will cut production time by at least 30%.
- Templates will also ensure that all users within a company are using the same source.
- Template files have the *.dwt extension.

WHAT ELEMENTS ARE INCLUDED IN A TEMPLATE FILE?

- These are the elements included in a template file:
  - Drawing units
  - Drawing limits
  - Grid and Snap settings
  - **OSNAP** settings
  - **POLAR** settings
  - Layers

- Linetypes
- Text Styles
- Dimension Styles
- Table Styles
- Layouts (including Border blocks and Viewports)
- Page Setups
- Plot Style tables

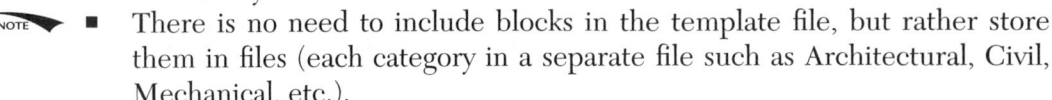

- There is no need to include blocks in the template file, but rather store them in files (each category in a separate file such as Architectural, Civil, Mechanical, etc.).
- You can't save Tool Palettes inside a template file as Tool Palettes are available for all files on a computer.

HOW DO YOU CREATE A TEMPLATE FILE?

- Start AutoCAD.
- Do the paperwork to prepare the above mentioned settings. This step may involve consultation with other people who operate AutoCAD in the company.
- Create a new file using the simplest template file **acad.dwt**.
- The new file will contain the minimum drawing requirements.
- Build inside this file all the above mentioned elements.
- Once you are done, select from the menu browser **File/Save As**. At **Files of type** select **AutoCAD Drawing Template (*.dwt)**, so AutoCAD will go directly to the **Template** folder in the AutoCAD folder.
- You can save this file in this folder, or you can create your own folder to accommodate all of your template files.
- It is highly recommended that you store your files in a different folder than the AutoCAD folders.
- You can create as many templates as you wish.
- If you want to edit an existing template simply do the following:
- Using the menu browser select **File/Open**. At **Files of type** select **Drawing Template (*.dwt)**.
- Open the desired template and perform the changes.
- Save it under the same name, or use a new name.

INQUIRY COMMANDS

In This Chapter

◊ Why we need Inquiry commands
◊ ID command
◊ DIST command
◊ AREA command
◊ LIST command

INTRODUCTION

- These commands are used to:
  - Identify a point coordinate.
  - Measure the distance between two points.
  - Calculate the area between points or of an object.
  - List information about an object.
- All of these commands are accessible from the **Ribbon**. Make sure you are at the **Tools** tab and using the **Inquiry** panel.

ID COMMAND

- This command is used to locate the coordinate of a point.
- Click the **ID Point** button.
- AutoCAD will display the following prompt:

```
Specify point:
```

- Click on the desired point, and AutoCAD will display something like:

```
X = 21.0000      Y = 11.5000      Z = 0.0000
```

DIST COMMAND

- This command is used to measure the distance between two points.
- Click the **Distance** button.
- AutoCAD will display the following prompt:

```
Specify first point:
Specify second point:
```

- Click on the two points desired, and AutoCAD will display something like:

```
Distance = 10.0000,  Angle in XY Plane = 0,  Angle from XY
Plane = 0
Delta X = 10.0000,  Delta Y = 0.0000,   Delta Z = 0.0000
```

AREA COMMAND

- This command is used to calculate the area between points or of an object.
- You can calculate area for:
  - Points, assuming there are lines connecting them.
  - Objects such as circles or polylines (closed or open).
- You can calculate two types of areas:
  - *Simple* area (single area).
  - *Complex* area (areas inside areas, and you want the net area).
- If you start the **Area** command and specify the points or select the object, AutoCAD will calculate simple area.
- To calculate the complex area, you have to start with either **Add** or **Subtract**.

- Click the Area button.
- AutoCAD will display the following prompt:

```
Specify first corner point or [Object/Add/Subtract]:
```

Specify first corner

- Calculating the simple area consists of counting points (assuming lines are connecting them). Specify the first point and AutoCAD will prompt:

```
Specify next corner point or press ENTER for total:
```

- Keep on doing the same thing up until you press [Enter]. The following message will appear:

```
Area = 33.3750, Perimeter = 23.6264
```

Object

- To calculate the area by selecting an object such as circle, polyline, etc., type **O**, or right-click and select **Object**. AutoCAD will prompt:

```
Select objects:
```

- Once you select the desired object, AutoCAD will report (the example is circle):

```
Area = 28.2743, Circumference = 18.8496
```

Add/Subtract

- You need these two modes in order to calculate Complex area, which is the area inside area, and you want the net area.
- Start with either one of these two modes, and AutoCAD will assume that you are starting with Area = 0.00. Hence, you will add the outer area, and then you can subtract the inner areas, or, you can subtract the inner areas, then add the outer area.
- Assume we started with **Add** mode. AutoCAD will prompt you:

```
Specify first corner point or [Object/Subtract]:
```

- You can specify area(s) using either points or objects. Whenever you are done, switch the mode to **Subtract** mode, and so on.
- While you are adding and subtracting AutoCAD will give you the current value of the area up until the last area added/subtracted.
- Once you are done press [Enter] twice, and AutoCAD will report to you the final value of the area.

LIST COMMAND

- This command is used to list information about a selected object without the ability to edit them.
- Click the **List** button.
- AutoCAD will display the following prompt:

```
Select objects:
```

- Select the desired object, and AutoCAD will list the following information (the example is circle):

```
CIRCLE      Layer: "0"
                 Space: Model space
                    Handle = 8d
  center point, X=  30.5000  Y=  13.5000  Z=   0.0000
            radius    3.0000
      circumference  18.8496
             area  28.2743
```

NOTE ➤ ■ The **Properties** command is much better, as you have the ability to edit any data you would like to change.

INDEX